The
I Hate
Corporate
America
R·E·A·D·E·R

The
I Hate
Corporate
America
R·E·A·D·E·R

HOW BIG COMPANIES FROM MCDONALD'S TO MICROSOFT ARE DESTROYING OUR WAY OF LIFE

EDITED BY CLINT WILLIS AND NATE HARDCASTLE

THUNDER'S MOUTH PRESS
NEW YORK

THE I HATE CORPORATE AMERICA READER:
How Big Companies from McDonald's to Microsoft Are Destroying Our Way of Life

Published by
Thunder's Mouth Press
An Imprint of Avalon Publishing Group Incorporated
245 West 17th St., 11th floor
New York, NY 10011-5300

AVALON
publishing group incorporated

ISBN 1-56025-635-4

Interior design by Paul Paddock

Printed in the U.S.A.

For activists everywhere

CONTENTS

INTRODUCTION

Corporations exert a troubling—make that horrifying—degree of control over every aspect of our lives: our work, our play, our entertainment, our health care, our food supply, our transportation, our environment, our government.

Worse, corporate power is growing. Americans who fear the power of big government have done what they could to reduce the role of government in our society—including its role as a brake on corporate power. These days, we have far more reason to fear the power of corporations, which—unlike governments—do not in any way reflect the will of the people.

True, corporations have shareholders. But few shareholders have a voice in corporate policy. Worse, corporate managers act on the assumption that the shareholders' best interests are served by the unbridled pursuit of short-term profit. This assumption is false.

Take the editors of this book. We hold shares in a number of companies, through our investments in retirement plans. Higher corporate profits tend to boost the value of our investments—and this increases the likelihood that we'll enjoy a comfortable and secure retirement.

Then again, the corporate pursuit of profits may kill us before we reach retirement age. We may die of cancer because of chemicals that profit-hungry corporations have poured into the environment. We may be killed in an automobile accident because liquor companies lobby against drunk driving laws. We may be poisoned by a piece of bad meat because the meat packing industry doesn't want to spend money to make our meat supply safer. We may be shot to death because gun makers fear gun control will cost them money. We may die on the job because our employers don't want to spend money on worker safety.

Or let's say we manage to reach retirement age. Along the way, corporate power will surely damage the quality of our lives in ways both subtle and obvious. We will find it increasingly difficult to locate a tomato that tastes like a tomato or a diner that makes real food. We will pay higher taxes to sustain a government that increasingly refuses to tax corporations—preferring to use workers' taxes to subsidize the corporate takeover of our public and private lives. Our political representatives will ignore our wishes to do the bidding of corporate contributors. We will continue to pay huge premiums for inadequate insurance policies—a reflection of a health care system designed to bolster corporate profits. We will lock our doors at night to keep out well-armed criminals who might be our friends and neighbors if corporations did their share to support our educational system. We will pay taxes to support wars driven by corporate agendas rather than our own beliefs or desires.

In return, we get higher returns on our 401(k)s— assuming we don't hold shares in the next Enron or Tyco or some dot.com flameout.

Hmmm. You know what? We think we're getting fucked—and so are you.

What can we—all of us—do about it? We need to create organizations and institutions to counteract corporate power. Community organizing groups, men's groups and women's groups, veterans groups, church groups—groups designed to bring us together in pursuit of something apart from profit. We need to stop bashing unions—without them, still more of us will join the working poor.

Institutions aside, we need to reclaim our power as individuals—at work and at home and in our communities. We can do that even in a corporate environment. I worked for a Fortune 500 company for a decade. My colleagues included some wonderful people who treated their coworkers with respect—and a few people who were willing to betray their fellow workers and sacrifice their own self-respect in pursuit of promotions or bigger cubicles. There were powerful incentives to behave badly—but most people resisted most of the time. I was impressed, and occasionally inspired.

Point is, even in a corporate environment there were always opportunities to behave generously and with courage—and when individuals seized them, they struck a blow against corporate power that otherwise threatened to overwhelm them. Such opportunities are available to us at work and at home and in our communities—opportunities to share our wealth, to help the powerless, to empower ourselves in our real guise, as human beings. Our hearts separate us from corporations, which are—literally—heartless.

Our minds also set us apart. Corporate power finds its way into our lives through fast food and video games and bad television. Those products profit corporations in two ways; they generate revenues and they put us to sleep. The best consumers and workers from a corporate point of view are mindless consumers and mindless workers.

Any corporate power is excessive. Corporations shouldn't have power; people—all of us—should have power.

How can we fight corporate power and achieve personal power? Our strategy *is* our salvation: We must wake up.

—Clint Willis

THEY LIE TO US

with a cartoon by Tom Toles

Normal human beings feel shame when they lie. Corporations, like psychopaths, are shameless. Corporate lies are becoming bigger, more sophisticated and more appalling. The lies conceal the harm corporations inflict upon the public; worse, misleading advertisements, bogus scientific studies and corporate-funded political events crowd out genuine discourse—and with it our best hope for a peaceful and democratic community.

The corruption of the biotech industry seems to know no bounds.

Rent-a-Mob
from TheEcologist.org (1/22/03)
Jonathan Matthews

The protesters were the poorest of the poor. Virtually all black and mostly women, the street traders and farmers conveyed an unpalatable message to the Earth Summit in Johannesberg. These were real poor people marching in the streets demanding development. Nothing surprising there. But a second glance revealed the demostraters were opposing the eco-agenda of the Greens in support of the biotech industry. This was the environmentalists' worst nightmare.

In the days that followed, the world's media latched on to the march. Seldom can the views of the poor, in this case a few hundred demonstrators, have been paid so much attention. Articles highlighting the march popped up the world over—in Africa, North America, India, Australia and Israel. In the UK The Times ran a commentary entitled "I do not need white NGOs to speak for me."

With the summit's passing, the Johannesburg march, far from fading from view, has taken on a deeper significance. Writing in the journal *Nature Biotechnology*, Val Giddings, a vice president at the Biotech Industry Organization (BIO), argued that the event marked "something new, something very big" that would make us "look back on Johannesburg as something of a watershed event—a turning point." What made the march so pivotal, he said, was that for the first time, "real, live, developing-world farmers" were "speaking for themselves" and challenging the "empty arguments of the self-appointed individuals who have professed to speak on their behalf."

PHONEY FARMER

To help give them a voice, Giddings singled out a statement made by one of the marchers, Chengal Reddy, the leader of the Indian Farmers Federation. "Traditional organic farming," Reddy said, "led to mass starvation in India for centuries . . . Indian farmers need access to new technologies and especially to biotechnologies."

Giddings also noted that the farmers expressed their contempt for the "empty arguments" of many of the Earth summiteers by honouring them with a Bullshit Award made from varnished cow dung. The award was given to the Indian environmentalist Vandana Shiva, in particular, for her role in "advancing policies that perpetuate poverty and hunger."

A powerful rebuke, no doubt. But if anyone deserves the cow dung, it is the president of BIO, for almost every element of the spectacle he described was carefully contrived and orchestrated.

Take Reddy, for instance, the "farmer" that Giddings quoted. Reddy is not a poor farmer, nor even the representative of poor farmers. Indeed, there is precious little to suggest he is even well-disposed towards the poor. The Indian Farmers Federation that he leads is a lobby of big commercial farmers in Andhra Pradesh. On occasion Reddy has admitted to knowing very little about farming, having never farmed in his life. He is, in reality, a politician and businessman whose family are a prominent right-wing force in Andhra Pradesh. (His father once famously said: "There is only one thing Dalits [members of the lowest caste] are good for and that is being kicked.")

If it seems doubtful that Reddy was in Johannesburg to help the poor speak for themselves, the identity of the march's organizers does not breed confidence. It is ironic, given the *Times'* headline, that the media contact on the organisers' press release was Kendra Okonski. The daughter of a U.S. lumber industrialist, Okonski has worked for various right-wing anti-regulatory NGOs—all funded and directed, needless to say, by "whites." These NGOs include the Competitive Enterprise Institute (CEI), a Washington-based think tank with a multi-million dollar budget that comes from such major U.S. corporations as BIO member Dow Chemicals. Okonski also runs the website Counterprotest.net, where her speciality is helping right-wing lobbyists take to the streets to mimic popular protesters.

Delving deeper, it is apparent that there was a network of organisations involved in events that surrounded the march.

BULLSHIT AWARD

It hardly needs saying that the Bullshit Award was far from the imaginative riposte of impoverished farmers to India's most celebrated environmentalist, as Giddings suggests. It was, in fact, the creation of another right-wing pressure group, the Liberty Institute, which is based in New Delhi and well known for its fervent support of deregulation, GM crops and Big Tobacco.

The Liberty Institute is part of the deceptively-named Sustainable Development Network (SDN) which was repsonsible for organising the Johannesburg rally. In

London the SDN shares its offices and key personnel (including Okonski) with the International Policy Network, a group which in Washington has the same address as the CEI. The SDN is run by Julian Morris, who also claims the title of environment and technology programme director for the Institute of Economic Affairs which has advocated that African countries should be sold off to multinational corporations in the interests of "good government."

The involvement of the likes of Morris, Okonski and Reddy does not mean, of course, that no "real" poor people were involved in the Johannesburg march. American journalist James MacKinnon witnessed the march first hand and saw many impoverished street traders, who seemed genuinely aggrieved with the authorities for denying them their usual trading places in the streets around the event. In the magazine *Adbusters* he reported that march organisers had played on this grievance by distributing a flyer that presented the march as a chance to demand "freedom to trade." The flyer made no mention of biotechnology, development or any other issue on the agenda of the Green Left.

For all that, there were some real farmers present as well. Mackinnon says he spotted some wearing anti-environmentalist T-shirts with slogans like "Stop Global Whining." This aroused his curiosity, since small-scale African farmers are not normally to be found among those jeering the "bogus science" of climate change. Yet here they were with slogans on placards and T-shirts: "Save the Planet from Sustainable Development," "Say No to Eco-Imperialism," "Greens: Stop Hurting the Poor" and "Biotechnology for Africa."

On approaching the protesters, however, MacKinnon

discovered that the props had been made available to the marchers by the organisers. He reported that when he tried to speak to some of the farmers about their pro-GM T-shirts, they could only smile. None of them could speak or read English.

Another irresistible question is how impoverished farmers—Giddings claims there were farmers from five different countries at the rally—afforded the journey to Johannesburg from as far away as the Philippines and India. Here, too, there is reason for suspicion.

In late 1999 the *New York Times* reported that a street protest against genetic engineering outside a Food and Drug Administration public hearing in Washington, D.C., was disrupted by a group of African-Americans carrying placards saying such things as "Biotech Saves Children's Lives" and "Biotech Equals Jobs." The paper reported that Monsanto's PR company Burson-Marsteller had paid a Baptist Church from a poor neighbourhood to bus in these demonstrators as part of a wider campaign to get groups of church members, union workers and the elderly to speak in favour of genetically engineered foods.

In this kind of rent-a-crowd approach, the industry's fingerprints are all over Johannesburg. Reddy, who for over a decade has featured prominently in Monsanto's promotional work in India, was brought to Johannesburg by AfricaBio which itself has been closely aligned with Monsanto's lobbying for its products.

HEART OF THE MATTER

And here lies the real key to the president of BIO's account of the march and specifically to the attack on Vandana Shiva. Monsanto and BIO want to project an image that the Third World accepts GM technology. That is why Monsanto's website used to be adorned with the faces of smiling Asian children. So when an Indian critic of the biotech industry gets featured as an environmental hero on the cover of *Time* magazine, as Shiva was recently, the brand is under attack and has to be protected.

The counterattack takes place through a contrarian lens, one that projects the attackers' vices onto their target. Thus the problem becomes not Monsanto using questionable tactics to push its products onto a wary Developing World, but malevolent agents of the rich world obstructing Monsanto's acceptance in a welcoming Third World. For this reason the press release for the Bullshit Award accuses Shiva of being "a mouthpiece of Western eco-imperialism." And the media contact for this symbolic rejection of neocolonialism? Okonski—an Amercian. In other words, the mouthpiece denouncing an Indian environmentalist as an agent of the West is . . . a Western mouthpiece.

The careful framing of the messages and the actors in the rally in Johannesburg provides one especially gaudy spectacle in a continuing fake parade. In particular, the Internet provides a perfect medium for such showcases, where the gap between the virtual and the real is easily erased.

Faking it

Take foodsecurity.net, which promotes itself as "the web's most complete source of news and information about global food security concerns and sustainable agricultural practices" and claims to be "an independent, non-profit coalition of people throughout the world." Despite its global reach, foodsecurity.net's only named member of staff is its African director Dr. Michael Mbwille, a Tanzanian doctor who is forever penning articles defending Monsanto and attacking the likes of Greenpeace.

The news and information at foodsecurity.net is largely pro-GM, often bitterly abusive, and boasts headlines like "The Villainous Vandana Shiva" and "Altered Crops Called Boon for Poor." When one penetrates beyond the news pages, the content is limited. A single message graces the message board, posted by myoung@bivwood.com, the domain name of the Bivings Group, an internet PR company that numbers Monsanto among its clients. There is also an event posting from an Andura Smetacek, recently identified by *The Guardian* as an e-mail front used by Monsanto to run a campaign of character assassination against its scientific and environmental critics.

The site is registered to one Graydon Forrer, currently the managing director of Life Sciences Strategies, a company that specialises in "communications programmes" for the bioscience industries. A piece of information that is not usually disclosed in Forrer's self-presentation is that he was previously Monsanto's director of executive communications. Indeed, he seems to have been working for the company in 1999, the same year the site of this "independent, non-profit coalition of people throughout the world" was first registered. And incidentally, foodsecurity's African director Dr. Mbwille is not in Africa at the moment. He is enjoying a sabbatical observing medical practice in St Louis, Missouri, the home town of the Monsanto Corporation.

WEB OF DECEIT

Foodsecurity.net is one of a whole series of websites with undisclosed links to biotech industry lobbyists or

PR companies. Although the president of BIO has this virtual circus oscillating about him, if he were really interested in hearing poor "live, developing-world farmers . . . speaking for themselves," he would need to look no further than Reddy's home state of Andhra Pradesh.

Here farmers and landless labourers were consulted as part of a "citizens' jury" on World Bank-backed proposals to industrialise local agriculture and introduce GM crops. Having heard all sides of the argument, including the views of Reddy, the jury unanimously rejected the proposals, which were likely to force more than 100,000 people off the land. Citizens' juries on GM crops in Brazil and the Indian state of Karnataka have come to similar conclusions, something that the president of BIO is almost certainly aware of.

But rainchecks on the real views of the poor count for little in a world where "something new, something very big" and "a turning point" in the global march towards our corporate future, turns out to be Monsanto's soapbox behind a black man's face.

The next time you read a newspaper article that cites a corporate source on a subject like global warming, remember this: Corporations don't care what happens to you or your grandchildren.

Global Warming Is Good for You

from *Trust Us, We're Experts!* (2001)

Sheldon Rampton and John Stauber

With the exception of nuclear war, it is hard to imagine a higher-stakes issue than global warming. The idea that industrial emissions of carbon dioxide and other greenhouse gases might lead to climate change has been seriously discussed among scientists since 1957. It first became a topic of public debate during the brutally hot summer of 1988, when Dr. James Hansen of NASA's Goddard Institute for Space Studies warned a congressional panel that human industrial activities were already exerting a measurable and mounting impact on the earth's climate. Hansen's testimony prompted *Time* magazine to editorialize that global warming's "possible consequences are so scary that it is only prudent for governments to slow the buildup of carbon dioxide through preventive measures." As subsequent years saw a succession of record global temperatures, climatologists became increasingly concerned by what their computer models were telling them. The most authoritative statement of these concerns is a November 1995 report issued by the Intergovernmental Panel on Climate Change (IPCC), a group of some 2,500 climatologists from throughout the world that advises the United Nations. It predicted "widespread economic, social and environmental dislocation over the next century" if action is not taken soon to restrict greenhouse gas emissions. To avert catastrophe, the IPCC has called for policy measures to reduce emissions of greenhouse gases by 20 percent below 1990 levels initially and ultimately reduce those emissions by 70 percent.

Automobile exhausts, coal-burning power plants, factory smokestacks, and other vented wastes of the industrial age now pump six billion tons of carbon dioxide and other "greenhouse gases" into the earth's atmosphere each year. They are called greenhouse gases because they trap radiant energy from the sun that would otherwise be reflected back into space. The fact that a natural greenhouse effect occurs is well-known and is not debated. Without it, in fact, temperatures would drop so low that oceans would freeze and life as we know it would be impossible. What climatologists are concerned about, however, is that increased *levels* of greenhouse gases in the atmosphere are causing more heat to be trapped. Concentrations of greenhouse gases in the atmosphere are currently at their highest level in 420,000 years.

"The basic science of global warming has not changed since the topic was raised earlier in this century," notes a December 1999 open letter by the directors of the U.S. National Oceanic and Atmospheric Administration and the British Meteorological Office. "Furthermore, the consensus of opinion has been growing, within both the scientific and the business communities. Our new data and understanding now point to the critical situation we face: to slow future change, we must start taking action soon. At the same time, because of our past and ongoing activities, we must start to learn to live with the likely consequences—more extreme weather, rising sea levels, changing precipitation patterns, ecological and agricultural dislocations, and the increased spread of human disease. . . . Ignoring climate change will surely be the most costly of all possible choices, for us and our children."

"There is no debate among statured scientists of what is happening," says James McCarthy, who chairs the Advisory Committee on the Environment of the International Committee of Scientific Unions. "The only debate is the rate at which it's happening." Between 1987 and 1993, McCarthy oversaw the work of the leading climate scientists from 60 nations as they developed the IPCC's landmark 1995 report.

There are, of course, areas of considerable outstanding dispute and genuine scientific uncertainty. No one knows how rapid or drastic global warming will turn out to be, or how severely it will affect food production, ocean levels, or the spread of disease. There is also debate over the extent to which global warming has already contributed to droughts, intense hurricanes, and environmental degradation such as coral bleaching. Given these uncertainties, it is difficult to talk of a "worst-case scenario," but the scenarios that are plausible include many that are dire enough. A number of these possibilities are discussed in Ross Gelbspan's book *The Heat Is On*. Gelbspan quotes the late Dr. Henry Kendall, a Nobel Prize–winning physicist, who worried that climate change could disrupt farming at a time when earth's growing population is already creating unprecedented demands on agriculture. "The world's food supply," Kendall said in 1995, "must double within the next thirty years to feed the population, which will double within the next sixty years. Otherwise, before the middle of the next century—as many countries in the developing world run out of enough water to irrigate their crops—population will outrun its food supply, and you will see chaos. All we need is another hit from climate change—a series of droughts or crop-destroying rains—and we're looking down the mouth of a cannon."

Gelbspan worries that a global disaster of this magnitude would not only mean mass starvation but would threaten the survival of democratic institutions, particularly in developing nations. "In many of these countries, where democratic traditions are as fragile as the ecosystem, a reversion to dictatorship will require only a few ecological states of emergency," he warns. "Their governments will quickly find democracy to be too cumbersome for responding to disruptions in food supplies, water sources, and human health—as well as to a flood-tide of environmental refugees from homelands that have become incapable of feeding and supporting them." This vision of the future—a starving world under martial law—is by no means inevitable, but the groups pushing for strong measures to curb global warming believe that the nightmare scenarios are plausible enough to justify invoking the precautionary principle.

For the oil, coal, auto, and manufacturing industries, warnings of this sort involve another kind of high stakes. Any measures to control emissions of greenhouse gases threaten their long-standing habits of doing business. They view scientists' conclusions about global warming with the same interest-driven hostility that the tobacco industry shows toward scientists who study lung cancer. Like the tobacco industry, they have pumped millions of dollars into efforts to debunk the science they hate. They have found little support, however, among the "statured scientists" to whom McCarthy refers—the people who are actually involved in relevant research and whose work has been published in peer-reviewed scientific journals. The global warming consensus among these scientists is so strong that the oil and auto industries have been forced far afield in their search for voices willing to join in their denial. What is remarkable, given this fact, is the extent to which industry PR has been successful in creating the illusion that global warming is some kind of controversial, hotly disputed theory.

LOBBYING FOR LETHARGY

In 1989, not long after James Hansen's highly publicized testimony before Congress and shortly after the first meeting of the UN's Intergovernmental Panel on Climate Change, the Burson-Marsteller PR firm created the Global Climate Coalition (GCC). Chaired by William O'Keefe, an executive for the American Petroleum Institute, the GCC operated until 1997 out of the offices of the National Association of Manufacturers. Its members have included the American Automobile Manufacturers Association, Amoco, the American Forest & Paper Association, American Petroleum Institute, Chevron, Chrysler, the U.S. Chamber of Commerce, Dow Chemical, Exxon, Ford, General Motors, Mobil, Shell, Texaco, Union Carbide, and more than 40 other corporations and trade associations. The GCC has also used "Junkman" Steven Milloy's former employer, the EOP Group, as well as the E. Bruce Harrison Company, a subsidiary of the giant Ruder Finn PR firm. Within the public relations industry, Harrison is an almost legendary figure who is ironically considered "the founder of green PR" because of his work for the pesticide industry in the 1960s, when he helped lead the attack on author Rachel Carson and her environmental classic *Silent Spring*.

GCC has been the most outspoken and confrontational industry group in the United States battling reductions in greenhouse gas emissions. Its activities have included publication of glossy reports, aggressive lobbying at international climate negotiation meetings, and raising concern about unemployment that it claims would result from emissions regulations. Since 1994 GCC alone has spent more than $63 million to combat any progress toward addressing the climate crisis. Its efforts are coordinated with separate campaigns by many of its members, such as the National Coal Association, which spent more than $700,000 on the global climate issue in 1992 and 1993, and the American Petroleum Institute, which paid the Burson-Marsteller PR firm $1.8 million in 1993 for a successful computer-driven "grassroots" letter and phone-in campaign to stop a proposed tax on fossil fuels.

These numbers may not seem huge compared to the billions that corporations spend on advertising. The Coca-Cola company alone, for example, spends nearly $300 million per year on soft drink advertisements. But the Global Climate Coalition is not advertising a product. Its propaganda budget serves solely to influence the news media and government policymakers on a single issue and comes on top of the marketing, lobbying, and campaign contributions that industry already spends in the regular course of doing business. In 1998, the oil and gas industries alone spent $58 million lobbying the U.S. Congress. For comparison's sake, environmental groups spent a relatively puny total of $4.7 million—on all issues combined, not just global warming.

Industry's PR strategy with regard to the global warming issue is also eminently practical, with limited, realistic goals. Opinion polls for the past decade have consistently shown that the public would like to see something done about the global warming problem, along with many other environmental issues. Industry's PR strategy is not aimed at reversing the tide of public opinion, which may in any case be impossible. Its goal is simply to stop people from mobilizing to do anything about the problem, to create sufficient doubt in their minds about the seriousness of global warming that they will remain locked in debate and indecision. Friends of the Earth International describes this strategy as "lobbying for lethargy."

"People generally do not favor action on a non-alarming situation when arguments seem to be balanced on both sides and there is a clear doubt," explains Phil Lesly, author of *Lesly's Handbook of Public Relations and Communications*, a leading PR textbook. In order for the status quo to prevail, therefore, corporations have a simple task: "The weight of impressions on the public must be balanced so people will have doubts and lack motivation to take action. Accordingly, means are needed to get balancing information into the stream from sources that the public will find credible. There is no need for a clear-cut 'victory.' . . . Nurturing public doubts by demonstrating that this is not a clear-cut situation in support of the opponents usually is all that is necessary."

IN THE BEGINNING THERE WAS ICE

As political theorist Goran Therborn has observed, there are three basic ways to keep people apathetic about a problem: (1) argue that it doesn't exist; (2) argue that it's actually a good thing rather than a problem; or (3) argue that even if it is a problem, there's nothing they can do about it anyway. Industry's first propaganda responses to the problem of global warming focused on the first line of defense by attempting to deny that it was happening at all. In 1991, a corporate coalition composed of the National Coal Association, the Western Fuels Association, and Edison Electrical Institute created a PR front group called the "Information Council for the Environment" (ICE) and launched a $500,000 advertising and public relations campaign to, in ICE's own words, "reposition global warming as theory (not fact)."

To boost its credibility, ICE created a Scientific Advisory Panel that featured Patrick Michaels from the Department of Environmental Services at the University of Virginia; Robert Balling of Arizona State University; and Sherwood Idso of the U.S. Water Conservation Laboratory. ICE's plan called for placing these three scientists, along with fellow greenhouse skeptic S. Fred Singer, professor emeritus of environmental sciences at the University of Virginia, in broadcast appearances, op-ed pages, and newspaper interviews. Bracy Williams & Co., a Washington-based PR firm, did the advance publicity work for the interviews. Another company was contracted to conduct opinion polls, which identified "older, less-educated males from larger households who are not typically active information-seekers" and "younger, lower-income women" as "good targets for radio advertisements" that would "directly attack the proponents of global warming . . . through comparison of global warming to historical or mythical instances of gloom and doom."

One print advertisement prepared for the ICE campaign showed a sailing ship about to drop off the edge of a flat world into the jaws of a waiting dragon. The headline read "Some say the earth is warming. Some also said the earth was flat." Another featured a cowering chicken under the headline "Who Told You the Earth Was Warming . . . Chicken Little?" Another ad was targeted at Minneapolis readers and asked, "If the earth is getting warmer, why is Minneapolis getting colder?"

"It will be interesting to see how the science approach sells," commented an internal memo by the Edison Electric Institute's William Brier. The campaign collapsed, however, after Brier's comments and other internal memoranda were leaked to the press. An embarrassed Michaels hastily disassociated himself from ICE, citing what he called its "blatant dishonesty."

Qualms notwithstanding, Michaels continues to benefit from his association with the fossil fuels industry. During an administrative hearing in Minnesota in May 1995, he testified that he had received $165,000 in funding during the previous five years from fuel companies, including $49,000 from the German Coal Association and funding from the Western Fuels company for a non-peer-reviewed journal that he edits called *World Climate Report*. Michaels has served as a paid expert witness for utilities in lawsuits involving the issue of global warming. He has written letters to the editor and op-ed pieces, appeared on television and radio, and testified before government bodies. He sits on the advisory boards of several industry-funded propaganda campaigns and is a "senior fellow" at the Cato Institute.

Other scientists who vocally defend the industry position

have similar entanglements. Robert Balling is a geologist by training whose work prior to 1990 focused on desertification and soil-related issues. Beginning with his work for the ICE campaign, he has received nearly $300,000 in research funding from coal and oil interests, some of it in collaborations with Sherwood Idso. According to Peter Montague of the Environmental Research Foundation, S. Fred Singer "is now an 'independent' consultant" for companies including ARCO, Exxon Corporation, Shell Oil Company, Sun Oil Company, and Unocal Corporation. Rather than conducting research, Singer "spends his time writing letters to the editor and testifying before Congress." Singer's Science and Environmental Policy Project (SEPP) was originally set up by the Rev. Sun Myung Moon's Unification Church, a frequent patron of conservative political causes. Although SEPP is no longer affiliated with Moon's cult, Singer's editorials frequently appear in the pages of the Unification Church–owned *Washington Times* newspaper.

With all of these side deals and front groups in place, the collapse of ICE didn't even slow industry's propaganda effort. The scientists who participated in the ICE campaign—Michaels, Balling, Idso, and Singer—have simply been recycled into new organizations with new names. As Gelbspan observes, this "tiny group of dissenting scientists have been given prominent public visibility and congressional influence out of all proportion to their standing in the scientific community on the issue of global warming. They have used this platform to pound widely amplified drumbeats of doubt about climate change. These doubts are repeated in virtually every climate-related story in every newspaper and every TV and radio news outlet in the country. By keeping the discussion focused on whether there really is a problem, these dozen or so dissidents—contradicting the consensus view held by the world's top climate scientists—have until now prevented discussion about how to address the problem."

SMOKE AND MIRRORS
In addition to the Global Climate Coalition, a host of other industry-funded front groups have entered the fray. Although the GCC leads the campaign against climate change reform, it collaborates extensively with a network that includes industry trade associations, "property rights" groups affiliated with the anti-environmental Wise Use movement, and fringe groups such as Sovereignty International, which believes that global warming is a plot to enslave the world under a United Nations–led "world government."

Groups participating in industry's global warming campaign have included the American Energy Alliance (consisting of the National Association of Manufacturers, the American Petroleum Institute, and Edison Electric Institute), the Climate Council (run by Don Pearlman, a fixture at climate negotiations around the world and a member of the oil-client-heavy lobby firm of Patton Boggs), the International Climate Change Partnership (whose members include BP, Elf, and DuPont), the International Chamber of Commerce and Citizens for a Sound Economy (a Washington-based lobby group whose funders include BMW, Boeing, BP, Chevron, GM, Mobil, Toyota, and Unilever). In 1997, international global warming treaty negotiations were held in Kyoto, Japan, prompting a bevy of industry groups to mobilize. Some of the participating groups were the following:

- *The Global Climate Information Project (GCIP)*, launched on September 9, 1997, by some of the nation's most powerful trade associations, spent more than $13 million in newspaper and television advertising. The ads were produced by Goddard*Claussen/First Tuesday, a California-based PR firm whose clients include the Chlorine Chemistry Council, the Chemical Manufacturers Association, DuPont Merck Pharmaceuticals, and the Vinyl Siding Institute. Goddard*Claussen is notorious for its "Harry and Louise" advertisement that helped derail President Clinton's 1993 health reform proposal. Its global warming ads used a similar fear-mongering strategy by claiming that a Kyoto treaty would raise gasoline prices by 50 cents per gallon, leading to higher prices on everything from "heat to food to clothing." The GCIP was represented by Richard Pollock, former director of Ralph Nader's group, Critical Mass, who has switched sides and now works as a senior vice president for Shandwick Public Affairs, the second-largest PR firm in the United States. Recent Shandwick clients include Browning-Ferris Industries, Central Maine Power, Georgia-Pacific Corp., Monsanto Chemical Co, New York State Electric and Gas Co., Ciba-Geigy, Ford Motor Company, Hydro-Quebec, Pfizer, and Procter & Gamble.
- *The Coalition for Vehicle Choice (CVC)*, a front group for automobile manufacturers,, launched its

own advertising campaign, including a three-page ad in the *Washington Post* that blasted the Kyoto climate talks as an assault on the U.S. economy. Sponsors for the ad included hundreds of oil and gas companies, auto dealers and parts stores, along with a number of far-right organizations such as the American Land Rights Association and Sovereignty International. CVC was originally founded in 1991 and has successfully prevented higher fuel-efficiency standards in U S. autos and trucks. From the beginning, it has been represented by Ron DeFore, a former vice president of E. Bruce Harrison's PR firm. Its budget in 1993 was $2.2 million, all of which came from the big three automakers—Ford, GM, and Chrysler.

• *The National Center for Public Policy Research*, an industry-funded think tank, established a "Kyoto Earth Summit Information Center," issued an "Earth Summit Fact Sheet," and fed anti-treaty quotes to the media through a "free interview locator service" that offered "assistance to journalists seeking interviews with leading scientists, economists, and public policy experts on global warming."

• *The Advancement of Sound Science Coalition (TASSC)*, headed by "Junkman" Steven Milloy, attempted to stimulate anti-treaty e-mail to President Clinton by promising to enter writers' names in a $1,000 sweepstakes drawing. Milloy's website also heaps vitriol on the science of global warming, including attacks on the American Geophysical Union, the American Meteorological Society, and *Nature* magazine.

• *The American Policy Center (APC)* worked to mobilize a "Strike for Liberty," calling on truckers to pull over to the side of the road for an hour and for farmers to drive tractors into key cities to "shut down the nation" as a protest against any Kyoto treaty. Signing the treaty, APC warned, would mean that "with a single stroke of the pen, our nation as we built it, as we have known it and as we have loved it will begin to disappear." APC also appealed to anti-abortion activists with the claim that "Al Gore has said abortion should be used to reduce global warming."

AUTOGRAPH COLLECTIONS

Waving petitions from scientists seems to be a favorite PR strategy of greenhouse skeptics. The website of S. Fred Singer's Science and Environmental Policy Project lists no fewer than four petitions, including the 1992 "Statement by Atmospheric Scientists on Greenhouse Warming," the "Heidelberg Appeal" (also from 1992), Singer's own "Leipzig Declaration on Global Climate Change" (1997), and the "Oregon Petition," which was circulated in 1998 by physicist Frederick Seitz. Thanks to the echo chamber of numerous industry-funded think tanks, these petitions are widely cited by conservative voices in the "junk science" movement and given prominent play by reporters.

The Heidelberg Appeal was first circulated at the 1992 Earth Summit in Rio de Janeiro and has subsequently been endorsed by some 4,000 scientists, including 72 Nobel Prize winners. It has also been enthusiastically embraced by proponents of "sound science" such as Steven Milloy and Elizabeth Whelan and is frequently cited as proof that scientists reject not only the theory of global warming but also a host of other environmental health risks associated with everything from pesticides in food to antibiotic-resistant bacteria. The Heidelberg Appeal warns of the "emergence of an irrational ideology which is opposed to scientific and industrial progress and impedes economic and social development" and advises "the authorities in charge of our planet's destiny against decisions which are supported by pseudo-scientific arguments or false and non-relevant data . . . The greatest evils which stalk our Earth are ignorance and oppression, and not Science, Technology and Industry."

The only problem is that the Heidelberg Appeal makes no mention whatsoever of global warming, or for that matter of pesticides or antibiotic-resistant bacteria. It is simply a brief statement supporting rationality and science. Based on the text alone, it is the sort of document that virtually any scientist in the world might feel comfortable signing. Parts of the Heidelberg Appeal in fact appear to *endorse* environmental concerns, such as a sentence that states, "We fully subscribe to the objectives of a scientific ecology for a universe whose resources must be taken stock of, monitored and preserved." Its 72 Nobel laureates include 49 who also signed the "World Scientists' Warning to Humanity," which was circulated that same year by the liberal Union of Concerned Scientists (UCS) and attracted the majority of the world's living Nobel laureates in science along with some 1,700 other leading scientists." In contrast with the vagueness of the Heidelberg Appeal, the "World Scientists' Warning" is a very explicit environmental manifesto, stating that "human beings and the natural world are on a collision course" and citing ozone depletion, global climate change, air pollution, groundwater depletion, deforestation, overfishing, and species extinction among the trends that threaten to "so alter the living world that it will be unable to sustain life in the manner that we know." More recently, 110 Nobel Prize–winning scientists signed another UCS petition, the 1997 "Call to Action," which called specifically on world leaders to sign an effective global warming treaty at Kyoto.

Like the Heidelberg Appeal, the Leipzig Declaration is named after a German city, giving it a patina of gray eminence. Signed by 110 people, including many of the signers of the earlier "Statement by Atmospheric Scientists," it is widely cited by conservative voices in the "sound science" movement and is regarded in some circles as the gold standard of scientific expertise on the issue. It has been cited by Singer himself in editorial columns appearing in hundreds of conservative websites and major publications, including the *Wall Street Journal, Miami Herald, Detroit News, Chicago Tribune, Cleveland Plain Dealer, Memphis Commercial-Appeal, Seattle Times,* and *Orange County Register.* Jeff Jacoby, a columnist with the *Boston Globe,* describes the signers of the Leipzig Declaration as "prominent scholars." The Heritage Foundation calls them "noted scientists," as do conservative think tanks such as Citizens for a Sound Economy, the Heartland Institute, and Australia's Institute for Public Affairs. Both the Leipzig Declaration and Seitz's Oregon Petition have been quoted as authoritative sources during deliberations in the U.S. Senate and House of Representatives.

When journalist David Olinger of the *St. Petersburg*

Times investigated the Leipzig Declaration, however, he discovered that most of its signers have not dealt with climate issues at all and none of them is an acknowledged leading expert. Twenty-five of the signers were TV weathermen—a profession that requires no in-depth knowledge of climate research. Some did not even have a college degree, such as Dick Groeber of Dick's Weather Service in Springfield, Ohio. Did Groeber regard himself as a scientist? "I sort of consider myself so," he said when asked. "I had two or three years of college training in the scientific area, and 30 or 40 years of self-study." Other signers included a dentist, a medical laboratory researcher, a civil engineer, and an amateur meteorologist. Some were not even found to reside at the addresses they had given. A journalist with the Danish Broadcasting Company attempted to contact the declaration's 33 European signers and found that four of them could not be located, 12 denied ever having signed, and some had not even heard of the Leipzig Declaration. Those who did admit signing included a medical doctor, a nuclear scientist, and an expert on flying insects. After discounting the signers whose credentials were inflated, irrelevant, false, or unverifiable, it turned out that only 20 of the names on the list had any scientific connection with the study of climate change, and some of those names were known to have obtained grants from the oil and fuel industry, including the German coal industry and the government of Kuwait (a major oil exporter).

SOME LIKE IT HOT

The Oregon Petition, sponsored by the Oregon Institute of Science and Medicine (OISM), was circulated in April 1998 in a bulk mailing to tens of thousands of U.S. scientists. In addition to the petition, the mailing included what appeared to be a reprint of a scientific paper. Authored by Arthur B. Robinson and three other people, the paper was titled "Environmental Effects of Atmospheric Carbon Dioxide" and was printed in the same typeface and format as the official Proceedings of the National Academy of Sciences (NAS). A cover note from Frederick Seitz, who had served as president of the NAS in the 1960s, added to the impression that Robinson's paper was an official publication of the academy's peer-reviewed journal.

Robinson's paper claimed to show that pumping carbon dioxide into the atmosphere is actually a *good* thing. "As atmospheric CO_2 increases," it stated, "plant growth rates increase. Also, leaves lose less water as CO_2 increases, so that plants are able to grow under drier conditions. Animal life, which depends upon plant life for food, increases proportionally." As a result, Robinson concluded, industrial activities can be counted on to encourage greater species biodiversity and a greener planet. "As coal, oil, and natural gas are used to feed and lift from poverty vast numbers of people across the globe, more CO_2 will be released into the atmosphere," the paper stated. "This will help to maintain and improve the health, longevity, prosperity, and productivity of all people. Human activities are believed to be responsible for the rise in CO_2 level of the atmosphere. Mankind is moving the carbon in coal, oil, and natural gas from below ground to the atmosphere and surface, where it is available for conversion into living things. We are living in an increasingly lush environment of plants and animals as a result of the CO_2 increase. Our children will enjoy an Earth with far more plant and animal life than that with which we now are blessed. This is a wonderful and unexpected gift from the Industrial Revolution."

In reality, neither Robinson's paper nor OISM's petition drive had anything to do with the National Academy of Sciences, which first heard about the petition when its members began calling to ask if the NAS had taken a stand against the Kyoto treaty. The paper's author, Arthur Robinson, was not even a climate scientist. He was a bio-chemist with no published research in the field of clima-tology, and his paper had never been subjected to peer review by anyone with training in the field. In fact, the paper had never been accepted for publication *anywhere*, let alone in the NAS Proceedings. It was self-published by Robinson, who did the typesetting himself on his own computer under the auspices of the Oregon Institute of Science and Medicine, of which Robinson himself was the founder.

So what is the OISM, exactly? The bulk mailing that went out to scientists gave no further information, other than the address of a post office box. The OISM does have a website, however, where it describes itself as "a small research institute" in Cave Junction, Oregon, with a faculty of six people engaged in studying "biochemistry, diag-nostic medicine, nutrition, preventive medicine and the molecular biology of aging." The OISM also sells a book titled *Nuclear War Survival Skills* (foreword by H-bomb inventor Edward Teller), which argues that "the dangers from nuclear weapons have been distorted and exagger-ated" into "demoralizing myths." Like the Institute itself, Cave Junction (population 1,126) is a pretty obscure place. It is the sort of out-of-the-way location you might seek out if you were hoping to survive a nuclear war, but it is not known as a center for scientific and medical research.

"Robinson is hardly a reliable source," observes journalist Ross Gelbspan. "As late as 1994 he declared that ozone depletion is a 'hoax'—a position akin to defending the flat-earth theory. In his newsletter, he told readers it was safe to drink water irradiated by the Chernobyl nuclear plant, and he marketed a home-schooling kit for parents concerned about socialism in the public schools.' "

None of the coauthors of "Environmental Effects of Atmospheric Carbon Dioxide" had any more standing than Robinson himself as a climate change researcher. They included Robinson's 22-year-old son, Zachary (home-schooled by his dad), along with astrophysicists Sallie Baliunas and Willie Soon. Both Baliunas and Soon worked with Frederick Seitz at the George C. Marshall Institute, a Washington, D.C., think tank where Seitz served as executive director. Funded by a number of right-wing foundations, including Scaife and Bradley, the George C. Marshall Institute does not conduct any original research. It is a conservative think tank that was initially founded during the years of the Reagan administration to advocate funding for Reagan's Strategic Defense Initiative—the "Star Wars" weapons program. Today, the Marshall Institute is still a big fan of high-tech weapons. In 1999, its website gave prominent placement to an essay by Col. Simon P. Worden titled "Why We Need the Air-Borne Laser," along with an essay titled "Missile Defense for Populations—What Does It Take? Why Are We Not Doing It?" Following the collapse of the Soviet Union, however, the Marshall Institute has adapted to the times by devoting much of its firepower to the war against environmentalism, and in particular against the "scare-mongers" who raise warnings about global warming.

"The mailing is clearly designed to be deceptive by giving people the impression that the article, which is full of half-truths, is a reprint and has passed peer review," complained Raymond Pierrehumbert, an atmospheric chemist at the University of Chicago. NAS foreign secretary F. Sherwood Rowland, an atmospheric chemist, said researchers "are wondering if someone is trying to hoodwink them." NAS council member Ralph J. Cicerone, dean of the School of Physical Sciences at the University of California at Irvine, was particularly offended that Seitz described himself in the cover letter as a "past president" of the NAS. Although Seitz had indeed held that title in the 1960s, Cicerone hoped that scientists who received the petition mailing would not be misled into believing that he "still has a role in governing the organization."

The NAS issued an unusually blunt formal response to the petition drive. "The NAS Council would like to make it clear that this petition has nothing to do with the National Academy of Sciences and that the manuscript was not published in the Proceedings of the National Academy of Sciences or in any other peer-reviewed journal," it stated in a news release. "The petition does not reflect the conclusions of expert reports of the Academy." In fact, it pointed out, its own prior published study had shown that "even given the considerable uncertainties in our knowledge of the relevant phenomena, greenhouse warming poses a potential threat sufficient to merit prompt responses. Investment in mitigation measures acts as insurance protection against the great uncertainties and the possibility of dramatic surprises."

Notwithstanding this rebuke, the Oregon Petition managed to garner 15,000 signatures within a month's time. Fred Singer called the petition "the latest and largest effort by rank-and-file scientists to express their opposition to schemes that subvert science for the sake of a political agenda."

Nebraska senator Chuck Hagel called it an "extraordinary response" and cited it as his basis for continuing to oppose a global warming treaty. "Nearly all of these 15,000 scientists have technical training suitable for evaluating climate research data," Hagel said. Columns citing the Seitz petition and the Robinson paper as credible sources of opinion on the global warming issue have appeared in publications ranging from *Newsday*, the *Los Angeles Times*, and *Washington Post* to the *Austin-American Statesman*, *Denver Post*, and *Wyoming Tribune-Eagle*.

In addition to the bulk mailing, OISM's website enables people to add their names to the petition over the Internet, and by June 2000 it claimed to have recruited more than 19,000 scientists. The institute is so lax about screening names, however, that virtually anyone can sign, including for example Al Caruba, the pesticide-industry PR man and conservative ideologue. Caruba has editorialized on his own website against the science of global warming, calling it the "biggest hoax of the decade," a "genocidal" campaign by environmentalists who believe that "humanity must be destroyed to 'Save the Earth.' . . . There is no global warming, but there is a global political agenda, comparable to the failed Soviet Union experiment with Communism, being orchestrated by the United Nations, supported by its many Green NGOs, to impose international treaties of every description that would turn the institution into a global government, superceding the sovereignty of every nation in the world."

When questioned in 1998, OISM's Arthur Robinson admitted that only 2,100 signers of the Oregon Petition had identified themselves as physicists, geophysicists, climatologists, or meteorologists, "and of those the greatest number are physicists." The names of the signers are available on the OISM's website, but without listing any institutional affiliations or even city of residence, making it very difficult to determine their credentials or even whether they exist at all. When the Oregon Petition first circulated, in fact, environmental activists successfully added the names of several fictional characters and celebrities to the list, including John Grisham, Michael J. Fox, Drs. Frank Burns, B. J. Honeycutt, and Benjamin Pierce (from the TV show *M*A*S*H*), an individual by the name of "Dr. Red Wine," and Geraldine Halliwell, formerly known as pop singer Ginger Spice of the Spice Girls. Ginger's field of scientific specialization was listed as "biology."

CASTING CALL

In April 1998, at about the same time that the OISM's petition first circulated, the *New York Times* reported on yet another propaganda scheme developed by the American Petroleum Institute. Joe Walker, a public relations representative of the API, had written an eight-page internal memorandum outlining the plan, which unfortunately for the plotters was leaked by a whistle-blower. Walker's memorandum called for recruiting scientists "who do not have a long history of visibility and/or participation in the climate change debate." Apparently, new faces were needed because the industry's long-standing scientific front men—Michaels, Balling, Idso, and Singer—had used up their credibility with journalists.

Walker's plan called for spending $5 million over two years to "maximize the impact of scientific views consistent with ours on Congress, the media and other key audiences." To measure success, a media tracking service would be hired to tally the percentage of news articles that raise questions about climate science and the number of radio talk show appearances by scientists questioning the prevailing view. The budget included $600,000 to develop a cadre of 20 "respected climate scientists" and to "identify, recruit and train a team of five independent scientists to participate in media outreach." (Unanswered, of course, was the question of how anyone who has been recruited and trained by the petroleum industry can be honestly described as "independent.") Once trained, these scientific spokesmodels would be sent around to meet with science writers, newspaper editors, columnists, and television network correspondents, "thereby raising questions about and undercutting the 'prevailing scientific wisdom.'"

"One of the creepiest revelations is that oil companies and their allies intend to recruit bona fide scientists to help muddy the waters about global warming," commented the *St. Louis Post-Dispatch*, seemingly unaware that this "third party" strategy had been part of the industry campaign from day one.

Hot Talk, Slow Walk

During the 1990s, Clinton-bashing was a common theme in industry's appeals to conservatives, using the argument that the global warming issue was a liberal attempt to replace private property with "socialism," "bureaucracy," and "big government." Particularly strong criticisms were leveled at then-Vice President Al Gore, who has spoken with occasional eloquence about the greenhouse effect and wrote about it in his book *Earth in the Balance*. Ironically, industry's attacks on Clinton and Gore helped conceal the Clinton administration's own complicity in the effort to prevent any effective regulations on greenhouse emissions.

On the eve of Earth Day in April 1993, Clinton announced his intention to sign a treaty on global warming, only to spend the rest of his two terms in office waffling and backpedaling. His "Climate Change Action Plan" of October 1993 turned out to be a "voluntary effort," depending entirely on the goodwill of industry for implementation. By early 1996, he was forced to admit that the plan was off track and would not even come close to meeting its goal for greenhouse gas reductions by the year 2000.

In June 1997, Clinton addressed the United Nations Earth Summit and pledged a sustained U.S. commitment to stop global warming. Painting a near-apocalyptic picture of encroaching seas and killer heat, he acknowledged that America's record over the past five years was "not sufficient. . . . We must do better and we will." Four months later, however, he announced that realistic targets and timetables for cutting greenhouse gas emissions should be put off for 20 years, prompting Australian environmental writer Sharon Beder to comment that "champagne corks are popping in the boardrooms of BP, Shell, Esso, Mobil, Ford, General Motors, and the coal, steel and aluminum corporations of the U.S., Australia and Europe. . . . The new limits are so weak, compared with even the most pessimistic predictions of what the U.S. would offer in the current negotiations, that two years of hard work by 150 countries towards reaching an agreement in December are now irrelevant."

During negotiations in Kyoto, the United States lobbied heavily and successfully to weaken the treaty's actual provisions for limiting greenhouse gases. The resulting treaty proposed a reduction of only 7 percent in global greenhouse emissions by the year 2012, far below the 20 percent cut proposed by the IPCC and European nations or the 30 percent reduction demanded by low-lying island nations that fear massive flooding as melting polar ice leads to rising sea levels. The United States also successfully won a provision that will allow countries to exceed their emission targets by buying right-to-pollute credits from nations that achieve better-than-targeted reductions.

Greenpeace called the resulting Kyoto treaty "a tragedy and a farce." It was condemned as "too extreme" by U.S. industry, declared dead on arrival by Senate Republicans, and praised by some environmental groups; and it provided all the political wiggle room that the Clinton administration needed to have its cake and eat it too. Clinton embraced the agreement but simultaneously said he would not submit it to the Senate until impoverished Third World nations agreed to their own cutbacks in greenhouse gas emissions.

There is a method to this madness that is well understood in Washington lobbying circles, although it is rarely discussed in public. By talking tough about the environment while sitting on the Kyoto treaty, Clinton and Gore were able to preserve their "green credentials" for political purposes while blaming the treaty's demise on anti-environmental Republicans and an apathetic public. For Democrats, it was a "win-win situation." They could stay on the campaign-funding gravy train by doing what their corporate donors wanted, while giving lip service to solving the problem. The December 12, 1997 *New York Times* reported that Clinton was "in the risk-free position of being able to make a strong pro-environmental political pitch while not having to face a damaging vote in the Senate. . . . One senior White House official . . . said it was possible that the treaty would not be ready for submission . . . during the remainder of Mr. Clinton's term in office "And indeed, this prediction proved correct. Industry's "lobbyists for lethargy" had succeeded.

STORMY WEATHER

While Nero fiddles, the burning of Rome is proceeding and even appears to be occurring faster than some climatologists expected. The twelve warmest years in recorded history have all occurred since 1983. The U.S. National Oceanic and Atmospheric Administration (NOAA) and the World Meteorological Association concurred that 1997 was the hottest year ever, only to be surpassed by 1998, which was in turn surpassed by 1999. In January 2000, the National Research Council of the National Academy of Sciences—Fred Seitz's former stomping grounds—issued a major report concluding that global warming is an "undoubtedly real" problem and is in fact occurring 30 percent faster than the rate estimated just five years earlier by the IPCC.

A series of extreme weather events also seemed to corroborate the IPCC's predictions. In 1998, a January ice storm caused widespread power outages in eastern Canada and the northeastern United States. In February, Florida was hit by the deadliest tornado outbreak in its history. April through June was the driest period in 104 years of record in Florida, Texas, Louisiana, and New Mexico, and May through June was the warmest period on record. Heat and dry weather caused devastating fires in central and eastern Russia, Indonesia, Brazil, Central America, and Florida. Massive floods hit Argentina, Peru, Bangladesh, India, and China, where the flooding of the Yangtze River killed more than 3,000 people and caused $30 billion in losses. Droughts plagued Guyana, Papua New Guinea, Pakistan, the Ukraine, Kazakhstan, and southern Russia. On October 4, 1998, Oklahoma was hit by 20 tornadoes, setting a national record for the most twisters ever during a single day. Three hurricanes and four tropical storms caused billions of dollars of damage to the United States. In late September, Hurricane Georges devastated the northern Caribbean, causing $4 billion in damages. A month later, Central America was devastated by Hurricane Mitch, Central America's worst natural disaster in 218 years, which killed more than 11,000 people and displaced another 2.4 million. In the Pacific, October's Supertyphoon Zeb inundated the northern Philippines, Taiwan, and Japan. Only eight days later, Supertyphoon Babs struck the Philippines, submerging parts of Manila.

In 1999, farmers in the northeastern and mid-Atlantic regions of the United States suffered through a record drought. A prolonged heat wave killed 271 people in the Midwest and Northeast. Hurricane Floyd battered North Carolina, inflicting more than a billion dollars in damages, while Boston marked a record 304 consecutive days without snow. In India, a supercyclone killed some 10,000 people. Torrential rains and mudslides killed 15,000 in Venezuela. Hurricane-force windstorms destroyed trees, buildings, and monuments in France, leaving more than $4 billion in damages. The South Pacific islands of Tebua Tarawa and Abunuea in the nation of Vanuato disappeared beneath the ocean, the first victims of the global rise in sea levels. The wave of catastrophes continued in 2000, with a prolonged drought in Kenya while wet, warm weather spawned billions of crop-threatening locusts in Australia and drought-driven fires devastated Los Alamos. The melting and fissuring of Antarctica's ice shelf, which first became dramatically evident in 1995, led in May 2000 to the calving of three enormous icebergs with a combined surface area slightly smaller than the state of Connecticut.

It is impossible, of course, to prove that any of these individual events was caused by global warming, but cumulatively the evidence is becoming harder to deny. As the evidence continues to mount, even some members of the oil industry have begun to defect. In 1999, the oil companies BP Amoco and Royal Dutch/Shell, along with Dow Chemicals, left the Global Climate Coalition and stated publicly that they now consider global warming a real, immediate problem. The following year saw similar moves from Ford, DaimlerChrysler, the Southern Company, Texaco, and General Motors. The DuPont corporation claims it will voluntarily cut emissions of greenhouse gases to 35 percent of their 1990 level by the year 2010.

"You can't stop climate change given what we're doing right now," said Michael MacCracken in February 2000. MacCracken is director of the National Assessment Coordination Office of the U.S. Global Climate Change Research Program, which was launched by President Bush in 1989. It is already too late to stop global warming, he said, due to the accumulated carbon-dioxide emissions that have already entered the atmosphere. The best that can be hoped for is to minimize the problem and adapt to the changes. In the United States, necessary measures will include changing the way water supplies are managed in the western United States, beefing up public health programs, building higher bridges, and rethinking massive environmental restoration projects.

For years, the PR apparatus of big coal and big oil persuaded many key decision-makers that global warming was a phantom—that it was not even happening. As the scientific data proving otherwise has accumulated, the contrarian line of argument has also shifted. Industry voices have begun to admit that the industrial greenhouse effect is real, and some are attempting to argue, like Arthur Robinson of the Oregon Institute of Science and Medicine, that it is actually a *good* thing—that it will enhance plant growth or that it will be of no consequence because the anticipated temperature changes will be relatively slight. Other voices are stepping forward with industry's standard lament, claiming that even if global warming is a bad thing, fixing the problem is impossible because it will cost trillions of dollars, ruin the economy, and eliminate jobs.

The Western Fuels Association (WFA), which provides coal to electrical utility companies, has been a major sponsor of efforts to respin the global warming debate. In the early 1990s, WFA backed the ICE campaign, which attempted to claim that the planet was actually cooling. Its more recent creations include the Greening Earth Society, which promotes that idea that increasing the amount of carbon dioxide in the atmosphere is "good for earth" because it will encourage greater plant growth. The Greening Earth Society has produced a video, titled "The Greening of the Planet Earth Continues," publishes a newsletter called the *World Climate Report*, and works closely with a group called the Center for the Study of Carbon Dioxide and Global Change. Each of these groups has its own separate website.

Another web venture is a "grassroots mobilization effort" created for WFA by Bonner & Associates, a Washington, D.C., lobby firm that specializes in "grassroots public relations"—a PR subspecialty that uses telemarketing and computer databases to create the appearance of grassroots public support for a client's cause. The "Global Warming Cost" website focuses on generating e-mail to elected officials. Between September 1997 and July 1998, WFA claims the site generated 20,000 e-mail messages to Congress opposing the Kyoto treaty. The way it works is simple. Visitors to the home page of the website are invited to click on an icon indicating whether they represent "business," "seniors," "farmers," "families," or "workers." This takes them to another Web page that requests their address and asks a handful of questions about the amount they spend on home heating, transportation, and other fuel costs. Based on this information, the website automatically generates a "customized" e-mail, directed to each senator and member of Congress in the visitor's voting area, asking them to "reject any effort to stiffen the United Nations Global Climate Change Treaty." It's all computerized, and the website makes no effort to verify that the resulting letter is accurate or even plausible.

Using the assumed name "George Jetson," for example, we plugged in an estimate that he currently spends

$24,166,666 per year on gasoline, electricity, heating oil, and natural gas. (After all, it takes a lot of energy to propel those flying cars.)

The computer promptly generated messages to our elected officials. "I am proud to be a worker which you represent," Mr. Jetson stated. "Estimates suggest I will personally see my cost for electricity, for natural gas, and for gasoline go up by $24,239,987.52 a year!"

It's nice to know that the democratic system works. Thanks to the miracles of modern computer technology and sophisticated PR, even cartoon characters can do their part to save America from the eco-wackos and their new-fangled scientific theories.

Disease Mongering

from *PR Watch* (1st Quarter, 2003)

Bob Burton and Andy Rowell

The bulk of the world's drug deals are not done secretively in dark alleyways or noisy nightclubs but involve government-approved drugs prescribed by doctors or bought over the counter in pharmacies and supermarkets.

The global pharmaceutical industry—which generated revenues of more than $364 billion in 2001—is the world's most profitable stock market sector. According to IMS Health, the leading drug industry market analyst, half the global drug sales are in the U.S. alone, with Europe and Japan accounting for another 37%.

While the common image of the legal drug industry is of workers in white lab coats, the reality is that public relations, marketing and administration commonly absorb twice the amount spent on drug research and development. During 2000 more than $13.2 billion was spent on pharmaceutical marketing in the U.S. alone.

Driving the annual double-digit growth in the legal drug supply are a band of specialist "healthcare" PR companies working for behemoths such as Pfizer, GlaxoSmithKline, Merck and Astra Zeneca. Heading the healthcare PR league table are Edelman, Ruder Finn and Chandler Chicco Agency in the U.S. and Medical Action Communications, Shire Health Group and Meditech Media in the UK.

"Medical education" includes cultivating and deploying sponsored "key opinion leaders" such as doctors. Patient groups too can be created or wooed to assist with "disease awareness campaigns" or provide emotionally charged testimony in favor of speedy regulatory approval of new drugs.

Other lucrative revenue streams for healthcare PR companies can include organizing events such as medical conferences that provide a platform for well-trained "product champions" to announce promising results of drug research. Such results can be reported by medical journalists—who can be hired by PR firms—in medical journals that they can create for their clients.

PR companies also undertake conventional lobbying strategies such as opposing restrictions on "direct to consumer" (DTC) advertising—currently allowed in the U.S. and New Zealand—that sells drugs using the same techniques used to sell products like toothpaste.

Add to the mix the usual grab bag of tricks in issue management for dealing with dissenting scientists or journalists and you have the world of healthcare PR.

BUZZ FOR DRUGS

According to Bob Chandler and Gianfranco Chicco, former staffers at the PR firm of Burson-Marsteller, the key to promoting drugs is creating "buzz." In 1997 Chandler and Chicco teamed up to found the Chandler Chicco Agency (CCA), which now boasts offices in New York and London and is ranked among the top healthcare PR companies.

CCA has plenty of experience creating "buzz," having launched Pfizer's $1 billion-a-year impotence drug, Viagra and the arthritis drug Celebrex for Pharmacia and Pfizer, which last year turned over $3.1 billion.

In a contributed article to the trade magazine *PharmaVoice,* Chandler and Chicco explained that "while buzz should always appear to be spontaneous, it should, in fact, be scientifically crafted and controlled as tightly as advertising in the *New England Journal of Medicine.*"

One of the reasons for Viagra's success, they explained, was "Pfizer's sensitive and responsible approach" to encouraging potential patients to talk openly about impotence. To create "disease awareness," they hired celebrities and public officials to talk publicly about "erectile dysfunction," their preferred terminology.

"The buzz spread through the media, virtually eliminating the taboo word 'impotence,'" they wrote. In the U.S., they hired former Vice President Bob Dole to endorse the product, turning Viagra into "success beyond a marketer's wildest dreams."

Impotence Australia (IA), Pfizer's front group down under, launched an advertising campaign with PR support from Hill & Knowlton. The campaign hit a snag, however, when its undisclosed ties to Pfizer were detailed in separate articles in *Australian Doctor* and the *Australian Financial Review*. Ray Moynihan, the author of the *AFR* story, revealed that Pfizer had bankrolled Impotence Australia to the tune of $200,000 Australian dollars (U.S. $121,000). In an interview with Moynihan, IA Executive Officer Brett McCann admitted, "I could understand that people may have a feeling that this is a front for Pfizer."

A later Impotence Australia advertising campaign featured Pele, the Brazilian soccer legend. "Erection problems are a common medical condition but they can be successfully treated. So talk to your doctor today . . . I would," Pele advised.

WHAT WOMEN WANT

While some PR firms work to gain media profile for their clients, others work hosing down bad publicity. In January 2003, for example, pharmaceutical companies were caught with their pants down when the *British Medical Journal* featured an article by Moynihan challenging the use of exaggerated statistics by corporate-sponsored scientists seeking to create a new medical "syndrome" called "female sexual dysfunction."

Moynihan's article was picked up by hundreds of other publications around the world, prompting a hasty response by Michelle Lerner of the bio-technology and pharmaceutical PR company HCC DeFacto. Lerner, a former business reporter for *Miami Today*, scrambled to mobilize "third party" allies. She dispatched an email to a number of women's health groups.

"We think it's important to counter [Moynihan] and get another voice on the record," the email stated. "I was wondering whether you or someone from your organisation may be willing to work with us to generate articles in Canada countering the point of view raised in the *BMJ*. This would involve speaking with select reporters about [female sexual dysfunction], its causes and treatments," she wrote.

As often happens in today's wired world, a copy of Lerner's email was forwarded to Moynihan. He contacted Lerner, who refused to disclose the identity of her client, stating that doing so would "violate ethical guidelines." When we contacted Lerner ourselves, she declined further comment and suggested that we interview HCC DeFacto Director Richard Cripps. All he would tell us, however, is that "I don't want to get into the specifics at this stage."

We also interviewed Moynihan, who expressed disgust with HCC DeFacto's crude campaign. "The participation of the corporate sector in that debate [on female sexual dysfunction] is extremely welcome if it is open. If they are going to try and get their message out there via small community groups without their fingerprints on it, that is just pathetic," he said.

Kathleen O'Grady, the editor of *A Friend Indeed*, a newsletter for Canadian women in menopause and midlife, was one of the recipients of Lerner's email. She told us that she was "surprised, and then very angry . . . They wanted to use our credibility to bolster their public relations. Under no circumstances would we ever agree to such an arrangement."

DISEASE AWARENESS

Writing for the *British Medical Journal*, Moynihan joined physicians David Henry and Iona Heath in warning that drug company marketing campaigns over-emphasize the benefits of medication. "Alternative approaches—emphasising the self-limiting or relatively benign natural history of a problem, or the importance of personal coping strategies—are played down or ignored," they wrote.

Conventional wisdom says that drugs are developed in response to disease. Often, however, the power of pharma PR creates the reverse phenomenon, in which new diseases are defined by companies seeking to create a market to match their drug.

A decade ago, the late journalist Lynn Payer wrote a book titled *Disease Mongering*, in which she described the confluence of interests of doctors, drug companies and media in exaggerating the severity of illness and the ability of drugs to "cure" them. "Since disease is such a fluid and political concept, the providers can essentially create their own demand by broadening the definitions of diseases in such a way as to include the greatest number of people, and by spinning out new diseases," she wrote.

Pharma PR practitioners are sometimes quite candid as they discuss the art of creating a need for a new product. "Once the need has been established and created, then the product can be introduced to satisfy that need/desire," states Harry Cook in the "Practical Guide to Medical Education," published by the UK-based *Pharmaceutical Marketing* magazine.

Sometimes patient groups are created out of whole cloth to boost a new drug that is about to emerge from a drug company's "pipeline." Most of the time, however, drug companies woo existing non-profit patient groups. "Partnering with advocacy groups and thought leaders at major research institutions helps to defuse industry critics by delivering positive messages about the healthcare contributions of pharma companies," explains Teri Cox from Cox Communication Partners, New Jersey, in a September 2002 commentary in *Pharma Executive*. Corporate-sponsored "disease awareness campaigns" typically urge potential consumers to consult their doctor for advice on specific medications. This advice works in tandem with corporate efforts to influence doctors, the final gatekeepers for prescription drugs.

According to Julia Cook of the Surrey-based Lowe Fusion Healthcare, potential "product champions" and "opinion leaders" in the medical fraternity are critical to influencing doctors' thinking. "The key is to evaluate their views and influence potential, to recruit them to specially designed relationship building activities and then provide them with a programme of appropriate communications platforms," Cook wrote in the "Practical Guide to Medical Education."

Recruiting potential supporters to an advisory committee, she says, allows time to develop a closer relationship and evaluation of how they can "best be used." However, a delicate touch is required. "Credibility can also be undermined by overuse," Cook warned. "If you front the same people to speak at your symposia, write publications, etc., they will be inevitably be seen as being in your pocket."

Obtaining favorable coverage in medical journals is also an important element in pharmaceutical marketing. An investigation by the *Journal of the American Medical Association* article found that it was a commonplace practice for articles to be "ghostwritten" for well-respected medical researchers.

Based in Oxford, England, 4D Communications is one of the PR firms that helps, in the words of its web site, to "mix experienced scientists with marketers and creatives to create memorable educational and commercial programmes." According to Emma Sergeant, 4D's managing director, PR companies can help with the "creation of authoritative journals." Indeed, drug company-sponsored publications are so lucrative that in 1995 Edelman established a subsidiary company, BioScience Communications, to "meet the education needs of major pharmaceutical firms."

Journals, though, can achieve far more than touting the benefits of a new drug. Publications can be used to create a market "by creating dissatisfaction with existing products and creating the need for something new," wrote Harry Cook from ICC Europe in a medical publishing guide. "Reprints [of journal articles] can be a very powerful selling tool, as they are perceived as being independent and authoritative." Indeed, this perception of independence and authority is precisely what healthcare PR uses to keep the public from realizing that much of what they see, hear and read about drugs originates from sources beset with conflicts of interest.

In creating or co-opting patient groups, hiring "product champions" and cultivating doctors, PR companies make it harder for citizens to obtain accurate, genuinely independent information to enable informed health decisions. While healthcare PR campaigns are undoubtedly effective in selling more drugs, they don't necessarily make for a healthy population.

The Clorox PR Crisis Plan

from *Toxic Sludge Is Good for You: Lies, Damn Lies and Public Relations* (1996)

John Stauber and Sheldon Rampton

Today, almost every company has in place a "Public Relations Crisis Management Plan" to anticipate and mitigate profit-threatening problems, and the Clorox Company is no exception. Chlorine, the active ingredient in its bleach, has been linked to a variety of health problems, including infertility, impaired childhood development, immune system damage, and cancer. Chlorine is also the basis of many persistent compounds including dioxin, Agent Orange herbicides, PCBs, and climate-destroying CFCs.

In 1991, in the face of a mounting campaign by Greenpeace for a "global phase-out" of chlorine, the Clorox Company turned to Ketchum Public Relations, a premier greenwashing firm. Ketchum's draft plan outlined strategies for dealing with a number of "worst-case scenarios," but failed to plan for the worst of all possible scenarios—the possibility that some conscientious objector would leak the plan to Greenpeace, which in turn provided it to us.

Below are edited excerpts from Ketchum's proposal to help Clorox "present a position that doesn't appear to be self-serving—sometimes using a disarming candor, other times presenting an understandable firmness." As corporations gear up for what one leading public relations advisor predicts will be a "wicked battle" over the chlorine controversy, the following text reveals the rigorous scripting behind their "disarming candor."

CRISIS MANAGEMENT PLAN FOR THE CLOROX COMPANY
1991 DRAFT PREPARED BY KETCHUM PUBLIC RELATIONS

. . . The environmental crises which could affect the Clorox Company can be planned for, strategies to address scenarios flowing from known issues of concern to the public can be established. . . . We have attempted to provide a 'crystal ball' pinpointing some of the issues which could arise over the next year. For each scenario we have suggested different levels of attention and response. . . .

SCENARIO #1:

. . . Greenpeace activists arrive at Clorox corporate headquarters with signs, banners, bull horns and several local television crews and proceed to launch a rally. The demonstrators hang a large banner . . . They release the results of a new "study" linking chlorine exposure to cancer. Two local network affiliates pick up the piece and go live to their noon news with a remote broadcast. AP Radio and the *San Francisco Chronicle* are on the scene and interview three unsuspecting Clorox employees, on their way to lunch, who agree that the safety of chlorine may be in question. . . .

Objective: Make sure this is a one-day media event, with no follow-up stories, that results in minimal short-term damage to Clorox's reputation or market position.

Strategies:

• Announce that the company will seek an independent, third-party review of the Greenpeace study and promise to report back to the media. . . . (Its primary value will be to cause reporters to question Greenpeace's integrity and scientific capabilities.)

• Reporters are invited into the company, without Greenpeace, for a news conference. . . .

• Team begins alerting key influentials, scientists, government environmental and health officials, and others previously identified as potential allies.

• Names of independent scientists who will talk about chlorine are given to the media. (These lists are assumed to already be on file as per Master Crisis Plan.)

• Regarding the employees who raised concerns . . . employee communications efforts will be improved.

• Survey research firm begins random telephone survey of 500 consumers to assess the impact of the event. Based on the results, available the next morning at 9, team will decide further steps. . . .

Scenario #2:

The movement back to more 'natural' household cleaning products is gaining momentum as consumers are eagerly looking for ways they can contribute to a cleaner planet. . . . A prominent newspaper columnist targets the environmental hazards of liquid chlorine bleach in an article, which is syndicated to newspapers across the country. The columnist calls for consumers to boycott Clorox products. Local chapters of Greenpeace take up the cause . . . A dramatic drop in sales of Clorox products within several weeks . . . Congress schedules hearings on the environmental safety of liquid chlorine bleach products . . .

This event is every company's worst nightmare, the company must be prepared to take aggressive, swift action to protect its market franchise. . . . The very future of the product and the company is at stake.

Objective: Restore Clorox's reputation and that of the product as quickly as possible.

Strategy: Use, wherever possible, actual rank and file employees and their families to act as spokespeople to support the company. . . .

• An independent scientist is dispatched to meet with the columnist and discuss the issue.

• Teams of scientists, independent or from Clorox or both, are dispatched . . . to conduct media tours.

• Arrange for sympathetic media, local, state and national governmental leaders, and consumer experts to make statements in defense of the product. . . .

• Advertising in major markets, using Clorox employees and their families who will testify to their faith in the product. . . .

• Advertising campaign: "Stop Environmental Terrorism,"

calling on Greenpeace and the columnist to be more responsible and less irrational. . . .

• Video and audio news release to affected markets.

• Enlist the support of the union and the national union leadership, since jobs are at stake.

• Determine if and how a slander lawsuit against the columnist and/or Greenpeace could be effective.

• Mass mailings to consumers in affected cities.

• If the situation truly grows desperate, the team agrees to consider the possibility of pulling the product off the market, pending a special review, assuming the review can be done quickly.

• Survey research is conducted daily to measure public reaction, changing attitudes, perceptions, etc.

Moderate Case Event: A nationally syndicated columnist attacks the household use of Clorox bleach as a hazard to the environment and calls for consumers to use 'safer' non-chlorine substitutes. . . . The article is picked up in newspapers in 25 major cities across the U.S., but otherwise generates no news. . . . Although consumers are asking questions, there is no loss of sales.

Objective: Prevent issue from escalating and gaining more credibility.

Strategy: Keep media interest minimal; prevent national or state government action.

Action Plan:

• Employee announcement is posted. . . .

• Media strategy Reactive/responsive as long as the interest remains light.

• The columnist is briefed on the environmental safety of liquid chlorine bleach.

• Media tours developed, but they rely more on a "Hints from Heloise" approach that only obliquely mentions that chlorine bleaches are useful and safe.

SCENARIO #3:

At least one scientist advisor to the chlorine industry has voiced concern that the National Toxicology Program analysts could conclude that chlorine may possibly be an animal carcinogen. In light of U.S. regulatory policy, a link with cancer could trigger public concern and harsh regulatory action against this important chemical.

Worst Case Event: The final NTP study analysis concludes that chlorine is, indeed, an animal carcinogen. On the same day of the NTP study announcement, Greenpeace holds a satellite news conference in Washington, New York and San Francisco to launch a concerted campaign to eliminate all use of chlorine in the United States. The news conference receives widespread national media coverage. A number of television reporters use a Clorox bottle to illustrate "dangerous" products produced with chlorine. The Environmental Protection Agency decides to reevaluate and severely tighten its regulations on the use of chlorine in manufacturing, causing . . . negative media coverage.

Objective: Working with other manufacturers and the Chlorine Institute, (1) forestall any legislative or regulatory action; and, (2) Maintain-customer and consumer loyalty.

Strategy: Demonstrate company's awareness that people are legitimately frightened and have questions that need answers, its commitment to getting those questions answered as quickly as possible, and its belief that chlorine does not pose a health hazard to people. . . . Where possible, ignore Greenpeace and don't give it credence. . . . Help people understand that Greenpeace is not among the serious players in this issue. . . .

• Through the Chlorine Institute, third-party scientific experts are brought to Washington to testify. . . .

• Because of advance planning, written material for reporters, customers, consumers and employees is in place with the specific target audiences clearly defined.

• Media briefing with key environmental and consumer reporters and with other interested media are held by industry, company, and independent spokespersons.

• Third-spokespeople are scheduled for major television and newspaper interviews.

• Industry generates grassroots letters to legislators calling on them to show restraint. Letters [are] designed to show that Greenpeace's overreaction is not causing widespread consumer concern.

• Through the Chlorine Institute, continue . . . consumer surveys to determine consumer attitudes and concerns and to develop clear, convincing messages.

• A hotline is established for consumers to call if they have questions.

THEY STEAL
FROM US

with a cartoon by Tom Toles

Corporate welfare and the privatization of public industries and public space—from air travel to national parks—reflect a fundamental falsehood at the heart of the corporate world. CEOs of Fortune 500 companies claim to be against big government. Truth is, corporations positively adore big government—the kind that provides them with subsidies and contracts, lets them trash the environment and exploit our national infrastructure, and helps them exploit workers and consumers.

Drug companies claim they must charge high prices on today's drugs to pay for research on tomorrow's drugs. Guess what: They're lying.

Plunder Drugs: Why Americans Believe They Have to Put Up with Pharmaceutical Profiteering

The Washington Monthly (3/1/04)

Shannon Brownlee

I have only two regrets over the life I led in my twenties. I should have gone on that sailing trip to the South Pacific with a group of entomologists seeking to study the insects on the exotic Marquesas Islands, instead of rushing back to college after my year off. My other regret is once back at school, I failed to heed the advice of the fellow graduate student who told all of us in the biology department at the University of California that we should scrape together every penny we had and invest in a startup biotechnology company called Amgen. Had I listened to him, I might be cruising the South Pacific in my own yacht instead of writing book reviews, because anybody who plunked down $100 in the mid-1980s on Amgen would have shares worth more than $1.5 million today.

Today, Amgen is the world's most successful biotechnology company, hailed regularly by Wall Street and the media as a shining example of the marriage between scientific ingenuity and the American entrepreneurial spirit. It is still headquartered in Thousand Oaks, Calif., the bedroom community of ranch houses and shopping malls an hour west of Los Angeles, where it was founded by a small group of scientists from UCLA in 1980. Back then, the company had no products, no warehouses, no laboratories—merely a handful of investors willing to bet that the fledgling firm could turn ideas into real drugs using recombinant DNA technology. Nine years later, Amgen launched its first product, Epogen, a genetically-engineered form of erythropoietin, one of the proteins made by the body that stimulates the production of red blood cells. Today, the company makes more than $5 billion a year, a third of which is profit, selling just three products. Epogen alone brings in over $1 billion, most of it from about 300,000 Americans on kidney dialysis, who would suffer debilitating anemia without it.

Epogen is truly a wonder drug. It eases many of the miserable symptoms that dialysis brings. But you don't have to be an economist to figure out that it is also incredibly expensive—among the most costly drugs on the market. The federal government picks up the tab for Epogen through the Medicare program that pays for dialysis. The company doesn't try to justify its high price on the basis of manufacturing costs; the recombinant DNA technology used to make Epogen is commonplace. And it long ago earned back its development expenses. Rather, as Merrill Goozner writes, the high price tag placed on Amgen products can only be justified as paying "for the scientists and technicians squirreled away in Thousand Oaks, who are busily searching for the next generation of wonder drugs."

Indeed, that is the mantra that the entire biotechnology and pharmaceutical industry begins chanting whenever the high price Americans pay for their medicine comes up. According to a 2001 Tufts University study—funded by the industry—it costs an average of $800 million to get a single new drug to market. But what biotech and Big Pharma companies don't tell you is that the vast majority of the new drugs they bring to market are "me-too drugs," new formulations of existing pharmaceuticals. They also don't tell you that they did not invest a dime in the basic research that produces the majority of breakthrough drugs.

Americans pay twice for the medications they take. First, their taxes go toward the federally-funded basic research that lies behind most such discoveries. The majority of new drugs are based on findings made by dedicated, hard-working, federally funded scientists in universities and government laboratories, not the research arms of drug companies. A recent congressional report found that of the 21 most important drugs introduced between 1965 and 1992, 15 were developed using knowledge and techniques from federally-funded research. Then the public pays astronomically for the drugs once they hit the market.

Why do we put up with the highest drug prices in the world? Because everybody from doctors to legislators, policy-makers, and patients has been bamboozled into believing that the breakthrough drugs of tomorrow will never materialize unless the drug industry makes an ungodly profit.

The $800 Million Pill is required reading for anybody who wants to understand the role Big Pharma and biotech companies play in driving up healthcare costs in America. This book does for drugs what *Fast Food Nation* did for fast food, peeling back the layers of science, clever accounting, and hype to expose the dark side of the nation's most profitable industry. Goozner, former chief economics correspondent for *The Chicago Tribune*, tells a series of deft and engaging stories about the discovery and development of a half dozen drugs. Amgen's block-buster blood booster Epogen, for instance, was the product of 20 years of slogging work by Eugene Gold-wasser, a soft-spoken, unassuming biochemist at the University of Chicago who in 1977 isolated the protein that formed the basis for the drug.

Then there's Roscoe Brady, the cell biologist who spent his entire career at the National Institutes of Health, taking apart the cellular machinery that lies behind a half-dozen rare genetic disorders and producing the proteins that would later lead to therapies. Brady's first discovery led directly to Ceredase, a drug for treating the devastating symptoms of Gaucher's Disease, which afflicts fewer than 10,000 people worldwide, generally killing them before they reach adulthood. Brady and his NIH colleagues helped Genzyme Corporation, which markets Ceredase, "overcome every obstacle it encountered in the development of [the drug]," Goozner writes. The company then turned around and charged patients as much as $350,000 a year for a drug they would have to take for the rest of their lives. When Congress called Genzyme to task for profiteering, the company's CEO, Henri Termeer, fired back in the pages of *The Wall Street Journal* that the company had every right to charge what the market would bear, because it had risked everything to develop Ceredase. "If we hadn't taken the first step, there would be no market, and no additional research on the disease," Termeer wrote, conveniently forgetting that Roscoe Brady and federal funds had done the lion's share of the work.

In the final third of the book, Goozner uses his skills as an economics and business reporter to full advantage, deconstructing industry accounting methods that allow it to count development costs twice over. He suggests changes to patent law which would close off loopholes that now lead companies to waste time and money squabbling among themselves over patent rights. As one Wall Street analyst quipped about Amgen, some pharmaceutical companies look like great legal departments that happen to make drugs on the side.

My personal favorite among Goozner's suggestions for reform is a new federally-funded institute, dedicated to tracking and comparing medications. I like this idea in part because I suggest the same thing in another magazine. But Goozner and I aren't the only ones who think the National Institutes of Health—or some other agency—should step up to the plate and fund the independent, unbiased research that is desperately needed by doctors, patients, and lawmakers who have been misled for too long into believing that America's health depends upon the pharmaceutical industry staying at the top of Fortune 500.

Corporations are happy with cuts in veterans' benefits, school budgets and health care programs—how else are you going to pay for corporate tax breaks? But they draw the line at cutting the budget for the Export-Import Bank. It's all about priorities, isn't it?

The Export-Import Bank: Corporate Welfare at Its Worst

CommonDreams.org (5/15/02)

Rep. Bernie Sanders

This country has a $6 trillion national debt, a growing deficit and is borrowing money from the Social Security Trust Fund in order to fund government services. We can no longer afford to provide over $125 billion every year in corporate welfare—tax breaks, subsidies and other wasteful spending—that goes to some of the largest, most profitable corporations in America.

One of the most egregious forms of corporate welfare can be found at a little known federal agency called the Export-Import Bank, an institution that has a budget of about $1 billion a year and the capability of putting at risk some $15.5 billion in loan guarantees annually. At a time when the government is under-funding veterans' needs, education, health care, housing and many other vital services, over 80% of the subsidies distributed by the Export-Import Bank goes to Fortune 500 corporations. Among the companies that receive taxpayer support from the Ex-Im are Enron, Boeing, Halliburton, Mobil Oil, IBM, General Electric, AT&T, Motorola, Lucent Technologies, FedEx, General Motors, Raytheon, and United Technologies.

You name the large multinational corporation, many of which make substantial campaign contributions to both political parties, and they're on the Ex-Im welfare line. Needless to say, many of these same companies receiving taxpayer support pay exorbitant salaries and benefits to their CEOs. IBM, for example, gave their former CEO Lou Gerstner over $260 million in stock options while they were lining up for their Ex-Im handouts.

The great irony of Ex-Im policy is not just that taxpayer support goes to wealthy and profitable corporations that don't need it, but that in the name of "job creation" a substantial amount of federal funding goes to precisely those corporations that are eliminating hundreds of thousands of American jobs. In other words, American workers are providing funding to companies that are shutting down the plants in which they work, and are moving them to China, Mexico, Vietnam and wherever else they can find cheap labor. What a deal!

For example, General Electric has received over $2.5 billion in direct loans and loan guarantees from the Ex-Im Bank. And what was the result? From 1975-1995 GE reduced its workforce from 667,000 to 398,000, a decline of 269,000 jobs. In fact, while taking the Ex-Im Bank subsidies, GE was extremely public about its "globalization" plans to lay off American workers and move jobs to Third World countries. Jack Welch, the longtime CEO of GE stated, "Ideally, you'd have every plant you own on a barge."

General Motors has received over $500 million in direct loans and loan guarantees from the Export-Import Bank. The result? GM has shrunk its U.S. workforce from 559,000 to 314,000.

Motorola has received almost $500 million in direct

loans and loan subsidies from the Ex-Im Bank. The result? A mere 56 percent of its workforce is now located in the United States.

In fact, according to *Time* magazine, the top five recipients of Ex-Im subsidies over the past decade have reduced their workforce by 38%—more than a third of a million jobs down the drain. These same five companies have received more than 60 percent of all Export-Import Bank subsidies. Boeing, the leading Ex-Im recipient, has reduced its workforce by more than 100,000 employees over the past ten years.

Here are a few examples of your Ex-Im taxpayer dollars at work:

The Export-Import Bank has provided an $18 million loan to help a Chinese steel mill purchase equipment to modernize their plant. This Chinese company has been accused of illegally dumping steel into the U.S.—exacerbating the crisis in our steel industry.

Since 1994, the Export-Import Bank has provided $673 million in loans and loan guarantees for projects related to the Enron Corporation, leaving taxpayers exposed to $514 million. The Ex-Im Bank approved a $300 million loan for an Enron-related project in India even though the World Bank repeatedly refused to finance this project because it was "not economically viable."

The Export-Import Bank is subsidizing Boeing aircraft sales to the Chinese military. According to the President of Machinists' Local 751: "Boeing used to make tail sections for the 737 in Wichita, but they moved the work to a military factory in Xian, China. Is this Boeing's definition of free trade, to have American workers compete with Chinese labor making $50 a month under military discipline?"

The Ex-Im Bank insured a $3-million loan to aid General Electric build a factory where Mexican workers will make parts for appliances to export back to the United States. This project is responsible for the loss of 1,500 American jobs in Bloomington, Indiana.

And on and on it goes. The bottom line is that if the Export-Import Bank cannot be reformed so as to become a vehicle for real job creation in the United States, it should be eliminated. American citizens have better things to do with their money than support an agency that provides welfare for corporations that could care less about American workers.

Corporations increasingly demand massive tax breaks and other subsidies in exchange for opening, say, a Dairy Queen or Wal-Mart in a particular town. State and local officials go along, giving up huge sums to land a few minimum-wage jobs for their constituents.

Money for Nothing
from *The Nation* (9/1/03)
Bobbi Murray

It was the dream of economic development that inspired officials in Caledonia, Minnesota, to give a Dairy Queen franchise a $275,000 tax subsidy in 1996. One problem: The largesse created exactly one job, at $4.50 an hour. The return on public investment wasn't much better in Pennsylvania a year later when the state—

led by then-Governor Tom Ridge—and the City of Philadelphia ponied up $307 million worth of incentives to persuade Kvaerner ASA, a Norwegian global construction company, to reopen a section of Philadelphia's moribund shipyard. That created 950 jobs that paid around $50,000 a year—not bad, until you calculate the cost to taxpayers: $323,000 per job.

Mercedes-Benz cadged $253 million in state and local incentives in 1993 to build a plant near Tuscaloosa, Alabama. The school in the adjacent small town of Vance lacks the funding to add permanent classrooms to meet capacity, while Mercedes employees enjoy a $30 million training center built at taxpayer expense. The jobs created cost the public $168,000 each.

Despite such boondoggles, it's been accepted as nothing less than gospel that public bodies must give out subsidies to private companies to fuel economic growth. State and municipal leaders dished out an estimated $48.8 billion in subsidies, tax breaks and other incentives to corporations in 1996, the last time the figure was calculated; a more recent figure would likely top $50 billion, says Greg LeRoy, founder of the Washington, D.C.-based Good Jobs First and author of *No More Candy Store: States and Cities Making Job Subsidies Accountable.*

The amount of money is even more mind-boggling in light of the fact that much of it is given away no strings attached—without any explicit agreement regarding the numbers and quality of jobs created, or even guidelines on environmental and community impact. "The stuff that corporations call economic development is pretty shabby if you kick the tires," LeRoy says.

In the quest for economic development, states and

regions lower their expectations on adherence to environmental regulations and what kinds of jobs are created,
frantically bidding each other up beyond the limits of
reason. Municipalities in Tennessee, Alabama, Arkansas
and Mississippi competed for a Toyota plant last year with
incentive packages as high as $500 million. Some of the
alluring offers included free land and the naming rights
for a sports stadium.

In 1998, then-New York City Mayor Rudy Giuliani
championed what may be the biggest subsidy package
ever—$1.4 billion in enticements to retain the New York
Stock Exchange in Manhattan after NYSE officials made
noises about moving to New Jersey. That state's Business
Employment Incentive Program had successfully lured
such big names as Goldman Sachs, Merrill Lynch and JP
Morgan from New York City by offering a total of $710
million in inducements over six years.

The taxpayer's tab on the NYSE deal included a $450
million land purchase, $480 million in cash and $160
million in tax incentives. The NYSE plan eventually unrav-
eled and was declared dead this past February, though taxpayers were still in for an estimated $109 million—just to
bail out.

Surprisingly, Giuliani's successor, Michael Bloomberg,
founder of capital's town crier, *Bloomberg News*, stood firm
against the NYSE decampment threat and has generally
been less than enthused about the notion of dishing out
money to retain companies in Manhattan. Before being
elected he said, "Any company that makes a decision as to
where they are going to be based on the tax rate is a company that won't be around very long."

Nevertheless, after 9/11, the public paid out some

eye-popping sums to retain companies in lower Manhattan. The Bank of New York got some $40 million, while American Express, whose building is adjacent to the World Trade Center site, got $25 million, even after company leaders had already elected to stay.

The money came from $2.7 billion in community development grants administered by the Lower Manhattan Development Corporation, a city/state collaboration that has already doled out some $1 billion to businesses affected by the attacks, including corporate giants. The Labor Community Advocacy Network to Rebuild New York (LCAN), a coalition of more than fifty unions, community organizations and environmental-justice groups, estimates that the terror attacks cost New York 80,000 to 100,000 jobs. LCAN representatives have been lobbying hard for the remaining $1.2 billion to be used to create 25,000 fully subsidized public-service jobs and 35,000 partially subsidized private-sector jobs.

Good Jobs New York (an affiliate of LeRoy's Good Jobs First) and LCAN have only begun to insert themselves into New York's subsidy debate, but their efforts are emblematic of a national movement that's grown up over the past decade to contest corporate welfare, push back-room deals into the light and attach strings to public economic development dollars. Hundreds of activists gathered in July 2000 in Baltimore to share strategies at a first-ever conference of its kind; in November, Good Jobs First and other leading accountability activists will join labor allies in Milwaukee to press these issues at the annual gathering of the AFL-CIO's Working for America Institute.

Activists call it a movement for "accountable economic

development," a phrase that doesn't begin to describe the dynamic range of political work going on, from a campaign in California to limit sprawl while bringing jobs and services to urban centers to a union lockout fight in Ohio, not to mention the widespread push to attach wage conditions to subsidy-based hires.

It's a sign of the times that few, if any, campaigns in the movement call for a subsidies cutoff. The role of government, under unflagging attack by the right for more than twenty years, has been increasingly supplanted by privatization, says Madeline Janis-Aparicio, co-founder and executive director of the Los Angeles Alliance for a New Economy. Opposition to subsidies is simply not winnable in most places, she argues, but public monies used for development give grassroots groups a chance to wedge into the debate and shape it from the beginning, to assess what a community really wants and fight for it.

Some development should be flatly opposed, she says. "There are times when a project is so bad, it should just be stopped in its tracks. Like Wal-Mart. It's a death star, killing all the local businesses." But in general she believes—as does the accountability movement as a whole—in a strategy of engagement. "Public investment is sometimes really needed in blighted communities," she says. "We need the right kind." To oppose all subsidies, she says, would be to "give up our place at the table."

For many organizations, the ground-floor fight is for information. Their battles center on local disclosure measures that require companies to reveal the figures on incentives received and jobs created. Public subsidies spew from so many spigots, it's often hard to identify all the sources and quantify the amount of public benefits any given company gets. The information provides the road map for subsequent accountability fights. Nine states now have some form of disclosure legislation that covers one or more subsidy programs.

The Minnesota Alliance for Progressive Action (MAPA), a coalition of twenty-eight organizations, pushed through the first and toughest disclosure law in 1995, which was subsequently strengthened even further. Minnesota's laws require public hearings that expose the details of subsidy agreements and provide an opening for demanding living-wage rules or other provisions. Beneficiary companies must make public their job-creation goals and wage structures, while the government body offering the subsidy has to report the amount and types of incentives it hands over. "We've got them on record if they're getting a bunch of money and giving nothing," says MAPA executive director Scott Cooper. MAPA is now working with organizations in North Dakota, Wisconsin and Iowa on crafting parallel disclosure legislation.

Stakes were high and the struggle grueling in Ohio three years ago, when an annual tax abatement to AK Steel became the target of a Steelworkers local. The county and city had granted AK Steel in Mansfield a $1.7 million annual tax abatement since 1993; in 1995 the local governments even lowered the hiring requirement from 1,140 workers to 700 and the payroll minimum from $49.3 million to $32.5 million.

So after AK Steel charged its 620 union workers with misconduct and locked them out, "The only way we could generate some economic leverage was to go after their tax abatement," says Tony Montana, a spokesperson for the United Steelworkers of America. The union argued that since the lockout brought AK way below its promised worker and payroll levels, the subsidy was vulnerable.

Unionists first launched a campaign in the summer of 2000 in support of a measure, Issue 7, that got on the ballot due to the signature-collecting work of scores of grassroots activists. The measure wouldn't have directly affected AK Steel's subsidy, but it would have reordered the way Mansfield doled out incentives, setting certain requirements for local hiring, a living wage and disclosure. It was soundly trounced in November after the mayor, the City Council president and the Chamber of Commerce joined forces to raise a $250,000 war chest to fight it. "It's symptomatic of a problem on a national scale," Montana says. "The City Council was more interested in making Mansfield a friendly place for business than making businesses live up to their promises."

Then the union carried the fight to the moribund Tax Incentive Review Council of Richland County, which is charged with overseeing some 200 local subsidies—but which had no regular open meetings and conducted most business by phone. Unionists revived the board, packed meetings of the City Council and county commissions, took their case to the media—and won. They forced the review council to commit to annual public meetings, which now attract great public interest. And in March 2002, the council reviewed AK Steel's performance and cut its subsidy by a third. That December AK Steel ended the lockout.

"It was a long, nasty struggle," Montana says, "and it's still not fully resolved." But, as far as subsidy accountability goes, "if we were able to do it in Mansfield with a bunch of locked-out workers and zero budget, we should be able to do it anywhere."

For grassroots accountability organizing, California is the gold standard. There, a decade-old pathfinder, the Los Angeles Alliance for a New Economy (LAANE), came up with a new accountability concept that has caught national attention in the movement: community benefits agreements. The agreements include job standards and more.

In 2001 LAANE leveraged $29 million in city subsidies to a mixed-use development in a struggling area of North Hollywood to win parks, a youth center and mitigation of problems caused by increased truck traffic. The developer also agreed to pay for fifty spots for low-income children at a planned childcare center and to provide free space for a community health clinic. A new grocery store will be required to sign a card-check neutrality agreement, making it easier for workers to organize, and 75 percent of the development's expected 2,000 retail and office jobs must be living wage. Finally, says Roxana Tynan, LAANE's director of accountable development, "the language around local hiring is the best and clearest that we have anywhere."

In three years, LAANE has negotiated a half-dozen such agreements, whose language is written directly into official city documents. For developers, says Tynan, "we are the pro-growth alternative. If they want to get past the NIMBYs they have to deal with us." Tynan says her hope is to take these individual victories and turn them into city policy.

California's Silicon Valley, once famed for its cyber-millionaires, has also experienced a boom in low-paid and temporary workers. An accountability group there called Working Partnerships USA negotiated a community-benefits package last year that mandated affordable housing, park space and wage standards as part of a housing and retail development in downtown San Jose. Amy Dean, a former labor leader and founder of Working Partnerships, says that winning in San Jose meant linking up with environmentalists who oppose suburban sprawl in the valley but who can be persuaded to support development that provides decent jobs and services in the urban core, where they are needed. "Many of them share our values and understand that 'smart growth,' absent equity, is elitist," Dean says.

Another accountability group, the East Bay Alliance for a Sustainable Economy (EBASE), won a ballot measure in March 2002 that set wage and other labor standards for jobs generated by the $1.9 billion expansion of the Oakland Port and airport. In San Diego, the Center for Policy Initiatives—at five years old, the youngest of California's accountability organizations—is laying the groundwork to challenge the city's head-snapping pace of subsidy approval.

Three years ago the four organizations formed a statewide alliance, the California Partnership for Working Families, with an eye toward pushing statewide policy initiatives. With four strong groups in key locations, the partnership offers the best hope yet for regional "no raid" agreements that will really stick. That would be groundbreaking. A few regions have attempted them before, Greg LeRoy says, citing one between New York, New Jersey and Connecticut in the early 1990s. "But they never really took," he says. "They had no binding authority—the minute a company would play one off against the other, they'd fall apart."

But each of the four groups in the California Partnership has developed what Amy Dean calls "a deep and rich base," built through scoring local wins. They all integrate research with organizing, which allows them to employ diverse tactics: generating large turnouts to hearings and actions and providing expert testimony based on a nuanced understanding of arcane development mechanisms.

Nationally, economic stress may create new openings for organizers. The current crisis in state budgets, the worst since the Great Depression, was certainly helped along by what LeRoy calls "subsidies enacted during the drunken-sailor binge of the late '90s." But fiscal austerity is also encouraging many state governments to rethink their subsidy policies. New Jersey, the feared raider of New York City jobs, suspended its Business Employment Incentive Program in February because of the state's budget crunch. The former Governor of Alabama, Don Siegelman, once an ardent proponent of corporate incentives, became an anti-subsidy crusader by the end of his term. State tax revenues from corporations in Alabama dropped by nearly half in 2001; 619 companies in the state paid no taxes at all in 2000, the result of past cut-throat incentives negotiations. Siegelman began barnstorming churches and unions, attacking corporate tax dodgers, calling them "Enrons and WorldComs."

An interesting connection. Even if most Americans are not aware that subsidy shakedowns debilitate local budgets, they do know the names of the corporate buccaneers who have wrecked retirement plans and kicked the slats out of an already wobbly economy. An agile accountability movement, able to leverage community benefits from economic development incentives—or block them, as the situation demands—has the potential to take advantage of this political opportunity, bringing a skeptical focus to local development and opening the lens to reveal the bigger picture as well.

Corporations like to portray themselves as patriotic—you'd think a bunch of CEOs kicked King George out of America, won the Civil War for the Union and then finished off Hitler all by themselves. But don't patriots pay their taxes?

Profits Trump Patriotism

from *Perfectly Legal: The Covert Campaign To Rig Our Tax System To Benefit The Super Rich—And Cheat Everybody Else* (2003)

David Cay Johnston

It was the last day of November 2001; the Internet bubble had burst on Wall Street, deflating the rest of the market. Gloom spread among executives who counted on rising share prices to make their stock options valuable. But a ray of hope, an antidote to the bear market, was being offered by the big accounting firm of Ernst & Young. It was pitching a get-rich-again scheme that worked *only* because the stock market was down.

Kate Barton, a partner in Ernst & Young's Boston office, smiled nervously as the Internet camera focused on her for a webcast pitch. Millions of dollars in extra fees were riding on Barton's success at persuading clients to act on the next big thing in corporate tax avoidance. So many Ernst & Young clients already were in the process of adopting the plan that Barton called it "a megatrend."

The plan was to have companies move the address of the corporate headquarters to Bermuda or another tax haven, such as the Cayman Islands or Panama. That way profits could be earned tax-free in the United States. Under a treaty with Barbados, U.S. profits could be converted into tax-deductible expenses that would become profits only when the money was accounted for offshore. The company's real headquarters would stay in the United States. The Bermuda headquarters would be nothing more than a mail drop.

This arrangement was all benefit and no cost to companies that bought the deal. The U.S. military would still be obligated to protect the company's physical assets in the United States. American courts would still enforce the contracts on which commerce depends. Companies making the move would continue to have complete access to the rich marketplace of the United States. And all of the other benefits of doing business in the United States—a well-educated workforce, research facilities, the FBI—would be available gratis, the costs shifted onto everyone else, who would have to make up the lost revenue.

On top of this came an extra benefit unique to the executives. They could make millions upon millions of extra dollars just by abandoning the United States, at least for tax purposes.

In taxspeak, Barton was proposing a *corporate inversion*. The move to a tax haven required turning inside out the usual structure of an American company with multinational operations. The parent company in the United States would first create a subsidiary in an offshore location, usually Bermuda. Then, in the inversion, the subsidiary was transformed into the corporate parent, making the American company a subsidiary of the new, offshore parent.

Under this new structure, what would otherwise be profits in the United States could be siphoned out of the country as tax-deductible payments to the corporate parent. The Bermuda parent, for example, could borrow capital and lend it to the American subsidiary. There were rules that prevented every dollar of what would otherwise be profit from being turned into interest payments. But there were other ways to turn profits in tax deductions. The Bermuda parent could impose a charge for management services. And it could collect royalties from the American corporate child for such things as use of the company's name and its logo.

With anxiety mangling her syntax, Barton explained to her viewers across cyberspace that "there is a lot of companies we are working with right now that are trying to migrate this through their board. It is a very positive technique. There are many companies that have inverted historically, including Tyco, Global Crossing and Ingersoll-Rand, just a whole bunch, and there is a lot of companies that we are working with, companies right now, that they are trying to migrate this through their board."

One of Barton's partners, Joe Knott, cheerily noted that companies that had already moved their headquarters offshore for tax purposes had received "very positive press" because their after-tax earnings improved. Barton added, "You can get financing and other aspects . . . so it's a real competitive advantage."

When the show's host broke in to observe that "It is hard to say that there'll be a downside to living in Bermuda," Knott corrected him: "The good part is this is substantially a paper transaction. You are not going to relocate bodies."

The host also posed an important question to the two partners of the Big Four accounting firm—"All this sounds positive; what is the downside?"

Barton said, "There are a lot of big issues that need to be worked through and that's why it is usually a long process that companies will go through analysis on. Some of the issues right now is patriotism. Is it the right time to be migrating a corporation's headquarters to an offshore location? That said, we are working through a lot of companies right now that it is—that the improvement on earnings is powerful enough that maybe the patriotism issue needs to take a back seat."

As Barton spoke of profits trumping patriotism, fires were still burning at Ground Zero, where 2,800 Americans had died in the September 11 Al Qaeda attacks that brought down the World Trade Center towers.

Kate Barton's firm, Ernst & Young, was not alone in recommending a Bermuda address. The law firm Baker & McKenzie was the first to discover this trick. The law firm Skadden Arps Slate Meagher & Flom and the investment houses Goldman Sachs and Lehman Brothers also tried to sell the idea to clients. Ingersoll-Rand's top tax officer, Gerald Swimmer, said all of the major investment houses and accounting firms had presented the idea to his company.

Barton's words were intended for a specific audience, the senior executives of large corporations. But 11 weeks after she spoke, her comments appeared on the front page of *The New York Times*. That set in motion a series of events that would focus attention on the issues of who benefits, and who pays, for maintaining America, on how far executives will go to escape taxes. These events also revealed how duplicitous politicians can be when constituents send a clear message that the politicians do not want to hear.

Barton's words also would lead to a break between the Republican rank and file in the House and their leadership in a floor vote, the only such split since Newt Gingrich and his Contract with America had brought the Republicans to control of the House in the 1994 elections. The tax savings from ostensibly moving a corporation's headquarters offshore are immense. Tyco estimated that it saved an average of $450 million each year after 1997, when it arranged to make Bermuda its tax headquarters while keeping its executive offices in the United States.

Bermuda charged Ingersoll-Rand just $27,653 a year to use it as a tax headquarters of convenience, a move that allowed the company to save $40 million in taxes to the United States the first year, an expected $60 million the second year and even larger sums in the future. Bermuda gave the same deal to Cooper Industries, a Houston industrial equipment maker that is a major Ingersoll-Rand competitor. Five Houston companies that drill wells and service the big oil companies—Global Santa Fe, Nabors Industries, Noble Drilling, TransOcean and Weatherford International—moved their tax address to Bermuda or the Cayman Islands in 2001 and 2002 and will pay little or no American corporate income tax in the future.

These companies were not required to have any offices in the tax haven country they now legally call their home. The laws of Bermuda explicitly prohibit these companies from doing any business there, lest they interfere with the profits earned by locals on their own enterprises or encourage more immigration to already packed little paradises. (Tyco did maintain a small office in Hamilton, Bermuda, because its inversion involved a historically Bermudian company.) David W. Devonshire, the chief financial officer of Ingersoll-Rand, explained that the New Jersey company's only presence in Bermuda is a mail drop. "We just pay a service organization" to accept mail, he said.

Most of the companies that call a Bermuda mailbox home for tax purposes also declare the company to be a legal resident of Barbados. Doing that lets them take advantage of a little known tax treaty with that Caribbean island country.

To qualify as corporate residents of Barbados, the companies merely need to have someone accept mail and answer the telephone there and to have the board of directors jet down once a year and meet on the resort island. Unlike in Bermuda, income is not tax-free in Barbados. It charges the corporations tax on a sliding scale at which the high point is 2.5 percent. The effective tax rate, the real tax big companies pay for making themselves Bermuda or Cayman Islands companies legally resident in Barbados, is 1 percent, as opposed to the U.S. rate of 35 percent.

Congress was not without experience about the use of what is known in taxspeak as *expatriation* to escape taxes. Frederick Krieble, a director of the sealants maker Loctite Corporation, Ernest Olde, owner of the Olde Discount securities brokerage, John Dorrance III, scion of the family that owns Campbell Soup, and Ken Dart, president of the foam cup maker Dart Container, had renounced their citizenship to escape taxes on the fortunes they made or inherited in the United States. Dart, who owed his fortune to American laws that let his firm patent every design detail of every foam cup the company ever made and then pursue competitors who made anything similar in the seemingly generic business of foam drinking cups, made Belize his country of convenience. He tried to move back to Sarasota, Florida, by becoming that country's consul there, but the Clinton administration rebuffed him.

These moves were defended by many of the same members of Congress who found nothing objectionable about the corporate moves to Bermuda. When legislation was proposed to require those renouncing their citizenship to pay up any taxes they owed before leaving, it was denounced by critics as an exit tax not unlike what the Soviet Union did when it stripped Jews leaving for Israel of their money.

Congress did pass a law, however, in 1996, that made people with wealth subject to American taxes for a decade after they renounced their citizenship. The law also limited the time they could spend in the United States to a few months.

What Congress did not do was approve any money to enforce that law. The results were predictable. In 2003 the staff of the congressional Joint Committee on Taxation reported that the IRS "generally has ceased all compliance" efforts to make sure those who renounced America paid the income, gift and estate taxes they owed. These tax dodgers also entered the United States whenever they wanted, staying for as long as they wanted. Not one expatriate covered by the law was turned away by the government at America's borders.

Congress was not the only place where no one paid attention to expatriation. H&R Block, the big income tax preparation firm, is the one company in America that cannot afford any tax scandal, but in 1999 it almost found itself in one. Block wanted to expand into the financial services business, selling stocks and investing the refund checks its clients get. To do this quickly it agreed to buy Olde Discount, which, like Block, had a mostly working-class clientele.

Even though Block sent Mark Ernst, its new president, down to meet with Olde at his home in the Cayman Islands, neither Ernst nor any of the lawyers and investment bankers working on the deal discovered that Olde had renounced his American citizenship. It would not have been hard to find out. The 1996 law requires the names of those who renounce their citizenship be published in the Federal Register, the official report of government actions. Block was saved from embarrassment only because Olde told the company at the last minute on the advice of his lawyer, who presumably worried that not disclosing could potentially expose Olde to some future legal action by Block.

No one knows if Olde paid the $137 million in capital gains taxes he owed when the $850 million deal closed. His spokesman, however, said Olde would pay any taxes required and had no objection to the capital gains taxes. Ernst said he got the strongest written pledge he could that Olde would pay. Yet even if Olde paid every dollar he owed, he still got a huge tax break. Under the 1996 law, if he lived for a decade after renouncing his American citizenship, he would not owe any estate taxes, although the Congressional report made clear that no one was enforcing the tax on people who died sooner.

When news of the corporate moves to Bermuda broke, the companies that were part of Barton's megatrend blamed the tax code for their actions. They whined about an injustice created by Congress taxing the worldwide income of corporations. Congress also taxes individual Americans on their worldwide incomes.

Many of these companies managed to get reporters and columnists and television newscasters to report that their overseas profits were being taxed twice, once by the foreign government and then again in the United States. There was just one small problem with that claim: it was false.

Congress gives companies and individuals a dollar-for-dollar credit for taxes paid to foreign jurisdictions. When Ingersoll-Rand was an American company and it paid a dollar of tax to the Czech government, it lowered by a dollar the taxes owed to the United States. Corporations complain that because of complex rules they cannot use every single dollar of credit each year. That is also true, but misleading. Each year more than 90 percent of available credits are used by corporations. Unused credits can be carried forward to use in future years. Many large companies also have lobbyists making sure that the policy of taxing worldwide income is kept, not abandoned.

In Congress a few members in both parties denounced the Bermuda moves as unpatriotic or characterized them as using a loophole that should be closed. A larger number asserted that the Bermuda moves showed that the United States should only tax profits earned in the United States or that the tax code was unfair to companies.

One of the most powerful members of Congress, Representative Dick Armey of Texas, went so far as to say that closing the Bermuda loophole would be wrong. "This is akin to punishing a taxpayer for choosing to itemize instead of taking the standard deduction," he said. Of course, itemizing generally does not reduce taxes to zero and it does not require people to adopt the fiction that they have moved to another country. And while itemizing deductions by individuals is explicitly allowed in the tax code, the Bermuda move was not approved in any statute. It worked by abusing the little known tax treaty between the United States and Barbados. When that treaty was being considered in the mideighties, at least six senators and representatives warned that it could be abused to pay zero taxes on corporate profits, but the Reagan administration dismissed this as so unlikely as not to be worth delaying approval of the agreement.

The Washington Times, the newspaper owned by the Reverend Sun Myung Moon, endorsed the Bermuda moves. In addition, it also published a column by Daniel Mitchell of the Heritage Foundation, who also worked with the tax cheats lobby, the Center for Freedom and Prosperity. Mitchell argued that keeping companies from acquiring a Bermuda mail drop to escape taxes would be similar to the Supreme Court's 1857 Dred Scott decision, which held that slaves did not gain their freedom by fleeing to non-slave states. That was too much for Senator Chuck Grassley, the Iowa Republican who led his party on the Senate Finance Committee. "Requiring a company to pay its fair share of taxes is not enslavement," replied Grassley, who is otherwise no fan of the current tax system, which he calls "immoral."

Grassley was a tax cutter, but was not in the thrall of

lobbyists who favored special tax treatment for their corporate clients. He was the only working farmer in the Congress, and his years of raising pigs kept him in touch with the idea that businesses should get to deduct real expenses, not ones manufactured by tricks like paying interest to a Bermuda address of convenience.

As for the Bermuda move, Grassley said that "there is no business reason for doing this, other than to escape U.S. taxation."

The real reason? "This is corporate greed."

Grassley held a Senate Finance Committee hearing to chastise Stanley Works, the Connecticut tool maker whose shareholders were being asked to approve a Bermuda move, and other companies. Holding up a saw with the bright yellow Stanley handle, Grassley denounced it and the others for "evading U.S. taxes and making profits off the taxes of middle-class Americans who are paying their taxes honestly."

The White House, quick to chastise individual Americans for remarks it felt lacked patriotism after the September 11 attacks, said nothing about the Bermuda moves and their effect on tax burdens. The White House had good reason not to criticize the Bermuda moves. When President Bush was a director of Harken Energy, a Texas oil drilling company, in 1989 it created an offshore subsidiary that would have allowed it to escape American taxes. During the five years that Vice President Dick Cheney was chief executive of Halliburton, the Dallas oil services and engineering company, it created at least 20 subsidiaries in the Cayman Islands.

When the administration finally did take a stand, it came from Mark Weinberger, chief of tax policy in the

Department of the Treasury. Siding with the corporate tax cheats, he blamed the tax code.

Weinberger, who before and after his government service made his living helping big companies to cut their taxes, said the moves to Bermuda and other tax havens showed that the American tax system was pushing companies to Bermuda. "We may need to rethink some of our international tax rules that were written 30 years ago when our economy was very different and that now may be impeding the ability of U.S. companies to compete internationally," he said. Weinberger said nothing critical of the companies.

There are many tax havens, but Bermuda was the haven of choice for several reasons, none of them related to its proximity to the United States or the American naval base there.

Under Bermuda law, shareholders have few rights to protect their property from executives and directors who divert company funds to themselves or use sweetheart contracts to enrich their friends. Conflicts of interest are tolerated far more under Bermuda law than in America.

Then there were two practical benefits of choosing Bermuda as a tax headquarters. Bermuda does not have law books that neatly organize and arrange the decisions of its court. Lawyers who want to know Bermudian case law must either ask their peers or go through the court decisions in the court clerk's office one case at a time. Even better from the point of view of managements who want to run companies as they see fit without interference from shareholders, there are no Bermuda law firms that specialize in representing plaintiffs against corporations. Bermuda is a country with a one-sided bar.

Of the companies seeking to join what Barton called

the megatrend of acquiring a Bermuda mail drop, only one, Stanley Works, was a household name. Its sturdy saws, planes and hammers with bright yellow handles could be found in most American homes and tool shops. Most of the companies that made the Bermuda move had little contact with consumers because they sold to other businesses. They had much less to worry about in terms of adverse public reaction than a firm like Stanley, whose profits depended not just on the quality of its tools, but on the positive attitude consumers had toward the company. If a company that was a household name could make the move, however, it meant—as Grassley said—Katie, bar the door.

Stanley was based in the Connecticut town of New Britain, a short drive from Hartford down a freeway whose route, locals say, was picked in part to pave over land that would otherwise have become Superfund sites, the soil contaminated with a century of industrial processing wastes.

New Britain used to greet visitors with a sign declaring itself Hardware Capital of the World, a place where huddled masses of immigrants yearning to be free came to the foundries and factories to do the dirty and dangerous work of forging, cutting and bending metal into tools. At many major corporations today, in high positions, the sons and daughters of New Britain can be found, some eager, and some not, to talk about their modest roots.

After World War II, the hardware companies in New Britain closed, one after another. The jobs moved first to states where people could be paid less and then, encouraged by tax rules set by Congress, overseas where workers could be hired for a few dollars a day. When only one big company was left, Stanley Works, the hardware capital sign came down.

Few companies can match the long-term success of Stanley Works. So prized are its tools that it has paid a dividend every 90 days since 1899. In July 1999 the company's new chief executive, John M. Trani, was invited to ring the opening bell at the New York Stock Exchange to mark a century of unbroken quarterly payments to investors. Four hours later Trani laid off 4,500 workers.

Trani had come from General Electric, where he ran its very profitable medical imaging division, and learned his business philosophy from chairman Jack Welch, whose way was to squeeze the pay and numbers of the rank and file and then richly reward executives. "Lean and mean," the critics called it. Trani saw in Stanley Works a fat and kindly company rich with opportunities.

Trani laid off thousands of machinists in Connecticut who made $14 an hour in cash and replaced them with workers in China who he said earned 25 to 30 cents an hour. Even with the cost of shipping metal parts in a UPS cargo jet now and then when production in China and inventory in America were not in perfect alignment, the cost of making products fell as much as 85 percent. Soon after his bell ringing, machinery in New Britain was being packed in grease and loaded onto ships bound for Shanghai so that less costly hands would work the levers.

"There are so many costs to be squeezed out of this company that it will take me years," Trani observed in an interview.

One day in 2001 Trani picked up his *BusinessWeek* magazine and read that Tyco International had cuts its taxes by $500 million by making Bermuda its nominal headquarters.

The article explained in part how profits could be stripped out of the United States as tax-deductible expenses. Trani told his chief financial officer to look into it. What he heard back was that there was no single step he could take to cut costs that would have anywhere near the financial gain of acquiring a Bermuda mailbox.

Stanley Works was almost ready to complete its Bermuda move when Barton's talk of patriotism taking a back seat to profits became news. All that was left was for shareholders to vote in favor of the plan. That posed a problem.

While institutions owned most Stanley shares, the men and women who worked at Stanley Works, or who had worked there, owned the margin of shares needed to approve the Bermuda move, which required a two-thirds majority of shares outstanding.

Workers who had loved the previous chief executive, who drove his pickup to union picnics, said Trani would not deign to speak with them. When he showed up at one event with a driver, the workers thought the man was a bodyguard and took offense.

Mayor Lucian J. Pawlak said the movement of jobs overseas, especially good-paying jobs for people with little education, was not Trani's fault, but part of a Faustian bargain that Congress had made in return for cheap imported goods. "We will be a much poorer city and America a much poorer country as companies move out jobs and machinery, pay less in taxes and take away the jobs that hard-working people without much education used to get their kids into college," the mayor said. But he said the workers did not see the distinction between policies set by the government and a company that was simply doing what made sense in light of those policies. Trani, he said, did nothing but fuel the anger of these workers and everyone else in town.

Trani was not unique in separating himself from the people who made his company profitable, in focusing on financial and production reports and not employees. He was part of a new era of corporate managers, many of them Welch acolytes, who never shook hands with anyone who got grease on theirs, even if they had wiped them clean when their one big chance came to meet the boss. They neither mingled with the people who made their companies' products nor did they appear to think much about their lives. The mayor said his city was left with the economic pollution of jobs going overseas, with people who had put their life into Stanley and had nothing left. "All those guys walking around with missing fingers and hunchbacks made Stanley, but Trani doesn't want to hear that."

Hardly anybody in New Britain wanted to do anything to help John Trani, especially after what he had done at the company's annual meeting in 2001, the first held outside New Britain.

Trani held the meeting in Columbus, Ohio. Union members and retirees hired buses and rode for 12 hours just to attend so they could complain about jobs going overseas. What transpired was an important lesson in how some chief executives regard the people who own the companies they run.

"Where is your American pride?" Nancy Mischaud asked.

"I look at it every day in the mirror. I'm proud to be an American. We just have a different view of the world."

Trani asked shareholders to trust him. "We're on a journey to becoming one of the world's best brands. It's a long journey, not a short trip," he said as he identified some of the 90 new products the company was making, most of them overseas. "The minute we deliver substantial growth in sales . . . we will see the stock price bump almost vertically for a little while. There's no doubt in my mind that we are on the right track."

Workers and retirees walked out grumbling about how they had to endure the lousy bus ride and that, after all that, Trani had cut them off, not even giving them respect as company owners. They said all he cared about was making money for himself. The residue of resentment Trani created at the Columbus meeting posed a problem for him a year later, when he was lobbying investment fund managers and others to vote approval for the Bermuda plan. The problem was that Trani could not win the vote without a big majority of shares held in the company 401(k) plan.

In a letter to employees and retirees, the company said that unvoted shares in the 401(k) plan would count as votes against the Bermuda plan. Many workers said that was just what they wanted so they tossed their proxy cards in the trash.

Then on the Saturday just five days before the vote, a second, undated letter began showing up in mailboxes. This letter stated that any unvoted shares would be voted by the 401(k) plan's trustee "in accordance with the trust agreement and applicable law." Many union members figured it was just more lawyer talk and ignored the letter. Even Donald D'Amato, president of the machinists union local, dismissed the letter as insignificant. At least at first.

On the day before the election, the union leaders suspected that something was up. A member said he had gotten a letter in the mail from the company that said something about the vote, though he didn't understand what it meant about how his shares in the 401(k) plan would be voted if he did not vote them himself. At the union office the officers and a secretary dug through their files for a copy of the 401(k) plan to see just what the plan said about voting rights. No one could remember ever seeing the plan document itself and D'Amato was not at all sure that, even if they did, he would be able to understand the legalese. When the scouring of files was done, it was clear that the union did not have the document. D'Amato slouched back in a stiff metal frame chair, looking overwhelmed, outwitted by men who he volunteered were smarter and better educated than he.

By the next morning, when time for the annual meeting came, the unionists were certain that whatever the document said, the company was somehow going to vote their shares for the Bermuda move. D'Amato figured many workers would take the usual two hours off to attend the annual meeting and could vote their 401(k) shares right then against the Bermuda move. But that morning, when some of the men started to shut down their machines, the foremen came around and told them that if they left, they were gone for the rest of the day—and with no pay. A few men glowered at the foremen and walked. Most, though, expecting that they would be laid off soon and needing to earn every dollar they could until then, quietly stayed at their stamping machines and lathes.

At the meeting in the company's auditorium, in a gracefully designed new building set in a picturesque hollow green with the leaves of manicured trees, portable metal detectors had been erected at the doors. Armed police were everywhere. For the first time in the history of the

159-year-old company, reporters were barred from its annual meeting. Executives escorted some men and women, the ones dressed in suits, around the security devices and into the auditorium. Everyone in the cheap clothes of the working class was made to empty their pockets and purses and, if the metal detectors went off when they passed through, they were pulled aside and fully scanned with wands. When the meeting started, those still in line waiting to get through security complained, but to no avail. Trani told of the glories of the company and how its future would be even better. When he took a few questions, one of those who got to speak was D'Amato, but he lacked Trani's way with words and his point was lost. To a shareholder who complained that this was the only chance for the owners to question their hired managers, Trani said an hour-long meeting, at which he spoke for more than 30 minutes, was all the time shareholders needed. Then Trani announced that shareholders had approved the Bermuda move with 85 percent in favor. "Our shareholders have strongly affirmed the benefits of reincorporation. The global playing field has been leveled and our company is now better able to compete," Trani announced. He said the Bermuda move would be finished by 4 P.M. the next day.

The Bermuda vote, it turned out, had not passed with 85 percent; that was just the margin of the shares that were voted. All of the 401(k) shares were voted, most of them by the trustee. Even so, the Bermuda plan, which needed a two-thirds majority, carried by the thinnest of margins, 67.2 percent of all shares.

D'Amato knew in his heart how Trani had gotten the winning votes. He walked outside where some reporters stood and said loudly, "They stole the election."

Some of the reporters had no idea who the heavyset middle-aged man in the warm-up jacket was or what he was talking about. They did not care to find out, either. They walked over to listen to Denise L. Nappier, Connecticut's state treasurer, who said she was appalled at Trani's arrogance in cutting shareholders off. "It was quite rude. I don't think that's the way to talk to the owners of the company."

There were about 7 million shares in the 401(k) plan and it turned out that the trustee cast unvoted shares in proportion to how all other votes were cast. That meant that had the unionists all voted their shares, then the Bermuda proposal would have lost by millions of shares.

At the White House, Ari Fleischer was asked if the president had any reaction. "Well, I can't comment on any— on one individual corporate action. But the president does feel very strongly that one of the reasons that we need to have trade laws enacted is so Americans will have incentives to create jobs here at home and to create trade opportunities for Americans here at home."

"That is a tax haven there, Ari," a reporter said in followup.

"Sonya," Fleischer said, moving on to another question.

Trani, however, was in a talkative mood, full of smiles and brimming with confidence. "Tomorrow. It will take effect tomorrow," the son of a Brooklyn longshoreman said with glee.

What about the charge that he had rigged the election, that he had tricked the unionists with the April 4 letter? He said the company had corrected that "little mistake" as soon as it was discovered. And what about the second letter's oblique phrasing? Did Trani think that machinists with at best a high school education understood the meaning of the words "in accordance with the trust agreement and applicable law"?

"They can read," Trani said, adding that no one but a few unhappy union members cared because there was nothing wrong with the election. Trani was wrong about that.

Among those who cared about the integrity of the election were Richard Blumenthal, the Connecticut attorney general, and Treasurer Nappier. Blumenthal's staff spent the afternoon drafting a lawsuit.

The next day Blumenthal's litigators filed a lawsuit accusing the company of using "misleading and deceptive information" to win the Bermuda vote. Then they invited Trani over to the New Britain courthouse for a private chat. Trani sent lieutenants, who listened for more than an hour as Blumenthal's prosecutors laid out their theory of how the election was rigged, of what they said had to have been a deliberate plan to trick the unionists. It was a legal strategy pregnant with implications because, were the Securities and Exchange Commission ever to conclude that the election had been rigged, then it could permanently bar anyone involved from being an executive of a company with publicly traded stock or debt. The prosecutors said that every aspect of how those letters to the 401(k) plan members were drafted would be examined. Every e-mail and note would be read, every telephone log reviewed and every executive and secretary questioned under oath.

Trani's lieutenants got the message. They phoned the boss with the bad news, telling him that, if he did not disavow the vote, it was clear that a judge would issue an order stopping the Bermuda move anyway.

Soon Blumenthal was on the steps of the modern New Britain courthouse. Behind him passed some young men with no jobs or prospects who had found themselves in trouble with the law and were coming to the courthouse to get their due process. Blumenthal announced that Stanley Works would not be going to Bermuda that day. "What we've done today is used the level of the law to stop an illegal act by Stanley Works," Blumenthal said, holding high a mahogany bubble level that a different chief executive had given him 10 years earlier for helping the company defeat a hostile takeover by the plastic container maker Newell Rubbermaid. "Stanley broke corporate governance laws that assure fairness, and there is evidence that Stanley Works broke federal securities laws. Stanley Works made a hammer with two heads. One was slipshod, and the other was dishonest. This victory is a major win for shareholder rights, but the debacle has decimated the company's credibility."

And what if the company sought a new vote? "We will critically scrutinize it to stop management's misleading statements about the move overseas," Blumenthal said. "Even before any revote, Congress should close the federal tax loophole that is motivating Stanley Works to abandon America and Connecticut."

Trani stayed in his office. The company issued a statement saying all was well with the vote but that "even the appearance of impropriety is unacceptable," and so there would be a second vote.

A month later, in June, a hearing on the Bermuda moves was held by a subcommittee of the House Ways and Means Committee at which the members treated Stanley Works as if it were toxic. The company, to the relief of the lawmakers, decided not to show up. Representative Kevin Brady, a Texas Republican who never met a tax he felt was reasonable, said that "no one on this panel is defending" the Bermuda moves.

Representative Scott McInnis of Colorado, a former cop who has also made a name for himself as a tax cutter, said he was appalled that corporations would even consider a move to Bermuda while a war against terrorism was being waged. "Focus for a moment on the young men and women who are fighting the war on terrorism" in Afghanistan, he said. "I would like to think that if these soldiers can shoulder their burden, we can expect our companies to shoulder their own fair share."

McInnis said that Trani had come to his Capitol Hill office to seek support for his company's move to Bermuda. McInnis handed Trani a small card imprinted with the names of American soldiers killed in the war in Afghanistan. "I told him to keep it in his wallet and to take it out and look at those names each time he talks about" using the Bermuda loophole to stop paying taxes.

When Trani was asked what he had done with the card, his spokesman issued a curious statement for a company that had in just a few years thrown thousands of Americans out of work and moved the machinery they used to China: "We believe keeping jobs in the U.S. is patriotic."

Some Republicans spoke more mildly than McInnis about the Bermuda move. But when Representative Mark Foley of Florida, a rising Republican star, referred to "apparently unpatriotic" corporations, he drew a retort from Representative Richard E. Neal, a Massachusetts Democrat and a leading enemy of corporate tax shelters and loopholes. "Mark, do you really think 'apparently' unpatriotic? I think they are unpatriotic."

Stanley Works pressed ahead with the revote and Blumenthal went back to court in July, saying that Stanley Works was misleading shareholders again. This time he tried to up the stakes by asking the SEC to investigate the company because its statement on the vote, called a prospectus, contained "conflicting and confusing statements" on how the rights of shareholders would be affected by a Bermuda move.

Stanley Works, in its prospectus for the revote, said that "despite differences, the corporate legal system, based on English law, is such that your rights as a Stanley Bermuda shareholder will be, in our view, substantially unchanged from your rights as a shareholder in Stanley Connecticut." Yet on another page, deep in the document, it said that "because of differences in Bermuda law and Connecticut law and differences in the governing documents of Stanley Bermuda and Stanley Connecticut, your rights as shareholders may be adversely changed if the reorganization is completed."

Accenture, the big global consulting firm, had earlier been much more blunt in telling shareholders the meaning of its formation under Bermuda law. "There is some doubt as to whether" Bermuda courts "would recognize or enforce judgments of U.S. courts against us or our officers or directors . . . or would hear actions against us."

Rigging an election was no small matter to Blumenthal. "The SEC may be focusing on the headline issues of corporate malfeasance and mismanagement" at WorldCom, Tyco International, Enron, Martha Stewart Living Omnimedia, ImClone Systems, Global Crossing and other companies just when it needed to focus on Stanley Works. "The real nuts and bolts of corporate accountability often depend on ordinary shareholders to enforce accountability on management," he said.

The SEC did nothing. It took the position that only a proposed prospectus on the vote had been filed.

Trani's determination to get a Bermuda mailbox would certainly be good for company shareholders. As it turns out, it would also be good for him.

While Americans like Ken Dart who renounced their citizenship did not have to pay what the critics called an exit tax, companies were required to settle their tax obligations on the way out. There were two ways to do this. One would be to tally up the embedded capital gains on the company's books and have the company pay the bill, which no one did. The other was to foist the obligation onto shareholders, who would owe capital gains taxes on the difference between the price they paid for their shares and their value on the day of the Bermuda move. As Kate Barton explained in her webcast, with the stock market down, it was a good time to make the move because shareholders would owe less.

Stanley Works estimated that shareholders overall would owe just $30 million in capital gains taxes because shares held in 401(k) plans, pension plans and charitable endowments were exempt from this rule and many shareholders in the tax system had owned their shares only a short time. Of course, the people of New Britain who had been buying shares for decades would be the hardest hit by the tax.

One person who would not be hit was Trani.

On the day he had planned to make the Bermuda move, Trani was the biggest individual shareowner, yet he would have owed less than $50,000 in taxes, which was a smaller sum than his weekly salary and bonus. Trani owned just 16,688 shares outright and therefore subject to tax and he said that to avoid paying any taxes he planned to give those shares to charity, a move that would reduce his federal income taxes by about $300,000.

Most of Trani's shares were either in his retirement accounts or in the form of stock options that he had not yet exercised. None of these shares would be taxable upon the acquisition of a Bermuda address.

Trani would, however, see his fortune rise on the day of the Bermuda move or soon after because he estimated that the move alone would increase the price of Stanley Works shares by 11.5 percent. That would make the shares in his retirement plan and his potential profits on his stock options jump by $17.5 million. Since he had said that the company would save $30 million the first year in taxes by the Bermuda move, it meant that Trani personally stood to gain 58 cents for every dollar of benefit to the company.

Over time Trani stood to make even more money for himself than the American government would lose in corporate income taxes. If after a Bermuda move the company's stock price doubled in eight years, then all shareholders would experience an increase in their wealth of $3.3 billion. The government stood to lose at least $240 million of corporate income taxes during that time.

Such an increase in the price of Stanley shares would mean a bigger salary and bonus for Trani. In addition, it would make it more likely that he would receive all the additional options he was eligible for under the company's stock option plan. If that happened, then he could pocket at least $385 million from exercising those options, or far more than the taxes the company would save. When these figures were published in *The New York Times* from its analysis of company disclosure statements, Trani issued a brief statement saying they were not correct, but he declined to provide more precise figures.

Trani was not alone in positioning himself for huge gains through a Bermuda move, shifting the immediate tax bill to shareholders and then cutting off revenue to the American government. Eugene M. Isenberg of Nabors Industries, H.John Riley Jr. of Cooper Industries, Herbert L. Henkel of Ingersoll-Rand, and Bernard J. Duroc-Danner of Weatherford International are among the chief executives who stood to also make huge gains because their companies had already made the Bermuda move.

At Nabors Industries of Houston, the world's largest operator of land-based oil drilling rigs, Isenberg stood to gain tens of millions of dollars each year because of the Bermuda-via-Barbados move. His stock options alone stood to gain $100 million in value, compensation lawyer Brian Foley calculated after reviewing the company's disclosure reports to shareholders.

Isenberg also stood to gain because of an unusual clause that gives him 6 percent of the company's cash flow, a measure of profits before certain expenses are deducted. With less money going to taxes, Nabors would have more money to pour back into the business, increasing its cash flow. Another unusual clause, Foley said, guaranteed Isenberg a payment of about $180 million if he decided to retire, became disabled or died.

Isenberg was already paid extraordinarily well. Nabors in 2000 had total revenues of $1.3 billion. Isenberg made $127 million, nearly 10 percent of that, mostly through exercising stock options. His compensation almost equaled the company's profits, which were $137 million, a simply astonishing compensation feat.

Meanwhile, the Bermuda issue was stirring in Congress. A spending bill came to the House floor only after Republican leaders stripped out the provision barring government contracts to companies that had a Bermuda tax address. The Democrats saw opportunity and pounced. For five hours, as viewers watched on C-SPAN, the Democrats lambasted the Republicans as "allies of corporate traitors."

Representative Lloyd Doggett, a Texas Democrat who for years has introduced bills to shut down corporate tax shelters, led the attack. "The Republicans' mantra to their corporate buddies is 'Friends don't let friends pay taxes,' " Doggett said.

Then Doggett, a former Texas Supreme Court justice, shifted gears, saying that the Democrats had become the guardians of business interests. "We need to take a pro-business stance and level the playing field so thousands of businesses that stay here and pay their fair share are not at a disadvantage" to those that avoid taxes through a Bermuda address, he said.

Doggett said that as he spoke, lobbyists for Accenture were in the Capitol working to make sure it could continue to get government contracts like the one it had to run the IRS Web site. Companies that renounce America for Bermuda can win such competitively bid contracts, Doggett said, because taxpaying companies have to bid higher to make a profit.

The Republicans insisted that they were as outraged as the Democrats about the Bermuda trick, but that the issue properly belonged before the Ways and Means Committee. "Allowing committees of jurisdiction their proper jurisdiction is the right thing to do," said David Dreier, a Californian.

After that debate President Bush finally spoke up. "I think we ought to look at people who are trying to avoid U.S. taxes as a problem," the president said. "I think American companies ought to pay taxes and be good citizens."

That day news broke that when President Bush was a Harken Energy director, it set up a Cayman Islands subsidiary to escape taxes. Ari Fleischer, the White House spokesman, said no taxes were avoided, which was true only because no oil was found and so no profits were earned.

A few weeks later another bill came up in the House, about whether companies with a Bermuda mailbox could hold contracts with the new Department of Security, the agency entrusted with keeping America safe from terrorists. The House Republican leadership favored giving Bermuda companies such contracts. The rank and file bolted. For the first time since the Republicans became the majority in 1995, the leadership lost control as 110 Republicans split with the leadership and voted to bar such contracts.

That was enough for Trani, who a few days later announced that Stanley Works would stop seeking shareholder approval to acquire a Bermuda address.

Just before the Congressional elections in the fall of 2002, eight months after the Bermuda story broke, the chief economist for the United States Chamber of Commerce, Martin Regalia, told a Senate hearing that Congress should not act in any way against companies that use the Bermuda tactic. The law requires companies to not waste corporate resources and companies may have a legal obligation to acquire a Bermuda mailbox if it means they can stop paying taxes. Companies that do not get a Bermuda mailbox could be sued, he said, although no such suits have been filed.

On the campaign trail the candidates heard a very different reaction from the relatively few voters they encountered. Among the few who actually attended campaign events, many raised the Bermuda issue, angry that corporations were shirking their obligations. But a funny thing happened after the elections, in which the Republicans won control of both the House and Senate. Congress voted to bar contracts to Bermuda mailbox companies—with a loophole that allowed their American subsidiaries to get contracts.

That was not all that the government did to favor Bermuda companies over those that remained loyal taxpayers. The Department of the Interior and other agencies had specifications for their office door—the kind that open automatically—that required the use of systems sold by Ingersoll-Rand, a Bermuda company. Stanley Works, which also made automatic doors and which was still an American company, was shut out of this government business.

The megatrend Kate Barton extolled has stopped, at least for now. But the underlying effort to enjoy the benefits of selling in America without sharing in the costs continues. A company does not need to make a high-profile move of its legal headquarters to escape American taxes. Sometimes just mailing a letter overseas can make American taxes vanish.

We choose not to educate or hire our young people; instead, we arrest them and turn them over to corporations, which have powerful financial incentives to neglect and abuse their youthful prisoners. Um, excuse me . . . can someone tell me. . . . What century is this? And where is Charles Dickens when we need him?

The At-Risk-Youth Industry
The Atlantic Monthly (12/1/02)
Jennifer Washburn and Eyal Press

I n August of 2000 the National Center for Children in Poverty, at Columbia University, released a study showing that despite the country's recent economic boom, 13 million American children were living in poverty— three million more than in 1979. For most Americans that was unsettling news, but for a small group of publicly traded companies it represented an opportunity. As the ranks of children living in poverty have grown during the past two decades, so have the ranks of juveniles filing through the nation's dependency and delinquency courts, typically landing in special-education programs, psychiatric treatment centers, orphanages, and juvenile prisons. These were formerly run almost exclusively by nonprofit and public agencies. In the mid-1990s, however, a number of large, multi-state for-profit companies emerged to form what Wall Street soon termed the "at-risk-youth industry."

The financial incentives were compelling. In 1997 Sun Trust Equitable Securities, one of the nation's leading investment firms, published a forty-five-page report titled "At-Risk Youth . . . A Growth Industry," which estimated that annual public spending on youth services amounted to

$50 billion. The report appeared shortly after Congress passed the 1996 Welfare Reform Act, which included a provision allowing for-profit companies to tap into child-welfare funds that had previously been reserved largely for nonprofit agencies.

The SunTrust report documented an array of disquieting social trends—including rising numbers of children living with single parents and in working-poor families that from the industry's perspective sounded like good news. "Not only has the raw number of abused and neglected children increased," SunTrust observed, "but . . . the rate of children reported as abused and neglected has increased from 28 per 1,000 children in 1984 to 43 per 1,000 in 1993." A diagram titled the "Privatization Spectrum" showed how companies could profit as children cycled "from the schoolhouse to the jailhouse," passing through one publicly funded, privately run facility after another. Arrows marked the flow of kids to companies offering programs in special education (a $32 billion market), child welfare ($12-$15 billion), and juvenile justice ($3.5 billion). No arrows indicated how these children might one day exit the system and lead ordinary lives.

Today, five years after the release of the Sun Trust report, the prospects for the at-risk-youth industry are less rosy. Claims that contracting out social services would improve efficiency and lower costs have not panned out—and the projected windfalls for private contractors have failed to materialize. Many state and local governments, however, continue to entrust social services to profit-driven companies. Examining the records of some of the industry's leaders highlights the substantial social costs of doing so.

Consider the Pahokee Youth Development Center, a 350-bed facility for "moderate-risk" youth, set on the northern edge of the Everglades and opened, in 1997, by Correctional Services Corporation, one of the nation's largest at-risk-youth companies. James Slattery, CSC's co-founder and CEO, promised that the facility would save taxpayers money while turning out "reformed, treated youths." But in 1998 an independent monitor assigned by the state found inadequate staff training and insufficient medical services, and the Florida Department of Juvenile Justice's inspector general confirmed numerous cases in which staff members had used "unnecessary and improper force" against youths.

CSC—which denied requests for interviews—seemed more interested in finding creative ways to maximize revenue than in rehabilitating kids. Although the state paid the company some $2.5 million a year to provide education, Pahokee failed to maintain proper student records, and for several weeks in the 1998 school year it held no classes whatsoever. A company document has revealed that CSC intentionally delayed the release of ten juveniles so as to maintain the head count, which determined payment. The following year, after Pahokee failed its second state quality-assurance review, CSC canceled its contract, and the facility was taken over be another company.

Children's Comprehensive Services is another case in point. CCS grew out of a Tennessee-based prison company named Pricor, which in 1994 was $10 million in debt. Five years later, in 1999, when CCS was at its peak, it had programs in fourteen states and annual revenues of $115 million. William J. Ballard, the company's CEO and the man largely responsible for the turnaround, is a businessman who specialized in mergers and acquisitions and came to CCS with, he says, "no background in treatment or education" of children. In 1998, at a CCS psychiatric-treatment center in Montana, two suicides and three attempted suicides occurred within fifteen days; allegations in a lawsuit brought by the State of Montana attributed the deaths to chronic understaffing, which investigations by three outside agencies seemed to support. (Children on suicide alert were left unsupervised.) Understaffing and low pay are common cost-cutting techniques among for-profit providers of social services, for whom staff salaries are by far the largest expense.

Ramsay Youth Services, based in Coral Gables, Florida, began as a chain of psychiatric hospitals. Luis Lamela, the president and CEO, is a businessman who worked for Florida's first licensed health-maintenance organization. The one thing Ramsay will never do, Lamela told us in an interview, is warehouse kids—yet he also spoke about Ramay's clients in language that might startle children's advocates. "It's a product-to-market approach," he explained. "We view everything as a product." He then opened a binder he called the "product-market matrix," in which charts displayed sex-offender programs, psychiatric-treatment centers, and other Ramsay services, all cross-listed with states where a rising demand for these services has been projected. Treating neglected children, Lamela said, is essentially no different from manufacturing widgets.

To be sure, problems in the youth-services field are by no means confined to the private sector. In both the mental-health and juvenile-justice fields, in fact, it was government's failure to provide adequate care that paved the way for privatization: a series of class-action lawsuits in the 1970s and 1980s forced states to shut down many abusive government-run mental-health institutions, and the 1974 Juvenile Justice and Delinquency Prevention Act provided states with federal funding to develop community-based treatment services as an alternative to incarceration with adults. A small contracting empire arose in response, with millions of dollars made available to private providers of services. During this first wave of privatization, contracts were awarded mostly to nonprofit and mom-and-pop organizations, many of which pioneered small, local programs in which staff members could develop close relationships with youths. Not until the 1990s did large, multi-state, for-profit companies—some, such as Wackenhut and Correctional Corporation of America, having earlier cut their teeth in the adult prison industry—become major players in the bidding process. They were enticed, in part, by the per diems attached to juveniles, which are higher than those for adults. (Juveniles are eligible for rehabilitative services such as education and mental health.)

When assessing the strength of these companies, Wall Street analysts have focused not on treatment methods or philosophy but on capacity. Investment reports highlight each company's recent acquisitions, referred to as "wins," and tally up the number of new "beds/slots." Although some companies do run a variety of smaller programs, industry leaders admit to a preference for large facilities. "I look at it in terms of size," Luis Lamela says. "What we look for is the achievement of economies of scale."

The trouble is that large-scale institutions rarely offer individualized treatment. According to Barry Krisberg, the president of the National Council on Crime and Delinquency, a substantial body of evidence shows that smaller programs are more conducive to rehabilitation. One NCCD study found that youths from Massachusetts, a state that runs mostly small-scale programs, had lower rates of recidivism than youths from California, which relies heavily on large institutions. In 2000 an array of leading advocacy groups, including the National Urban League and the American Youth Policy Forum, issued a report calling for a shift in resources away from large-scale, prison-like facilities and toward community-based, early-stage treatment and prevention programs. "Along with large facilities comes too few staff for too many kids," Krisberg says. "Administrators start to resort to stringent security measures—shakedowns, lockdowns—and the facility starts to look and feel like a prison . . . There's replication of the conflicts in the streets."

Not only can privatization lead to abuses but it doesn't even necessarily save money. In Alabama, for example, after a 1993 federal court order required that the state improve rehabilitative services for juvenile delinquents, the Department of Youth Services quickly turned to the private sector. Among the companies that won contracts were Ramsay, CCS, and an Alabama-based company named Three Springs. Henry Mabry, the state's finance director at the time, told us that he first grew suspicious in 1999, when the DYS, whose budget nearly tripled from 1993 to 1998, approached him with a request for $24 million in supplemental funding over the next two years. Shocked at the amount of the request, Mabry examined the contracts and discovered not only that empty beds were available in less costly, state-run facilities but also that there were huge disparities in funding rates: some providers, including CCS, were being paid as much as $142 a day per child, whereas others received less than $70.

Almost every private contract issued by Alabama's Department of Youth Services from 1994 to 1998 was awarded without any request for proposals or competitive bids; state records show that Ramsay, CCS, and Three Springs were all clients of the Bloom Group, a powerful Montgomery lobbying firm. And James Dupree, who had been the director of the DYS during the peak period of privatization, became a lobbyist for Bloom shortly after leaving public office, in September of 1998.

CCS was at one point even paid to provide services for children in Alabama who were never under its care: in 1998 a CCS boot camp served an average monthly population of 10.66 children but was paid a flat rate to serve forty. In February of 1999 the Regional Alliance 4 Children, an umbrella group of children's advocates and judges in southern Alabama, learned of this from an internal DYS memo indicating that the department had doubled the program's funding despite a history of problems, including poor staff training and psychological abuse of children. The author of the memo, a monitor named Alan Dodson, expressed disbelief that the state was allotting CCS additional funding, given that during the previous year CCS had served barely a quarter of the children it was paid to serve. Judge Charles Fleming, a member of the Regional Alliance, found the increase particularly baffling in view of the fact that Pathway, a local family-owned program with an excellent reputation, was on the brink of closing for lack of funds. Fleming and other prominent children's advocates, including Sue Bell Cobb, an Alabama judge who chairs the

Children First Foundation, say that, unfortunately, Mabry and the current administration failed to clean up the DYS bidding process, depriving Alabama of much needed programs for at-risk youth.

Such problems arise in state after state. As Elliot Sclar, a professor of urban planning at Columbia, points out in his book *You Don't Always Get What You Pay For: The Economics of Privatization* (2000), states often fail to conduct internal cost assessments to determine what private contractors should be paid, even though there is clear evidence that companies frequently tailor their bids to accord with such assessments. Many states also invest inadequately in monitoring.

Monitoring youth services has become especially challenging in recent years, because in the mid-1990s government agencies began shipping juveniles across state lines. In 1999 Florence Simcoe, a former clinical director at Century HealthCare, which operated treatment centers for mentally disturbed children in Phoenix, told the *Chicago Tribune* that she marketed her company's services to officials in Illinois. At-risk children, she said, were "bodies that we got $300 a day for." Barry Krisberg highlights the problem. "We have less regulation of the interstate commerce in troubled kids than of meat products," he says.

If the track records of both government and for-profit providers are unimpressive, how should we care for our troubled young people? A visit we paid to Youth Environmental Services, a residential treatment program in Hillsborough County, Florida, suggest one path.

YES is a thirty-five-bed facility operated by Associated Marine Institutes, one of the oldest nonprofits in the juvenile-justice field. It houses kids who are moderate-risk offenders—the same category as those assigned to Pahokee when Correctional Services Corporation ran the facility. Unlike many other juvenile-delinquent programs, YES has no fences or locked doors. "I've been in facilities where just to man the security devices—watching cameras, unlocking doors—takes twenty-five employees," Bob Weaver, the head of AMI, says. "We achieve security at our programs by investing in people and keeping staff levels high." YES has one staff member for every three youths. AMI runs numerous other programs along the same model, with intensive staffing, no fences, and an emphasis on rehabilitation. AMI's YES program ranked near the middle of the pack in a 2001 study by the Florida Department of Juvenile Justice, which analyzed costs and recidivism rates; six of AMI's other programs ranked among the top ten most effective in the state.

Back in the early, heady days of the at-risk-youth industry, it seemed likely that nonprofit providers would soon be forced out of business. Their inability to obtain capital from investors or to lobby lawmakers (because of their tax-exempt status) appeared to place them at a competitive disadvantage. But nonprofits have resources that for-profits do not—volunteers, charitable donations, freedom from investors' demands. Although some nonprofit and mom-and-pop providers have engaged in abuse and profiteering of their own, in general they have a stronger commitment to community-based rehabilitation programs than their for-profit counterparts. In many cases, too, nonprofits have grown out of the same communities as the kids they serve. This can motivate them to ride out economic downturns, and they can maintain services without having to worry about quarterly earning reports.

Five years ago Wall Street had almost limitless hopes for the at-risk-youth industry, but times have changed. Although all but one of the at-risk-youth companies we spoke with in our initial research are still in operation (the exception is CCS, which was bought out in January of 2002 and is now part of Keys Group Holding), their profits have stagnated, their stock prices have fallen, and current prospects for growth are uncertain. The problem, according to Bob Weaver, is a basic one: "There just isn't enough money in serving these kids to deliver quality and still turn a profit."

Our programs to privatize prisons are supposed to save us money. They don't—but that's the least of it.

Gilded Cage: Wackenhut's Free Market in Human Misery

from *The Best Democracy Money Can Buy* (2003)

Greg Palast

One of the hottest stock market plays of the 1990s was the investment in hotels without doorknobs: privately operated prisons. And the hottest of the hot was a Florida-based outfit, Wackenhut Corporation, which promised states it would warehouse our human refuse at bargain prices. In 1999, I thought it worth a closer look.

That year, New Mexico rancher Ralph Garcia, his business ruined by drought, sought to make ends meet by signing on as a guard at Wackenhut's prison at Santa Rosa, New Mexico, run under contract to the state. For $7.95 an hour, Garcia watched over medium-security inmates. Among the "medium security" prisoners were multiple murderers, members of a homicidal neo-Nazi cult and the Mexican Mafia gang. Although he had yet to complete his short training course, Garcia was left alone in a cell block with sixty unlocked prisoners. On August 31, 1999, they took the opportunity to run amok, stabbing an inmate, then Garcia, several times.

Why was Garcia left alone among the convicts? Let's begin with Wackenhut's cutrate Jails "R" Us method of keeping costs down. They routinely packed two prisoners into each cell. They posted just one guard to cover an entire "pod," or block of cells. This reverses the ratio in government prisons—two guards per block, one prisoner per cell. Of course, the state's own prisons are not as "efficient" (read "cheap") as the private firm's. But then, the state hadn't lost a guard in seventeen years—where Wackenhut hadn't yet operated seventeen months.

Sources told me that just two weeks prior to Garcia's stabbing, a senior employee warned corporate honchos that the one-guard system was a death-sentence lottery. The executive's response to the complaint? "We'd rather lose one officer than two."

How does Wackenhut get away with it? It can't hurt that it put Manny Aragon, the state legislature's Democratic leader, on its payroll as a lobbyist and used an Aragon company to supply concrete for the prison's construction.

"Isn't that illegal?" I asked state senator Cisco McSorley. The Democratic senator, a lawyer and vice chairman of the legislature's judiciary committee, said, "Of course it is," adding a verbal shrug, "Welcome to New Mexico."*

Wackenhut agreed to house, feed, guard and educate an inmate for $43 a day.

But it can't. Even a government as politically corroded as the Enchanted State's realized Wackenhut had taken them for a ride. New Mexico found it had to maintain a costly force of experienced cops at the ready to enter and lock prisons down every time Wackenhut's inexperienced "green boots" lost control. A riot in April 1999 required one hundred state police to smother two hundred prisoners with tear gas—and arrest one Wackenhut guard who turned violent. The putative savings of jail privatization went up in smoke, literally.

The state then threatened to bill Wackenhut for costs if the state had to save the company prison again. In market terms, that proved a deadly disincentive for the private company to seek help. On that fateful August 31, during a phone check to the prison, state police heard the sounds of the riot in the background. Wackenhut assured the state all was well. By the time the company sent out the Mayday call two hours later, officer Garcia had bled to death.

Why so many deaths, so many riots at the Wackenhut prisons? The company spokesman told me, "New Mexico has a rough prison population." No kidding.

---

* Tell me about it, Senator. In 1985, I was hired by New Mexico's attorney general to look into a merger agreement between the state's electric and gas companies. As the daisy chain of self-dealing by corporate chiefs and politicos began to unravel, the AG's office gave me $5,000 to bury my files and leave the state. I did; it's the only time I've ever taken a dive to the mat on an investigation. There, I've confessed.

My team at the *Observer* obtained copies of internal corporate memos, heartbreaking under the circumstances, from line officers pleading for lifesaving equipment such as radios with panic buttons. They begged for more personnel. Their memos were written just weeks before Garcia's death.

Before the riots, politicians and inspectors had been paraded through what looked like a fully staffed prison. But the inspections were a con because, claim guards, they were ordered to pull sixteen- and twenty-hour shifts for the official displays.

One court official told me that Wackenhut filled the hiring gap, in some cases, with teenage guards, several too young to qualify for a driver's license. And because of lax background checks, some ex-cons got on the payroll.

A few kiddie guards and insecure newcomers made up for inexperience by getting macho with the prisoners, slamming them into walls. "Just sickening," a witness told me in confidence. Right after the prison opened, a pack of guards repeatedly kicked a shackled inmate in the head. You might conclude these guards needed closer supervision, but that they had. The deputy warden stood nearby, arms folded. One witness to a beating said the warden told the guards, "When you hit them, I want to hear a *thunk*." The company fired those guards and removed the warden—to another Wackenhut prison.

Conscientious guards were fed up. Four staged a protest in front of the prison, demanding radios—and union representation. Good luck. The AFL-CIO tagged Wackenhut one of the nation's top union-busting firms. The guards faced dismissal.

Senator McSorley soured on prison privatization. New

Mexico, he says, has not yet measured the hole left in its treasury by the first few months of Wackenhut operations. After the riots, the company dumped 109 of their problem prisoners back on the government—which then spent millions to ship them to other states' penitentiaries.

Still, let's-get-tough pols praise Wackenhut's "hard time" philosophy: no electricity outlets for radios, tiny metal cells, lots of lockdown time (which saves on staffing). And, unlike government prisons, there's little or no schooling or job training, no library books, although the state *paid* Wackenhut for these rehab services.

The company boasted it could arrange for in-prison computer work, but the few prisoners working sewed jail uniforms for thirty cents an hour. Most are simply left to their metal cages. Brutality is cheap, humanity expensive—in the short run. The chief of the state prison guards' union warns Wackenhut's treating prisoners like dogs ensures they lash out like wolves.

Wackenhut Corporation does not want to be judged by their corrections affiliate only. Fair enough. Following the *Exxon Valdez* disaster in Alaska, an Exxon–British Petroleum joint venture wiretapped and bugged the home of a whistleblower working with the U.S. Congress. This black-bag job was contracted to, designed by, and carried out by a Wackenhut team.

Wackenhut did not have a very sunny summer in 1999. Texas terminated their contract to run a prison pending the expected criminal indictment of several staff members for sexually abusing inmates. The company was yanked from operating a prison in their home state of Florida. Mass escapes in June, July and August threatened Australian contracts. In New Mexico, Wackenhut's two prisons, which had barely been open a year, experienced numerous riots, nine stabbings and five murders, including Garcia at Santa Rosa. Wackenhut's share price plummeted.

But there was a ray of hope for the firm. At the end of Wackenhut's sunless summer, between the fourth and fifth murder in New Mexico, the office of Britain's Home Secretary announced he would award new contracts to the company. Wackenhut opened a new child prison in County Durham one month after Texas prosecutors charged executives and guards at Wackenhut's juvenile center with "offensive sexual contact. Deviant sexual intercourse and rape were rampant and where residents were physically injured, hospitalized with broken bones."

Based on its stellar performance in the United States, Wackenhut has become the leading operator of choice in the globalization of privatized punishment.

It wasn't a convict but an employee who told me, "My fifteen months in the prison were hell on earth. I'll never go back to Wackenhut." Those sentiments need not worry the company so long as they are not shared by governments mesmerized by the free market in human misery.[*]

---

[*] Following my initial report on Wackenhut, I was flooded with whistleblowers, insiders and professionals in the incarceration "industry" who piled papers on me, internal company and government documents from three continents, pleading that I keep their names concealed. To be honest, I hated it. I felt weighed down, responsible and guilty as hell because I couldn't report it. There was the story of Wackenhut's juvenile center in Louisiana, where guards beat a seventeen-year-old boy so severely that part of his intestines leaked into his colostomy bag. But that's not exactly attractive television. Editor after editor said, "No thanks."

THEY OWN OUR DEMOCRACY

with a cartoon by Pat Oliphant

It's horrifying that corporations can contribute to political campaigns—it's worse than giving them the vote. Corporations do not have inalienable rights; they do not care about liberty, justice or freedom; they don't care who wins the next war; they are simply an organizational tool designed to amass and safeguard wealth. So why are they running our country?

Michael Jewell offers graphic (literally and figuratively) evidence that our democracy is bought and paid for by the likes of Halliburton.

USA, Inc.:
The Corporate-Government Tapestry of George W. Bush
(2003)

Michael A. Jewell

Our republic was created with the knowledge that the centralization of power is a threat to the freedom of individuals. We are committed to our story that in the United States, power lies in our hands, that our three-branch system of government protects us from the tyranny of greed, that our lawmakers represent us—living, breathing, individual persons—and that our domestic and foreign policies are largely driven by the compassion of real persons for real persons.

But for decades we have heard warnings concerning the influence of corporations on national and foreign policy. As early as 1961, Dwight Eisenhower cautioned: "In the counsels of Government, we must guard against the acquisition of unwarranted influence, whether sought or unsought, by the Military Industrial Complex. The potential for the disastrous rise of misplaced power exists, and will persist. We must never let the weight of this combination endanger our liberties or democratic processes."

USA,INC., the chart on pages 138 and 139, emerged out of an attempt to uncover the actual motivation behind our invasion of Iraq. Although we consistently encounter references to the power that corporations have acquired, the tapestry of corporate-government relationships illustrated by this chart provides stunning insight into the degree to which corporations have become embedded within our government. The story told by this picture is not the story told in our nation's high schools.

Some centralization of power is necessary to maintain cultural stability. Corporations contribute to the efficiency and productivity of our economy. But surely any observer of this picture of corporate-government relationships would be tempted to wonder:

1. Have corporations gained too much influence?

2. Do corporations with board members on governmental organizations (or quasi-governmental organizations such as the U.S. Defense Policy Board) secure unfair leverage in the marketplace?

3. Has corporate influence displaced the voices of citizen voters, thus threatening the integrity of our democracy?

4. Do the agendas of corporations mirror the agendas of individual citizens?

5. How thorough is this weave of relationships between corporations and government?

READING THE CHART

All lines indicate an intimate *and* positive relationship. Like lines on an electronic schematic, they represent flow of power.

Lines between individuals and corporations indicate present or past participation in the company indicated;

usually the individual is a member of the company's board of directors.

Lines between individuals indicate an intimate professional history or relevant friendship (for instance, Colin Powell was once a racquetball partner of Ambassador Bandar of Saudi Arabia, while the ambassador's relationship with G.H.W. Bush is so close that he has been called "Bandar Bush" by the ex-president).

Lines between corporations indicate past or present business relationships (for example, the Saudi bin Laden Group's relationship to both Bechtel and Carlyle).

Corporations (enclosed by ovals) surround the chart. For the most part, these corporations are in the energy, defense, and communications industries. Fox News is honored for its ties to the Project for The New American Century (PNAC) and its role as a voice for the conservative right. A small oval indicates a subsidiary company.

Names surrounding corporations indicate board members.

The Defense Policy Board (USDPB) forms the hub location on our chart because it centrally locates and redistributes power between the energy and defense industries and the Defense Department and the White House. The USDPB has gained increased influence in the Bush administration and advises the Secretary of Defense on foreign policy.

Its members are selected by the Defense Department and its meetings are classified. Many of its members are on the boards of companies that stand to earn fortunes from the policies that these members advocate.

The Center for Public Integrity notes that "The board (USDPB) consists of 30 members, at least 9 of whom are linked to companies that have won more than $76 billion in defense contracts in 2001 and 2002." Represented on the board are: Boeing, TRW, Northrop Grumman (through Johnston & Associates), Lockheed Martin, Booz Allen Hamilton, Symantec Corp., Technology Strategies and Alliance Corp., Polycom Inc. and many others.

Members who are particularly influential and/or tied to the defense industry include:

- *Kenneth Adelman*, former aide to Defense Secretary Donald H. Rumsfeld.
- *Richard Allen*, senior counselor to APCO Worldwide, registered lobbyist for Alliance Aircraft, former national security advisor.
- *Barry M. Blechman*, founder and president of DFI International, a consulting firm for government as well as the private sector.
- *Gen. (Ret.) Ronald R. Fogleman*, on the board of several defense-related companies including Rolls-Royce North America, North American Airlines, AAR Corporation and the Mitre Corp. President and CEO of the Bar J Cattle Company. Chairman and CEO of Durango Aerospace, Inc..
- *Newt Gingrich*, CEO of the Gingrich Group. Former Speaker of the House. Senior fellow at the American Enterprise Institute. Analyst for Fox News. Zealous critic of the Department of State and its propensity for diplomacy and dialogue in foreign relations.
- *Gerald Hillman*, managing director of Hillman Capital Corp. On the board of Trireme.
- *Adm. David Jeremiah*, director or advisor for several corporations that do business with the Defense Department. These corporations have been awarded billions of dollars in contracts with the

Pentagon. Has ties with Mitre Corporation and Technology Strategies & Alliances Corporation.

• *Henry Kissinger*, former Secretary of State. Chairman of Kissinger Associates, an international consulting firm. Former consultant to Unocal oil company.

• *Adm. (Ret.) William Owens*, co-chief executive officer and vice chairman of Teledesic LLC. On the board of Symantec. Former president of Science Applications International Corporation.

• *Richard Perle*, (See below.)

• *James Schlesinger*, chairman of the Mitre Corporation. Former director of the Central Intelligence Agency.

• *Gen. (Ret.) Jack Sheehan*, senior vice president of Bechtel, which received one of the largest contracts created by the American invasion of Iraq.

• *Chris Williams*, works for Johnston & Associates, whose clients have included Boeing, TRW, and Northrop Grumman. Works as a registered lobbyist for defense companies.

• *James Woolsey*, vice president of Booz Allen Hamilton. A principal of the Paladin Capital Group. Former Director of the CIA.

• *Richard Perle* earns a central position on our chart because of his pivotal role as both a leading voice in the PNAC and in the U.S. Defense Policy Board (he was recently forced to step down as chairman of the USDPB under allegations of corruption, but remains a member). His experience includes:

> • Board member of Autonomy Corporation, which receives homeland securities contracts from the government.

- Managing partner of Trireme, a venture-capital company which invests in companies dealing in technology, goods, and services that are of value to homeland security and defense.
- As a member of Trireme and the PNAC and chairman of the USDPB, Perle secretly met with the Saudi businessmen Adnan Khashoggi and Harb Seleh al-Zuhair in an alleged attempt to secure contracts for Trireme (he denied this motive for the meeting).
- Subject of a 1983 *New York Times* investigation into allegations that he recommended that the Army buy weapons from an Israeli company from whose owners he had, two years earlier, accepted a fifty-thousand-dollar fee.
- Member of the Board of Advisors of Foundation for Defense of Democracies (FDD), a Far-Right defense oriented organization. (Other members are William Kristol, Charles Krauthammer, and Gary Bauer).
- Former Assistant Secretary of Defense for international security policy.
- An FBI summary of a 1970 wiretap described Perle discussing classified information with someone at the Israeli embassy. In 1983, newspapers reported that he received substantial payments to represent the interests of an Israeli weapons company. Perle denied conflicts of interest, insisting that, although he received payment for these services after he had assumed his position in the Defense

Department, he was between government jobs when he worked for the Israeli firm.

The PNAC (Project for the New American Century), like the USDPB, occupies an important place on the chart. The PNAC is an activist conservative "educational institution" developed in the early 1990s and comprised of corporate board members, CEO's, powerful government employees, and conservative writers. Intimately connected to the religious right, to the USDPB, and to the White House, the PNAC since its inception has lobbied for a United States foreign policy based on preemptive invasion. Throughout the last decade it has been persistent in its cry for an American invasion of Iraq.

Although its policies were rejected by the Clinton Administration, the PNAC has found a friend in George W. Bush. Bush—with Dick Cheney, a PNAC founding member—has cynically exploited a series of attacks on American interests (including the World Trade Towers and the Pentagon) by Saudi Arabian nationals to pursue the PNAC agenda.

Particularly influential past and present PNAC members include:

- *Vice President Dick Cheney,* a PNAC founder and past CEO to Halliburton, who served as Secretary of Defense for Bush Sr.
- *I. Lewis Libby,* Cheney's top national security assistant.
- *Secretary of Defense Donald Rumsfeld,* also a PNAC founding member, along with four of his chief aides including:
  - *–Deputy Secretary of Defense Paul Wolfowitz,* served in the Reagan and George H. W. Bush administrations.

–*Eliot Abrams*, prominent member of Bush's National Security Council, who was pardoned by Bush Sr. after being convicted of withholding information in the Iran/Contra scandal.

–*John Bolton*, who serves as Undersecretary for Arms Control and International Security in the current Bush administration.

–*Randy Scheunemann*, President of the Committee for the Liberation of Iraq, Trent Lott's national security aide, and advisor to Rumsfeld on Iraq in 2001.

–*Bruce Jackson*, Chairman of PNAC, past vice president of Lockheed Martin.

–*William Kristol*, noted conservative writer for the *Weekly Standard*, a magazine associated with Fox News Network and owned by conservative media mogul Rupert Murdoch. Kristol also is a political contributor for Fox News.

Saudi Arabia earns a place on our chart because Saudi citizens have been nearly exclusively responsible for terrorism directed toward the United States (including the attacks on 9/11). Therefore to understand why we have invaded Iraq it is necessary to understand why we have *not* invaded Saudi Arabia.

There are no surprises here. The Ambassador of Saudi Arabia ("Bandar Bush") has close personal ties with the Bush family, and was a racquetball partner of Colin Powell. Saudi Arabia has a trillion dollars invested in the American stock market and another trillion dollars in American banks. They hold the major source of emergency oil reserves in the world. And, of course, Saudi companies have close business ties to American corporations. For instance, the Saudi bin Laden Group is a major investor in Carlyle, an employer of George H. W. Bush. (As a leading manufacturer of military hardware, Carlyle is in the position to earn millions of dollars as a result of the decisions that G. H. W. Bush's son makes. And incidentally, George W. used to serve on the board of Caterair, a subsidiary of Carlyle.)

CORPORATIONS, CONFLICTS OF INTEREST, AND THE THREAT TO OUR DEMOCRACY

Ironically, corporations are non corporeal. They are reifications: concepts experienced and treated as concrete entities. And although by law they possess the rights of a person, corporations do not have minds and thus cannot feel compassion. They are not attached to place nor are they imbued with specific content. Staff and management can be replaced, ownership can change hands, office headquarters can be moved, logos can be replaced, subsidiaries can be absorbed and sold—even corporate names can be changed. Yet through all of these incarnations, corporate entities carry on.

Since corporations lack hearts and minds, their goals are limited to maximum profit and maximum growth. And even though corporations are populated by real persons, as employees those persons are expected to represent the agenda of the corporation in which they work. This explains the behavior of tobacco companies, of the Exxon Corporation after the Valdez oil spill, and of Union Carbide after "it" poisoned 200,000 people in Bhopal, India. These companies are presumably managed by responsive and compassionate people who love their relatives, engage in genuine dialogue with others, experience themselves as part of humanity, and function with codes of ethics that recognize the sanctity of life. Yet these companies consistently turn a blind eye to the damage, the suffering, and the death that they cause.

Possessing hearts and minds, individuals behave (and vote) out of a complex fabric of ideological, emotional, selfish, *and* selfless motivations. Most Americans assume that the policies of their government will represent that complex fabric of being. But as mere legal concepts, corporations do not reflect the motives of live individuals and they are not guided by the same ethical and moral standards as are our citizen voters. As corporate influence in our government increases it displaces the influence of our citizens; as domestic and foreign policies increasingly satisfy the wishes of corporations those policies decreasingly reflect the wishes of voters. *Even when consistent with the wishes of voters, policies dictated by corporations are corporate policies and not the policies of citizens.*

The problem with which Americans are now confronted is not party-specific. That our voices have been massively displaced in the media, in the election process and in government by the voice of corporations is a reflection of decades of growing corporate influence. However, the administration of George W. Bush has unabashedly adopted the agendas and the policies of the Project for the New American Century and of defense and energy industry corporations. This neoconservative and corporate juggernaut has had its way with the world and with the American people. That the vice president, the president, the president's father, and nearly the entire team of policy makers in an administration are tied to either the largest defense and energy industry corporations in the world, and/or to an ethnocentric, self-righteous, and militaristic "educational organization" like the PNAC indicates that it is time that voters reevaluate the wisdom of offering mere reifications such enormous power and influence throughout the culture.

The threat that corporations pose to our democracy is clear. The tapestry of government/corporate influence illustrated by *USA, INC.* is not a democracy of the people. It is not the democracy envisioned by our forefathers. It is not the democracy in which we imagine that we live. Rather, this tapestry illustrates an integration of church (of commodity) and state within which our voices are often barely heard.

I am a mountaineering guide and instructor. I researched and designed this chart in less than three months in my spare time. The original version has been edited to fit available space. Thus, the relationships illustrated by the chart are merely "the tip of the iceberg." A thorough treatment of the subject would create a far more complex picture. An enterprising researcher and programmer might consider developing a program that would centralize any of the organizations on the chart (rather than just the USDPB) and then reference the relationships indicated. Such a program would not only illustrate the flow of power in this administration but it would offer an opportunity to compare the flow of power in future administrations and thus track the history and development of corporate influence in our government.

The following chart on pages 138 and 139 was designed by Michael A. Jewell.

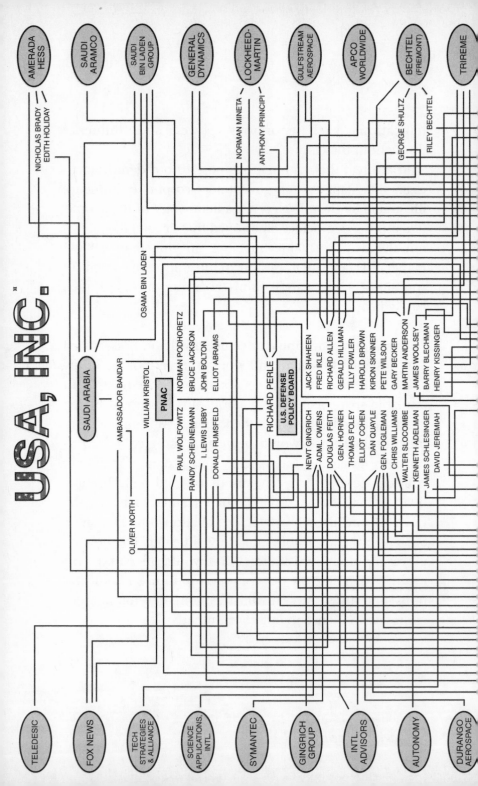

War profiteering is nothing new at Halliburton—but they're getting better at it.

Houston, We Have a Problem: An Alternative Annual Report on Halliburton

(April 2004)

CorpWatch

Halliburton, the largest oil-and-gas services company in the world, is also one of the most controversial corporations in the United States. The company has been the number one financial beneficiary of the war against Iraq, raking in some $18 billion in contracts to rebuild the country's oil industry and service the U.S. troops. It has also been accused of more fraud, waste, and corruption than any other Iraq contractor, with allegations ranging from overcharging $61 million for fuel and $24.7 million for meals, to confirmed kickbacks worth $6.3 million. Halliburton is also currently under investigation by the Department of Justice.

Perhaps most importantly, Halliburton has friends in the highest of places: Vice President Dick Cheney was Halliburton's CEO prior to his taking office in 2000, and he continues to receive annual payments from the company in excess of $150,000. While CEO at Halliburton from 1995 to 2000, Cheney took advantage of his extensive relationships with U.S. government agencies and world leaders that he developed during his tenure as secretary of defense under President George Bush Senior. Through these ties, he helped the company win billions of dollars in government contracts to provide services to the U.S.

military and billions more from international lending institutions for projects ranging from coal mines in India to oil fields in Chad and Colombia.

Now that Cheney has become the U.S. vice president, even more money has flooded into Halliburton's coffers. In 2003 Halliburton earned $3.9 billion from contracts with the U.S. military, a dizzying 680 percent increase over the $483 million it earned in 2002. In Iraq, Halliburton's contracts are worth three times those of Bechtel, its nearest competitor.

Halliburton saw a barrage of criticism in 2003. The company has a much longer history of scandal. Since 1919, when Earle P. Halliburton founded the company with patented technology stolen from his former employer, Halliburton has been involved in controversial oil drilling projects around the world. It was found guilty of fixing the prices of marine construction in the oil industry over a 16-year period in the Gulf of Mexico, and it paid out more than $90 million in claims and fines in the 1970s. In 2002, the company admitted that one of its employees in Nigeria was caught attempting to bribe a tax inspector for $2.4 million.

Over the years, Halliburton has been subject to charges of war profiteering and cronyism. During the Vietnam War, Halliburton's construction-and-engineering subsidiary, Brown & Root Services, was heavily criticized for war-profiteering and lax controls. In 1982, the General Accounting Office (GAO) reported that the company lost accounting control of $120 million and that its security was so poor that millions of dollars worth of equipment had been stolen.

In 1966 Donald H. Rumsfeld, then a Republican member of the House of Representatives from Illinois, demanded to know about the 30-year association between Halliburton Chairman George R. Brown and Lyndon B. Johnson. Brown had contributed $23,000 to the President's Club while the Congress was considering whether to continue another multimillion-dollar Brown & Root Services project. "Why this huge contract has not been and is not now being adequately audited is beyond me. The potential for waste and profiteering under such a contract is substantial," Rumsfeld said.

Since the Vietnam War, Halliburton's military contracts have only increased, and the company is under more scrutiny. As Halliburton President and CEO David J. Lesar acknowledged in a recent television spot responding to taxpayer concerns about its Iraq contracts, "You've heard a lot about Halliburton lately." But we certainly haven't heard everything. Halliburton's public-relations machine emphasizes that the company is "proud to serve our troops," but it fails to mention the myriad ways in which Halliburton has proven itself to be one of the most unpatriotic corporations in America.

This report will document Halliburton's track record in violating many of the values that Americans hold dear, from a belief in human rights and democracy to an interest in transparency and accountability. It covers Halliburton's blatant use of political connections and campaign contributions to win contracts that have allowed it to profit from the war on terrorism as well as the war in Iraq. The report also provides numerous case studies of Halliburton's business dealings with some of the most odious and corrupt regimes in the world. Many of these business deals were subsidized with corporate welfare checks from the World Bank and the U.S. Export-Import Bank (ExIm).

Halliburton's Lesar insists that "criticism is OK." "We can take it," he says. The question is, can the company study the criticism and translate it into ethical, transparent, and accountable business practices? Judging from its track record as documented in this report, it is unlikely that Halliburton will transform its claims of patriotism from sound bites into substance. This report concludes with recommendations that, if enacted, would ensure that Halliburton no longer rips off Iraqis nor the U.S. public. Without such changes, the firm's government contracts should be terminated, and Congress should ensure that our taxpayer dollars no longer go to truly unpatriotic companies such as Halliburton.

HALLIBURTON AND THE MILITARY
Halliburton is one of the ten largest contractors to the U.S. military with several lucrative deals in Iraq: It earned $3.9 billion from the military in 2003, a dizzying 680 percent more than in 2002, when the company brought in just $483 million from the military. Halliburton's business in Iraq is three times as much as Bechtel, its nearest competitor. Just how Halliburton has won so many lucrative contracts from the military can be attributed to one man—its former CEO and current U.S. Vice President Dick Cheney, a lifelong politician in Washington, D.C., who practically invented the modern system of outsourcing American military work.

Early Contracts
Cheney's role began in 1988, when he was named secretary of defense after the election of George Bush Senior.

The end of the Cold War brought with it expectations of a peace dividend, and Cheney's mandate was to reduce forces, cut weapons systems, and close military bases. Over the next four years, Cheney downsized the total number of U.S. soldiers to their lowest level since the Korean War. He also sought private companies to pick up some of the jobs left vacant by the military downsizing.

As a company with a history of military contracting—Halliburton subsidiary Kellogg Brown & Root (KBR) has been building bases and warships for the military since World War II—Halliburton was a natural choice for many of these contracts. In 1990, the Pentagon paid Halliburton $3.9 million to draw up a strategy for providing rapid support to 20,000 troops in emergency situations. After reading the initial Halliburton report, the Pentagon awarded Halliburton another $5 million to complete the plans for outsourcing support operations.

In August 1992, the U.S. Army Corps of Engineers chose Halliburton to implement a plan the company had drawn up under a contract called Logistics Civil Augmentation Program (LOGCAP). The contract gave the government an open-ended mandate and budget to send Halliburton anywhere in the world to support military operations. Although the Pentagon had often used private contractors, this was the first time it had relied so heavily on a single company. For Halliburton, the deal was sweet: The profit margins were lower than they were for private-sector jobs, but there was a guaranteed profit of between 1 percent and 9 percent. Working under this new contract in December 1992, Halliburton began providing assistance to the U.S. troops overseeing the humanitarian crisis in Somalia, putting employees on the ground within 24 hours of the first U.S. landing in Mogadishu. By the time Halliburton left in 1995, it had become the largest employer m the country, having contracted out most of the menial work while importing experts for more specialized needs.

Cheney Joins Halliburton

In 1992, when Bill Clinton was elected president, Cheney's political fortunes at the Pentagon came to an end. But his political connections paid off in the private sector. After spending an obligatory year outside the government-industrial complex (government employees are not allowed to work for the companies they may have done business with for 12 months after leaving their jobs), Cheney landed a position with Halliburton in 1995. This was no ordinary job: Despite the fact that he brought with him no experience in corporate America, Cheney was hired to lead Halliburton as chief executive officer. What he did bring with him was a trusty Rolodex of political cronies and his former chief of staff, David Gribbin, whom he appointed as chief lobbyist for the company.

Under Cheney, the company's contracts and subsidies from the federal government multiplied. For example the ExIm and its sister U.S. agency, the Overseas Private Investment Corporation (OPIC), guaranteed or made direct loans totaling $1.5 billion to Halliburton. That came on top of approximately $100 million the government banks insured and loaned in the five years before Cheney joined the company. During Cheney's tenure, Halliburton also won $2.3 billion in U.S. government contracts, almost double the $1.2 billion it earned from the government in the five years before he arrived.

Not everything was smooth during Cheney's tenure as CEO. In 1997, Halliburton lost the lucrative LOGCAP deal to Dyncorp, a private military contractor that hires out former soldiers and police officers for training and security operations. The financial impact was short-lived, however, because the Pentagon turned right around and hired Halliburton as an additional contractor, paying the company more than $2 billion dollars to manage almost every aspect of the logistical operations at the bases in the former Yugoslavia. Halliburton's role began from the minute that soldiers touched down in Kosovo, where they were met not by their commander but by Halliburton workers who assigned them to barracks and told them where to pick up their gear. The company sent the government extravagant bills for this work. According to a February 1997 study by the General Accounting Office, an operation that Halliburton told Congress in 1996 would cost $191.6 million had ballooned to $461.5 million a year later. Examples of overspending included billing the government $85.98 per sheet for plywood that cost $ 14.06 per sheet in the United States. The company also billed the Army for its employees' income taxes in Hungary.

A subsequent GAO report, issued in September 2000, found many instances of waste: the agency calculated that Halliburton could save $85 million just by buying instead of leasing power generators. The GAO also found that many of Halliburton's staff were idle most of the time, and that its housekeeping staff were cleaning offices up to four times a day.

Cheney Returns to Washington
When the presidential elections got underway in 2000, candidate George Bush Junior asked Cheney to suggest a

running mate, and Cheney modestly recommended himself. When Bush accepted his offer, Cheney quit Halliburton and asked chief lobbyist Gribbin to join him. Gribbin became director of congressional relations for the Bush-Cheney transition team, where he managed the confirmation process for newly nominated cabinet secretaries.

When Cheney and Gribbin left their positions at Halliburton, the company hired an equally well-connected successor. Admiral Joe Lopez, Cheney's close confidante and the former commander-in-chief of the U.S. Navy's Southern Forces Europe, became Halliburton's chief lobbyist. Lopez's first job at Halliburton was a $100 million contract to secure 150 U.S. embassy and consulate buildings around the world against terrorist attacks. In March 2002, the Center for Strategic and International Studies, a private think tank, appointed Lopez to the bi-partisan Commission on Post-Conflict Reconstruction, a group established to develop specific proposals to enhance U.S. participation in international reconstruction efforts in war-torn regions such as Afghanistan, Bosnia, and Kosovo. Other members of the commission included seven senators and representatives from the U.S. Congress, including three members of the Senate Armed Services Committee, no doubt useful friends to Lopez when it came to cashing in on military contracts for Halliburton.

Halliburton's War on Terrorism
With Halliburton's political connections firmly in place and its groundwork laid for military work, the company was perfectly positioned to win more military contracts when Bush announced his "war on terrorism." In

December 2001, when Dyncorp's 5-year LOGCAP contract ran out, Halliburton was awarded a new 10-year LOGCAP contract to support the military anywhere in the world with no pre-set spending limit.

On April 26, 2002, three employees of Halliburton arrived at the Khanabad airbase in central Uzbekistan to begin the first civilian takeover of a U.S. military base in the Afghanistan "theater of operations." Within two weeks, the number of Halliburton employees had swelled to 38, and by June 10, Halliburton employees replaced the 130 military personnel that oversaw day-to-day support services at the two Force Provider prefabricated military bases, which housed more than 1,000 soldiers from the Green Berets to the 10th Mountain Division. Soon, Halliburton employees, who wore khaki pants, black or blue golf shirts and baseball caps, greeted new troops arriving at the base and assigned them to sleeping quarters. Kellogg Brown & Root (KBR) employees were also in charge of laundry, food, general base camp maintenance, and airfield services. Within months, the company took over operations of the Bagram and Kandahar bases in Afghanistan. (Today, Halliburton bills $1.5 million a week to feed 13,000 troops at five dining facilities in Bagram airfield and in Kabul, importing meats from Philadelphia, fruits and vegetables from Germany, and sodas from Saudi Arabia and Bahrain.) Around the same time that Halliburton began work in Afghanistan, other military contract offers quickly poured in. In April 2002, the U.S. Navy hired Halliburton to construct detention centers for prisoners-of-war captured in Afghanistan in 2001. To do this job, the company hired 199 Filipino welders, fabricators, and carpenters through the Manila-based company Anglo-European Services. In less than 24 hours, Anglo-European Services did a job that normally takes two to three months, processing and approving travel and working papers of the skilled laborers. These new employees were immediately flown to Cuba and housed in enormous tents, where they were not allowed access to television, radio, or newspapers, and were allowed to call their families for no more than two minutes at a time. One worker said that while the food was good and the pay sufficient—they were given $2.50 an hour for 12 hours a day, seven days a week—they lived like prisoners. "We had our own guards and could not leave our compound," he said.

Halliburton Joins Iraq Effort

By late 2002, the Pentagon decided that Halliburton could take on an even greater role in the "war on terrorism" and offered the company a plum job: preparing for the war in Iraq. As the White House mounted pressure on Saddam Hussein, the Army Corps of Engineers asked Halliburton to get several new bases in the Kuwaiti desert ready for a possible invasion. In September 2002 approximately 1,800 Halliburton employees began setting up tent cities for tens of thousands of soldiers and officials who would soon enter the country. Within a matter of weeks, the company's employees turned the rugged desert north of Kuwait City into an armed camp that would eventually support some 80,000 foreign troops that were preparing for the upcoming war in Iraq. Halliburton also worked north of Iraq, hiring approximately 1,500 civilians to work for the U.S. military at the Incirlik military base near the city of Adana, where they supported approximately 2,000 U.S. soldiers monitoring the no-fly zone above the 36th parallel in Iraq.

Overcharging In Iraq

On March 19, 2003, the United States and Britain invaded Iraq and vanquished the army of Saddam Hussein in three weeks. Halliburton employees accompanied the troops and quickly began building bases, cooking food, and cleaning toilets. The company's LOGCAP contract was expanded to include hiring engineers to help put out oil well fires and repair the dilapidated oil fields.

The next big contract was to help provide fuel to the U.S. occupation. Although Iraq sits on the world's second largest known reserves of crude oil, its refining capacity is woefully inadequate. As a result, Halliburton was asked to import gasoline from neighboring Turkey and Kuwait— work that prompted a wave of criticism about overspending.

In December 2003, two Democratic members of Congress, Henry Waxman and John Dingell, issued a report claiming that Halliburton was charging the Army an average of $2.64 per gallon of oil, and sometimes as much as $3.06. By comparison, the Defense Department's Energy Support Center had been doing a similar job for $1.32 per gallon, and SOMO, an Iraqi oil company, was doing the same job for just 96 cents a gallon. Between May and late October 2003, Halliburton spent $383 million for 240 million gallons of oil—an amount that should have cost taxpayers as little as $230 million.

"I have never seen anything like this in my life," Phil Verleger, a California oil economist and consultant, told the *New York Times*. "That's a monopoly premium—the only term to describe it. Every logistical firm or oil subsidiary in the United States and Europe would salivate to have that sort of contract." A couple of days later, the *Wall*

Street Journal revealed that Halliburton's subcontractor supplying the fuel, Altanmia, a firm owned by a prominent Kuwaiti family, was not an oil transportation company but an investment consultant, real-estate developer, and agent for companies trading in military, nuclear, biological, and chemical equipment. According to the paper, Richard Jones, the U.S. ambassador to Kuwait and the deputy to Paul Bremer, the head of the U.S. occupation in Iraq, asked officials at Halliburton and the Army Corps of Engineers to complete a deal with Altanmia for future gasoline imports, even if the company couldn't agree to lower rates. In January, Halliburton revealed that it had fired two employees who had taken $6 million in kickbacks from an unnamed Kuwaiti subcontractor for the oil delivery contracts.

Halliburton officials say they immediately told the Pentagon about the problem. "Halliburton internal auditors found the irregularity, which is a violation of our company's philosophy, policy, and our code of ethics," a Halliburton spokeswoman said. "We found it quickly, and we immediately reported it to the inspector general. We do not tolerate this kind of behavior by anyone at any level in any Halliburton company." Around the same time, a new problem surfaced: A previously undisclosed memo from a branch office of the Defense Contract Audit Agency labeled as "inadequate" Halliburton's system for accurately estimating the cost of ongoing work. The memo was sent to various Army contracting officials, and Pentagon officials said they subsequently rejected two huge proposed bills from Halliburton—including one for $2.7 billion—because of myriad "deficiencies." In a briefing to Congress last February, GAO officials described a lack of

sufficient government oversight of the Halliburton contract. Some of the monitoring was conducted by military
reservists with only two weeks' training, and one $587-
million contract had been approved in 10 minutes based
on only six pages of documentation. In another case, the
GAO reported that Halliburton was overestimating the
cost of a project worth billions of dollars. The company
initially told the government it would cost $2.7 billion to
provide food and other logistics services to the military in
Iraq. But following questioning by the Defense Department, company officials slashed the estimate for the work
to $2 billion without explaining how they had arrived at
the new figure.

As a result of these claims, the Defense Criminal Investigation Service, a federal agency, launched an ongoing
investigation into the fuel overcharging, and Halliburton
officials announced that they would suspend billing the
government. The company also stopped payment to its
subcontractors for invoices totaling $500 million.

Unanswered Questions

Despite these investigations into alleged over-charging,
Halliburton's unique role as sole provider of support services to the U.S. military has not been called into question
by the government. One fundamental question still must
be asked: Has the military taken what was clearly intended
to be a cost-saving emergency measure and turned it into
a boondoggle that will end up costing taxpayers more
than we would have paid under the original system?

Secondly, has this system of outsourcing military work
changed the dynamic of war? Sam Gardiner, a retired Air
Force colonel who has taught at the National War College,

estimates that if it was not for companies like Halliburton, the U.S. military would need twice as many solidiers in Iraq. "It makes it too easy to go to war," he told *The New Yorker.* "When you can hire people to go to war, there's none of the grumbling and the political friction." He noted that much of the grunt work now contracted out to firms like Halliburton was traditionally performed by reserve soldiers, who often complain the loudest.

Finally, we also need to ask if this massive contract was a sweetheart deal for the well-connected company.

OPERATION HALLIBURTON:

A LOOK INSIDE THE COMPANY'S DAY-TO-DAY PRACTICES IN IRAQ

Ever since Halliburton scored its first military contract in Iraq in 2003, the company has suffered criticism over its practices as a contractor. Here's a look at some of the ways in which Halliburton's daily work doesn't measure up.

Dirty Dishes, Dirty Books

In late 2003, NBC news aired a story about Halliburton's unsanitary kitchen practices. According to NBC, the Pentagon has repeatedly warned Halliburton that the food it served to U.S. troops in Iraq was "dirty," as were the kitchens it was served in. The Pentagon reported finding blood all over the floor; dirty pans, grills, and salad bars; and rotting meats and vegetables in four military messes that Halliburton operates in Iraq.

Even the mess hall where Bush served troops their Thanksgiving dinner was dirty in August, September, and October, according to NBC. Halliburton's promises to improve "have not been followed through," according to the Pentagon report that warned "serious repercussions may result" if the contractor did not clean up.

In December 2003, Halliburton told NBC that it had served 21 million meals to the 110,000 troops at 45 sites in Iraq. But military auditors have begun to suspect that the company might be overcharging the government millions of dollars. In February, the *Wall Street Journal* reported that Halliburton may have overcharged taxpayers by more than $16 million for meals to U.S. troops serving to Operation Iraqi Freedom for the first seven months of 2003. In July 2003, for instance, Halliburton billed for 42,042 meals a day but served only 14,053 meals daily.

Melissa Norcross, a spokesperson for Halliburton's Middle East region, defended the company's practices with an explanation from Randy Harl, CEO of Halliburton subsidiary, Kellogg, Brown & Root: "For example, commanders do not want troops 'signing in' for meals due to the concern for safety of the soldiers; nor do they want troops waiting in lines to get fed." Norcross also claimed that the "dirty kitchen" problems have been taken care of, and the facilities have since passed subsequent inspections.

Cheap Labor

According to the military, the government outsources work to Halliburton in order to save money in certain areas such as labor. "When we go contract, we don't have to pay health care and all the other things for the employees; that's up to the employer," explained Major Toni Kemper, public affairs director at the Incirlik base in Turkey.

But Halliburton's labor practices are questionable: Instead of paying expensive U.S. soldiers, Halliburton

imports cheaper Third World workers through subcontractors. For example, Kuwait-based Al Musairie company
supplies South Asian workers to set up temporary military
bases in Iraq; Kuwait-based Al Kharafi supplies South
Asian workers for the oil fields; and Saudi Arabia-based
Tamimi Corporation supplies South Asian cooks for the
military chow halls in Iraq.

These South Asian workers get approximately $300 a
month—including overtime and hazard pay. This is twice
as much as the Iraqi workers who make $150 a month,
but far below the $8,000 per month Halliburton pays
unskilled workers from Texas. Halliburton and the military justify the wage discrepancy by arguing that they do
not trust local workers to do certain jobs, fearing that they
might poison, kick out, or kill their colonial bosses.

But this huge disparity in wages has sparked resentment
from local workers, Hassan Jum'a, the leader of the South
Oil Company union in Iraq, staged strikes to kick out the
foreign workers. The company's anti-labor practices elsewhere have also spurred controversy. In the Philippines,
Halliburton was slapped with a $600 million lawsuit for
refusing to allow workers hired for the construction of a
204-unit detention camp at Guantanamo Bay, Cuba, to
form a union.

A Former Halliburton Employee Blows the Whistle on Overspending

Henry Bunting, a Vietnam veteran who worked as a purchasing and planning professional for a number of companies, went to work for Halliburton at the Khalifa resort
in Kuwait in early May 2003. He quit in mid-August

because he was "completely worn out" from working 12-to 16-hour days.

On February 13, 2004, Burning testified before a panel of Senate Democrats about his experience purchasing products for Halliburton, Bunting brought with him an embroidered orange towel used at an exercise facility for U.S. troops in Baghdad that he said Halliburton insisted on buying for $5 apiece, rather than spending $1.60 each for ordinary towels.

He described what he observed during the purchasing of the towels: "There were old quotes for ordinary towels. The MWR (Morale, Welfare, Recreation) manager changed the requisition by requesting upgraded towels with an embroidered MWR Baghdad logo. He insisted on this embroidery, which you can see from this towel. The normal procurement practice should be that if you change the requirements, you re-quote the job. The MWR manager pressured both the procurement supervisor and manager to place the order without another quote. I advised my supervisor of the situation but resigned before the issue was resolved. I assume the order for embroidered towels was placed without re-quoting."

Senator Richard Durbin (D-Ill), who was attending the hearing, did a quick calculation and determined that the additional cost for the embroidered towels would have paid for 12 suits of body armor, which were in short supply for soldiers who were sent to Iraq.

According to Bunting and other whistle-blowers who spoke on condition of anonymity, Halliburton officials routinely insisted that the buyers use suppliers that had worked for the company in the past, even if they didn't offer the best prices. While it is common for companies to use reliable suppliers rather than the cheapest provider, the buyers quickly discovered that the suppliers weren't reliable. One whistleblower speculated that these were favors to suppliers that Halliburton had used in Bosnia.

Bunting explained to the senators that there are three levels of procurement staffing at Halliburton: "Buyers are responsible for ordering materials to fill requisitions from Halliburton employees. We would find a vendor who could provide the needed item and prepare a purchase order. Procurement supervisors were responsible for the day-to-day operation of the procurement section. The procurement, materials, and property manager was a step above them.

"A list of suppliers was provided by the procurement supervisor. It was just a list of names with addresses and telephone numbers. We were instructed to use this preferred supplier list to fill requisitions. As suppliers were contacted, commodities/product information was added. However, we found out over time that many of the suppliers were noncompetitive in pricing, late in quoting, and even later in delivery."

"While working at Halliburton, I observed several problematic business practices. For purchase orders under $2,500, buyers only needed to solicit one quote from one vendor. To avoid competitive bidding, requisitions were quoted individually and later combined into purchase orders under $2,500. About 70 to 75 percent of the requisitions processed ended up being under $2,500. Requisitions were split to avoid having to get two quotes."

* * *

HALLIBURTON AROUND THE WORLD

> *"The problem is that the good Lord didn't see fit to put oil and gas reserves where there are democratically elected regimes friendly to the interests of the United States."*
> —Dick Cheney, then-CEO of Halliburton, 1996

> *"We hope Iraq will be the first domino and that Libya and Iran will follow. We don't like being kept out of markets because it gives our competitors an unfair advantage."*
> —John Gibson, chief executive of Halliburton's Energy Service Group 2003.

Halliburton has created partnerships with some of the world's most notorious governments in countries such as Angola, Burma, and Nigeria.

U.S. lawmakers, human rights activists and the company's own shareholders want to know how Halliburton has been able to sidestep federal laws aimed at keeping U.S. companies from doing business in countries that support terrorism, including Iran—a member of the Bush administration's so-called "axis of evil." This section examines some of Halliburton's work with these regimes around the world.

Nigeria

In May of 2003, Halliburton reported to the Security Exchange Commission (SEC) that company employees made $2.4 million in "improper payments" to officials of Nigeria's Federal Inland Revenue Service in 2001 and 2002 "to obtain favorable tax treatment." "Based on the findings of the investigation we have terminated several employees," Halliburton said in the filing, adding that none of its senior officers was involved. But the *Houston Chronicle* later pointed out, "left unanswered is how a 'low-level employee' could channel that much money from the company to the pockets of a corrupt official."

The second case, also associated with Halliburton's activities in Nigeria, is more complicated and potentially much more controversial. It dates back to the early 1990s, and involves an international consortium of four companies led by Halliburton subsidiary Kellogg Brown & Root. The other companies involved are from France (Technip), Italy (Snamprogetti SpA), and Japan (Japan Gasoline Corp.). Together, the companies formed a joint venture called TSKJ, which won a lucrative contract from international oil companies to build a large liquefied natural gas (LNG) plant on Bonny Island in the eastern Niger delta.

According to news reports the TSKJ incorporated a subsidiary (LNG Services) in the Portuguese tax-haven Madeira. LNG paid at least $180 million for "commercial support services" into a score of offshore bank accounts controlled by Gibraltar-based TriStar Corporation. Jeffrey Tesler, a British lawyer connected to Halliburton and the only TriStar official that could be identified, in turn allegedly transferred the money through TriStar and another set of bank accounts that he controlled in Switzerland and Monaco. It is not known where the money ultimately ended up, but Tesler was reportedly also a financial adviser to Nigeria's late dictator, General Sani Abacha. Georges Krammer, a former top Technip official, has testified to French investigators that Halliburton imposed Tesler as an intermediary over the objections of Technip.

French police launched a preliminary probe into the French company's activities in October 2002. In June 2003, the prosecutor in the preliminary investigation saw enough merit in the case to assign it to Renaud van Ruymbeke, a French anti-corruption investigating judge with a reputation for probity and independence. Van Ruymbeke opened a formal investigation in October 2003 and suggested that he may summon Cheney to France to be questioned. The Nigerian government, the U.S. Justice Department, and the SEC have also opened their own investigations.

Saddam's Iraq

During the 2000 campaign, Cheney claimed he saw Iraq differently than the other countries. In an August 2000 segment of ABC's *This Week* news program, he told Sam Donaldson, "I had a firm policy that I wouldn't do anything in Iraq—even arrangements that were supposedly legal. We've not done any business in Iraq since U.N. sanctions were imposed on Iraq in 1990, and I had a standing policy that I wouldn't do that."

Yet the *Washington Post* reported in January 2001 that, according to oil industry executives and confidential UN records, Halliburton held stakes in two companies—Dresser Rand and Ingersoll-Dresser Pump—which signed contracts to sell more than $73 million in oil production equipment and spare parts to Iraq from the first half of 1997 to the summer of 2000—while Cheney was chairman and CEO of the company. Apart from complying with the law, the executives told the Post, there was no specific policy related to the issue at Halliburton, as Cheney had claimed.

"Most American companies were blacklisted" by the Iraqi regime, a UN diplomat told *The New Yorker.* "It's rather surprising to find Halliburton doing business with Saddam. It would have been very much a senior-level decision, made by the regime at the top."

Halliburton's presence in Iraq ended in February 2000. The company was also among more than a dozen American companies that supplied Iraq's petroleum industry with spare parts and retooled its oilrigs when U.N. sanctions were eased in 1998.

Iran

In 1995, President Clinton passed an executive order barring U.S. investment in Iran's energy sector. In 1996, Congress passed the Iran-Libya Sanctions Act, which seeks to punish non-U.S. oil companies that invest $20 million or more in either country, and which has been a source of friction with key U.S. allies, including France, Germany, Russia, and the UK.

In a letter to New York City's fire and police pension fund managers, who used Halliburton's shareholder meetings to question the company's involvement in Iran, Halliburton explained that Halliburton Products and Services, a Cayman islands company headquartered in Dubai, made more than $39 million in 2003 (a $10 million increase from 2002) by selling oil-field services to customers in Iran.

When investigators from the CBS news show *60 Minutes* visited the Cayman Islands address where Halliburton Products and Services is incorporated, they discovered a "brass plate" operation with no employees. The company's agent—the Calidonian Bank—forwards all of the company's mail to Halliburton's offices in Houston—an indication that key business decisions are made in Houston and not Dubai or the Cayman Islands. The news show also reported that Halliburton's operations in Dubai share the same address, telephone, and fax numbers as Halliburton Products and Services—indicating that the companies do not function separately.

Other companies have ceased their operations in Iran after shareholders began to raise questions. ConocoPhillips, for instance, agreed to cut its business connections with Iran and Syria in February 2002. But Halliburton has yet to announce any changes in its policies and maintains that its operations do not violate any laws.

In February, Halliburton disclosed that the Treasury Department's Office of Foreign Asset Control had reopened a 2001 inquiry into the company's operations in Iran. Meanwhile, in early March the SEC's new Office of Global Security Risk announced that it would be hiring five full-time staff to look at companies with ties to rogue nations.

In the meantime, Halliburton has been lobbying heavily against the sanctions. During Cheney's tenure, Halliburton was a leading member of USA Engage, a lobbying group of some 670 companies organized to oppose U.S. unilateral sanctions policies. Since 2001, USA Engage has continued to work against the sanctions, working with sympathetic individuals within the Bush administration, including Cheney's chief of staff, I. Lewis Libby. USA Engage is headed by Don Deline, Halliburton's top

Washington lobbyist. "We're encouraged by what several administration officials have said so far about sanctions," Dehne said in 2001, adding that he hopes the energy task force will "broadly address sanctions."

Libya

Some of the most significant sanctions against doing business with Libya were put in place by President Reagan in 1986, in response to the Qaddafi regime's use and support of terrorism. Those sanctions ban most sales of goods, technology, and services to Libya. They provide for criminal penalties of up to 10 years in prison and $500,000 in corporate and $250,000 in individual fines.

Despite these sanctions, Halliburton subsidiary KBR has worked in Libya since the 1980s. The company helped construct a system of underground pipes and wells that purportedly are intended to carry water. But according to Rep. Henry Waxman (D-CA), "some experts believe that the pipes have a military purpose. The pipes are large enough to accommodate military vehicles and appear to be more elaborate than is needed for holding water. The company began working on the project m 1984 and transferred the work to its British office after the 1986 embargo."

In 1995, Halliburton was fined $3.8 million for re-exporting U.S. goods through a foreign subsidiary to Libya in violation of U.S. sanctions. The company reportedly sold oil-drilling tools (pulse neutron generators) that critics, including former U.S. Rep. John Bryant of Dallas suggested could be used to trigger nuclear bombs.

As is the case with the company's business in Iran, Halliburton works in Libya through foreign subsidiaries. In

March 2004, Halliburton reported to the SEC that it continues to own "several non-United States subsidiaries and/or non-United States joint ventures that operate in or manufacture goods destined for, or render services in Libya. "News reports indicate that Halliburton Germany GmbH is involved in Libya. Meanwhile, in 2003 U.S. government officials warned RWE, the second-largest German utility, that it could face sanctions against its U.S. operations if it does not scale back plans for a project in Libya.

UN sanctions on Libya were lifted on September 12, 2003. Unilateral U.S. sanctions continue to remain in force, although the Bush administration says it is considering lifting them because of the country's renunciation of nuclear ambitions. In February, the White House lifted a 23-year-old ban on Americans traveling to Libya and said U.S. companies that had been in Libya before the sanctions can start negotiating their return, pending the end of the trade ban. Halliburton was in Libya before the ban.

Burma

Halliburton's engagement in Burma began as early as 1990, two years after a brutal military regime (SLORC) took power by voiding the election of the National League for Democracy, the party of Aung San Suu Kyi. In the early 1990's, Halliburton Energy Services joined with Britain-based Alfred McAlpine to provide pre-commissioning services to the Yadana pipeline.

To facilitate the Yadana pipeline's construction, the Burmese military forcibly relocated towns along the onshore route. According to the U.S. Department of Labor, "credible evidence exists that several villages along the route were forcibly relocated or depopulated in the months before the production-sharing agreement was signed."

According to EarthRights International (ERI), the Yadana and Yetagun pipeline consortia—Unocal, Total, and Premier—knew of and benefited from the crimes committed by the Burmese military on behalf of the projects. An ERI investigation concluded that construction and operation of the pipelines involved the use of forced labor, forced relocation, and even murder, torture, and rape. In addition, as the largest foreign investment projects in Burma, the pipelines will provide revenue to prop up the regime, perhaps for decades to come.

In 1997, after Dick Cheney joined Halliburton, the Yadana field developers hired European Marine Services (EMC) to lay the 365-kilometer offshore portion of the Yadana gas pipeline. EMC is a 50-50 joint venture between Halliburton and Saipem of Italy. Early in his tenure as Halliburton CEO, Cheney also signed a tentative deal with the government of India to bring Burmese gas to Indian customers.

Shortly before the 2000 election, Cheney defended Halliburton's involvement in Burma by pointing out that the company had not broken the U.S. law imposing sanctions on Burma, which forbids new investments in the country. "You have to operate in some very difficult places and oftentimes in countries that are governed in a manner that's not consistent with our principles here in the United States," Cheney told Larry King. "But the world's not made up only of democracies."

Angola
Halliburton has benefited from $200 million in ExIm support for oil field developments in the enclave of

Cabinda. According to a March 2004 Global Witness report, "new evidence from IMF documents and elsewhere confirm previous allegations made by Global Witness that over $1 billion per year of the country's oil revenues—about a quarter of the state's yearly income—has gone unaccounted for since 1996. Meanwhile, one in four of Angola's children die before the age of five and one million internally displaced people remain dependent on international food aid."

The watchdog group blamed "political and business elites" with "exploiting the country's civil war to siphon off oil revenues. Most recently, evidence has emerged in a Swiss investigation of millions of dollars being paid to President Dos Santos himself. The government continues to seek oil-backed loans at high rates of interest which are financed through opaque and unaccountable offshore structures. A major concern exists that Angola's elite will now simply switch from wartime looting of state assets to profiteering from its reconstruction."

Bangladesh
In a 1996 deal witnessed by Bangladesh's then-Prime Minister Sheik Hasina and Britain's Prime Minister John Major, Cheney and UK-based Cairn Energy signed a gas purchase and sales agreement with state-owned Petrobangla. Halliburton took a 25 percent stake in the offshore Sangu field in exchange for building a pipeline to the coast.

Ever since, Halliburton and Cairn Energy have pressed Bangladesh's government to drop a ban on the export of its natural gas, even though four of five people in the country have no access to electricity, and even though proven gas reserves can only supply another 20 years of domestic consumption. The World Bank, which has financed the Sangu field, joined the side of Halliburton: It has determined that Bangladesh is too poor to consume gas at global market prices. Bangladesh, one of the world's poorest countries, has accumulated a debt in payments to Halliburton and Cairn, and now, says the Bank, the country must pay this bill by mortgaging its future.

"Bangladesh's gas reserves are a major potential source of foreign exchange earnings, if opposition to their export can be overcome," reads a recent Bank country strategy. "Prospects for further investment depend on the government's willingness to allow gas exports without which the limited domestic market demand will hold back exploration and production."

The U.S. government, too, is pressuring Bangladesh to drop its export ban. In August 2003, U.S. Ambassador Harry K. Thomas asserted, "We would like to see a certain amount of natural gas to be exported, in an honest and transparent manner. Your Finance Minister [Saifur Rahman] has said about turning Bangladesh into a middle-income country, and this is one way of achieving that."

But former World Bank chief economist Joseph Stiglitz sees this kind of pressure as antithetical to his former employer's alleged reason to exist: to eliminate global poverty. Stiglitz advised Bangladesh to preserve, not export, its gas reserves. "It is better for Bangladesh to keep its gas reserve for the future," he told reporters in August 2003. "Gas reserve is your security against any volatility of energy prices on the international market. One should be very careful about the pace of extraction. If you exploit your reserves quickly, you will have to be dependent upon imports later."

Western Siberia

In 2000, Halliburton CEO Dick Cheney personally lobbied ExIm to finance Halliburton's deal to equip the Samotlor oil field. He was able to overcome objections raised by the U.S. State Department.

The State Department initially rejected the loan package in December 1999. While objections to the loans were diverse, including the brutal military campaign in Chechnya, Secretary of State Madeleine Albright particularly cited corruption as the key concern meriting the invocation of the Chafee Amendment. This little known and rarely used legal provision allows the secretary of state to block ExIm financing deemed to violate the "national interest." "Our principal interest was promoting the rule of law in Russia," said a State Department official.

In a meeting with Alan Larson, the U.S. undersecretary of state for economic, business, and agricultural affairs, Cheney reportedly emphasized the impact the financing package delay would have on his company. Albright backed down.

A State Department official said the decision turned after the U.S. "opened a dialogue with the Russian government to impress upon them the need to address weaknesses in Russia's legal framework that led to the abuses in this case." (Interestingly Larson was the only Clinton appointee at the State department to keep his job when the Bush-Cheney team took over in 2000.)

Kazakhstan

Halliburton is a contractor in three major oil developments—Uzen, Karachaganak, and Alibekmola—that have sustained President Nursultan Nazarbayev's notorious autocratic rule. "It's almost as if the opportunities [in Kazakhstan] have arisen overnight," Cheney marveled in 1998.

The Karachaganak "opportunity," later supported by a $120 million loan from the World Bank's International Finance Corporation, arose from corruption, according to a recent indictment handed down by U.S. prosecutors.

On April 2, 2003, a federal grand jury in New York indicted U.S. businessman James Geffen on charges that he bribed Kazakh officials in two Karachaganak-related transactions: "Mobil Oil's 1995 agreement to finance the processing and sale of gas condensate from the Karachaganak oil and gas field" and "Texaco and other oil companies' purchase of a share in the Karachaganak oil and gas field in 1998."

Azerbaijan

Dick Cheney lobbied to remove congressional sanctions against aid to Azerbaijan—sanctions imposed because of concerns about ethnic cleansing. Cheney said the sanctions were the result only of groundless campaigning by the Armenian-American lobby. In 1997, KBR bid on a major Caspian project from the Azerbaijan International Operating Company.

CORPORATE WELFARE AND POLITICAL CONNECTIONS

In 2000, *The Chicago Tribune* quoted a Halliburton vice president, Bob Feebler, saying, "Clearly Dick gave Halliburton some advantages. Doors would open."

Doors did open for Halliburton while U.S. Vice President Dick Cheney was the company's CEO—especially doors in Washington. While Cheney was in charge of Halliburton, he parlayed political connections and taxpayer assistance into a dramatic global expansion that was fueled through corporate welfare. These corporate welfare checks, paid for by U.S. taxpayers, came in the form of subsidies from the World Bank Group, ExIm, and other international lending institutions.

No corporation has benefited more from World Bank fossil fuel extractive project financing than Halliburton. Since 1992, the Bank approved more than $2.5 billion in finance for 13 Halliburton projects. ExIm is an even more significant financier of Halliburton's global expansion. Since 1992, ExIm's board has approved more than $4.2 billion for 20 Halliburton projects. Other U.S. taxpayer-financed institutions, including OPIC and regional development banks, tossed in another $1.1 billion for Halliburton-related projects, bringing the overall total U.S. taxpayer-supported finance for Halliburton's overseas projects since 1992 to more than $7.8 billion.

These institutions support Halliburton projects that span the world, from the coal mines of India to the oil fields of Chad and Colombia. Some of these corporate welfare projects are now under government investigation, such as the Nigeria LNG plant, where not only are Halliburton representatives accused of corrupt transactions, they are also accused, by Nigerian activists, of complicity in the violent suppression of dissent and relocation of Bonny Islanders. This project received $235 million in financial support from ExIm and the African Development Bank in 2002.

Sources of Halliburton Corporate Welfare, 1992–2004

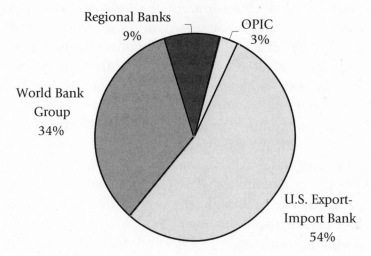

When the World Bank and ExIm become involved in Halliburton projects, they provide a cloak of legitimacy to the company's business deals with some of the worlds most unsavory governments. Additionally, the entire practice of providing government loans for fossil fuel development is under fire, even from the World Bank itself. A vast body of evidence shows that public money is being used to perpetuate an industry that is at the root of climate change, wars, corruption, and a widening gap between rich and poor. These systemic troubles led a January 2004 World Bank-commissioned study, the *Extractive Industries Review*, to recommend that the Bank get out of the oil extraction business altogether.

Campaign Contributions and Lobbying
Cheney's extensive political connections and ties to Halliburton are not the only way Halliburton opens doors

in Washington. Halliburton, along with other energy corporations, has been one of the most steadfast supporters of the Bush administration. There are more "Pioneers" (individuals who have committed themselves to generating $100,000 or more in hard money contributions for Bush) from energy company executives than any other economic sector.

Even among this stalwart industry, Halliburton stands out. The company has contributed over $1.1 million in soft money and donations since 1995. Halliburton's Political Action Committee (PAC) contributed more than $700,000 to federal candidates over the last five election cycles. Halliburton also made $432,375 in soft money contributions beginning in 1995 and ending in November 2002 when the Bipartisan Campaign Reform Act took effect and banned the national parties and federal candidates from raising such money.

In addition to contributing to specific political candidates, Halliburton has spent $2.6 million lobbying public officials since 1998, employing well-connected lobbyists with extensive histories in the Defense Department and on congressional oversight committees. One former Halliburton lobbyist, David Gribbin, served as Dick Cheney's administrative assistant during his tenure in the House of Representatives and as assistant secretary for legislative affairs under Cheney in the Pentagon. Another lobbyist, Donald Deline, served as legislative counsel to Cheney when he was secretary of defense and later became counsel to the Senate Committee on Armed Services.

Halliburton gave $376,952 in contributions during the 2000 presidential election cycle and will likely spend a similarly large amount in the upcoming presidential election.

Every presidential election cycle usually sees a spike in contributions from many industries, including energy and energy services. This year especially, companies like Halliburton will likely be relying heavily on PAC contributions to ensure a Congress favorable to its needs.

HALLIBURTON PAC & SOFT MONEY EXPENDITURES[*]
January 1, 1995 through December 31, 2003

PAC		Soft	
Democrats	Republicans	Democrats	Republicans
$44,500	$710,002	$0	$432,375
$754,502		$432,375	

[*]Soft money refers to contributions made outside the limits and prohibitions of federal law, including large individual and direct corporate and union contributions. It includes donations by executives and/or affiliates. The ban on soft money raising by national parties went into effect on November 6, 2002. While many companies make contributions to both political parties, over 94 percent of Halliburton's hard money contributions since 1995 have gone to Republicans. All of Halliburton's soft money contributions went to the Republican Party. (Hard money refers to contributions raised by candidates, the parties, or other political committees subject to federal contribution limits and disclosure requirements.) PAC refers to a political-action committee established and operated by individuals, organizations, corporations, or labor unions that solicits hard money contributions from members or executives to support or oppose federal candidates.

THEY OWN OUR DEMOCRACY

HALLIBURTON PAC, SOFT MONEY & LOBBYING EXPENDITURES
January 1995 through December 2003

Election Cycle	Lobbying Expenditures*	PAC & Soft Money Contributions**	Total
1995-1996	$218,000	$218,000	
1997-1998	$540,000	$354,175	$894,175
1999-2000	$1,200,000	$376,952	$1,576,952
2001-2002	$600,000	$163,250	$763,250
2003	$300,000	$75,500	$375,500
Total	$2,640,000	$1,187,877	$3,827,877

*Lobbying reports available only for the years 1998 through 2003.
**Soft money includes donations by executives and/or affiliates. The ban on soft money went into effect on November 6, 2002.

CONCLUSION AND RECOMMENDATIONS

On May 19, Halliburton will hold its annual shareholders meeting in Houston, Texas. David Lesar, Halliburton's CEO, has said, "One day, I believe, we will look back on 2003 as a watershed year when we took steps to become a leaner, tougher organization and continued to put ourselves in position to win in the years ahead." 2003 is also the year when Halliburton will, beyond a doubt, have established itself as one of the most unpatriotic corporations in America.

As documented in this report, Halliburton's track record in Iraq is scandalous, from the company's failure to live up to the terms of its contract to its overcharging millions of dollars to U.S. taxpayers Elsewhere in the world, Halliburton's practices are similarly abhorrent, and include bribing political officials, dodging taxes through the use of offshore subsidiaries, and side-stepping federal laws in order to do business with some of the most corrupt and brutal regimes in the world.

But Halliburton is embedded in the Bush administration, the company has continued to receive lucrative government contracts despite its unethical and illegal business practices. It is the leading partner among the "coalition of the billing" in Iraq and the sole provider of support services to the U.S. military.

Rather than being rewarded for its unethical and possibly illegal behavior, Halliburton should be held accountable for its past and current practices. The Pentagon's decision to refer Halliburton's actions to the Justice Department for a criminal investigation is commendable and an important first step. However, a much broader inquiry is needed into the politics of contract decisions and the performance of corporations that have been given billions of taxpayer dollars.

The following recommendations are directed to Halliburton's executives and shareholders as well as U.S. policy makers. If enacted, they would go a long way toward protecting U.S. taxpayers and Iraqis from fraud, waste, and corruption by Halliburton. They would also show the American public that Halliburton and American politicians take seriously our concerns about war profiteering and corporate cronyism. As Congressman James Leach said in January of this year: "It's not a partisan issue, the public has a right to expect that its resources are carefully dispersed and honestly spent."

Recommendations for Halliburton

• **Bring your employees home from Iraq.** Halliburton's presence in Iraq is angering qualified Iraqis who are being denied contracts to do the work themselves and endangering Halliburton's own employees. It's also clear, from the confirmed case of bribery to the allegations of overcharging, that Halliburton is unable to properly oversee its work in Iraq to ensure that Iraqis and American taxpayers are not being ripped off. It's time to bring the company home from Iraq.

• **End the veil of secrecy—release the Iraq contract details to the public.** Americans deserve to know how our tax dollars are being spent. And certainly we want our legislators, who are charged with oversight of public contracts, to have access to the Iraq reconstruction contracts. Halliburton should immediately make public the details of its contracts in Iraq and the bidding process by which they were awarded.

• **Stop doing business with dictators.** By doing business with dictators and corrupt regimes around the world, Halliburton not only supports and provides credibility to those regimes, it profits from the suffering of people in those countries. Being a patriotic company means supporting human rights. Halliburton should end its business dealings with Iran, Libya, Kazakhstan, and other countries that violate the human rights of their citizens.

• **Be a good corporate citizen—pay your taxes.** Doing business in the United States means paying taxes to support the infrastructure that makes it possible for U.S. businesses to operate. Halliburton must stop using overseas subsidiaries to dodge its U.S. tax obligations.

- **Cut financial ties to Vice President Dick Cheney.** It is an unbelievable conflict of interest for Halliburton, the number one beneficiary of Iraq "reconstruction" contracts, to be paying more than $150,000 annually to a vice president who pushed for and promotes the very war from which Halliburton is profiting. At the very least, Halliburton shareholders should demand a halt in payment of Cheney's deferred compensation until all federal investigations concerning accounting fraud and bribery that happened during his tenure as CEO are resolved.

- **Respect your workers.** Pay your workers a fair wage, provide decent working conditions especially in war situations, and allow your workers to form unions as well as to access courts and dispute resolution mechanisms in the United States.

Recommendations for U.S. Policy Makers

- **Cancel Halliburton's Iraq contracts.** Enact a contract suspension and debarment standard that disqualifies any company from being eligible for contracts if it has committed three major violations of law within the last five years, or which is currently under criminal investigation for activities similar to those involved in the prospective contract. Enough evidence has been accumulated to merit the cancellation of Halliburton's Iraq contracts, including reports about Halliburton's shoddy work in Iraq, its possible overcharges to the government of some $85 million, ongoing investigations of accounting fraud and bribery in Nigeria, and confirmed kickbacks worth more than $6 million. Halliburton is also being investigated by the Justice Department for possible criminal wrongdoing related to its Iraq contracts. It's time for the U.S. government take action to protect both Iraqis and U.S. citizens from Halliburton's unethical practices.

• **Investigate and penalize war profiteering.** Congress should immediately pass the War Profiteering Prevention Act (H.R. 3673/S. 1813), which would prohibit profiteering and fraud relating to military action, relief, and reconstruction efforts in Iraq. Congress should also enact legislation introduced by Representative James A Leach (R-Iowa), which would establish a select oversight committee to investigate the awarding and carrying out of government contracts in Iraq and Afghanistan, similar to the Truman Committee of World War II.

• **Ensure transparency and accountability in government contracting.** U.S. government agencies should prevent the type of cronyism that has allowed companies like Halliburton to cash in their political connections for lucrative contracts. The bidding process for U.S. government contracts in Iraq and elsewhere should be open and transparent. Companies like Halliburton that have repeatedly violated federal laws should be banned from receiving government contracts.

• **Let Iraqis rebuild their own country and make their own decisions about the future of their economy.** Qualified Iraqi businesses are hungry to take over the work that Halliburton has been doing unsatisfactorily and at a fraction of the cost. The Iraqi people deserve to be the first bidders on contracts to rebuild their country rather than being prohibited from bidding as is currently the case. Iraqis should also be making the decisions about who is awarded rebuilding contracts, not to mention all other decisions regarding future control of the Iraqi economy.

• **Overturn Executive Order 13303.** In May 2003, President Bush quietly passed Executive Order 13303, entitled 'Protecting the Development Fund and Certain Other Property in Which Iraq Has an Interest.' According to whistleblowers who have seen this order, it allows "U.S. oil companies in Iraq blanket immunity from lawsuits and criminal prosecution" and "appears to provide immunity against contractual disputes, discrimination suits, violations of labor practices, international treaties, environmental disasters, and human rights violations. Even more, it doesn't limit immunity to the production of oil, but also protects individuals, companies, and corporations involved in selling and marketing the oil as well." Therefore, Halliburton, which was in charge of Iraqi oil distribution and thus has assets that can be traced back to Iraqi oil, becomes immune from any kind of prosecution, even if it engages in criminal behavior in the United States.

• **End corporate welfare.** The World Bank, U.S. Export-Import Bank, the Overseas Private Investment Corporation, and other international lending institutions should stop subsidizing Halliburton's

fossil fuel development projects, which have per-
petuated climate change, wars, corruption, and a
widening gap between rich and poor.

• **Take the money out of politics.** Attempts by
companies like Halliburton to manipulate the
political process with millions of dollars in campaign contributions will only be thwarted when the
corrupting influence of money is taken out of our
political system. Federal funding of political campaigns would ensure that Halliburton's claim that
they get their contracts because of "what they know,
not who they know" rings true.

How would you be punished for financing terrorism? Citigroup (annual revenues: $100 billion) was fined $2,925. And so it goes . . .

Trading with the Enemy
from *The Nation* (4/23/03)
Matt Bivens

C itigroup stands judged of financing terrorism. The penalty: $2,925. ChevronTexaco violated sanctions against Iraq. The penalty: $9,000. The North Carolina-based International Union of Pure and Applied Chemistry broke U.S. laws that prevent proliferation of weapons of mass destruction. It was fined $500, the same as the penalty for littering in Kentucky.

Sometimes a light rebuke is appropriate. Perhaps, despite the weighty topics of terrorism and mass destruction, these were misdemeanors at heart, and it was totally proper for lawyers on both sides to quietly settle on the gentlest of punishments. But it's hard to say for sure, because in each of the 59 cases of trading with the enemy tersely reported by the Treasury Department's Office of Foreign Assets Control [OFAC], no details are provided beyond the country involved and the penalty assessed—no dates, no specifics, no nothing. Even that miserly data we have only because Public Citizen and the Corporate Crime Reporter newsletter teamed up to pry it free.

Should we give the Bush Administration the benefit of the doubt, and assume the judgments are appropriately restrained? Fine. There's still a glaring contrast with the harsh treatment meted out to individuals accused of similar crimes. Six Yemeni-Americans in their 20s were arrested in September outside Buffalo, New York, and described by George Bush as an "al-Qaeda cell" in his State of the Union address. But even the attorney prosecuting the case has said there's no evidence they were involved in any violent plot (!), and the prosecution strategy to paper over that gaping hole in their case seems to be to terrify the young men into plea bargains. Or consider the U.S. citizen who was never accused of any crime, never tried in a court—but one day was incinerated by the CIA, and then, post-mortem, declared an "enemy combatant."

"When individual Americans are accused of helping terrorists, they're thrown in jail and their names are dragged through the mud," sums up an observer on CBS's Market Watch business news. "But when multinational corporations like Wal-Mart, Dow Chemical, ExxonMobil and Amazon.com agree with government prosecutors that they have violated laws that prohibit doing business with enemy states, the news is buried on an obscure government Web site."

Corporations have a vested interest in election outcomes. Good thing they sell the voting machines, huh?

Diebold's Political Machine

from MotherJones.com (3/5/04)

Bob Fitrakis and Harvey Wasserman

Soccer moms and NASCAR dads come and go, but swing states are always in fashion. And this year, Ohio is emerging as the most fashionable of the bunch. Asked recently about the importance of Ohio in this year's presidential campaign, one veteran of Buckeye State politics told *Salon*, "Ohio is the Florida of 2004."

That label sounds ominously accurate to the many who are skeptical of computerized voting. In addition to being as decisive as the 2000 polling in Florida, they worry this year's vote in Ohio could be just as flawed. Specifically, they worry that it could be rigged. And they wonder why state officials seem so unconcerned by the fact that the two companies in line to sell touch-screen voting machines to Ohio have deep and continuing ties to the Republican Party. Those companies, Ohio's own Diebold Election Systems and Election Systems & Software of Nebraska, are lobbying fiercely ahead of a public hearing on the matter in Columbus next week.

There's solid reason behind the political rhetoric tapping Ohio as a key battleground. No Republican has ever captured the White House without carrying Ohio, and only John Kennedy managed the feat for the Democrats. In 2000, George W. Bush won in the Buckeye State by a scant four percentage points. Four years earlier, Bill Clinton won in Ohio by a similar margin.

In recent years, central Ohio has been transformed from a bastion of Republicanism into a Democratic stronghold. Six of Columbus' seven city council members are Democrats, as is the city's mayor, Michael Coleman. But no Democrat has been elected to Congress from central Ohio in more than 20 years, and the area around Columbus still includes pockets where no Democrat stands a chance. One such Republican pocket is Upper Arlington, the Columbus suburb that is home to Walden "Wally" O'Dell, the chairman of the board and chief executive of Diebold. For years, O'Dell has given generously to Republican candidates. Last September, he held a packed $1,000-per-head GOP fundraiser at his 10,800-square-foot mansion. He has been feted as a guest at President Bush's Texas ranch, joining a cadre of "Pioneers and Rangers" who have pledged to raise more than $100,000 for the Bush reelection campaign. Most memorably, O'Dell last fall penned a letter pledging his commitment "to helping Ohio deliver its electoral votes to the President."

O'Dell has defended his actions, telling the *Cleveland Plain Dealer* "I'm not doing anything wrong or complicated." But he also promised to lower his political profile and "try to be more sensitive." But the Diebold boss' partisan cards are squarely on the table. And, when it comes to the Diebold board room, O'Dell is hardly alone in his generous support of the GOP. One of the longest-serving Diebold directors is W.R. "Tim" Timken. Like O'Dell, Timken is a Republican loyalist and a major contributor to GOP candidates. Since 1991 the Timken Company and members of the Timken family have contributed more than a million dollars to the Republican Party and to GOP presidential candidates such as George W. Bush. Between

2000 and 2002 alone, Timken's Canton-based bearing and steel company gave more than $350,000 to Republican causes, while Timken himself gave more than $120,000. This year, he is one of George W. Bush's campaign Pioneers, and has already pulled in more than $350,000 for the president's reelection bid.

While Diebold has received the most attention, it actually isn't the biggest maker of computerized election machines. That honor goes to Omaha-based ES&S, and its Republican roots may be even stronger than Diebold's.

The firm, which is privately held, began as a company called Data Mark, which was founded in the early 1980s by Bob and Todd Urosevich. In 1984, brothers William and Robert Ahmanson bought a 68 percent stake in Data Mark, and changed the company's name to American Information Services (AIS). Then, in 1987, McCarthy & Co, an Omaha investment group, acquired a minority share in AIS.

In 1992, investment banker Chuck Hagel, president of McCarthy & Co, became chairman of AIS. Hagel, who had been touted as a possible Senate candidate in 1993, was again on the list of likely GOP contenders heading into the 1996 contest. In January of 1995, while still chairman of ES&S, Hagel told the Omaha *World-Herald* that he would likely make a decision by mid-March of 1995. On March 15, according to a letter provided by Hagel's Senate staff, he resigned from the AIS board, noting that he intended to announce his candidacy. A few days later, he did just that.

A little less than eight months after steppind down as director of AIS, Hagel surprised national pundits and defied early polls by defeating Benjamin Nelson, the state's popular former governor. It was Hagel's first try for public office. Nebraska elections officials told *The Hill* that machines made by AIS probably tallied 85 percent of the votes cast in the 1996 vote, although Nelson never drew attention to the connection. Hagel won again in 2002, by a far healthier margin. That vote is still angrily disputed by Hagel's Democratic opponent, Charlie Matulka, who did try to make Hagel's ties to ES&S an issue in the race and who asked that state elections officials conduct a hand recount of the vote. That request was rebuffed, because Hagel's margin of victory was so large.

As might be expected, Hagel has been generously supported by his investment partners at McCarthy & Co.— since he first ran, Hagel has received about $15,000 in campaign contributions from McCarthy & Co. executives. And Hagel still owns more than $1 million in stock in McCarthy & Co., which still owns a quarter of ES&S.

If the Republican ties at Diebold and ES&S aren't enough to cause concern, argues election reform activist Bev Harris, the companies' past performances and current practices should be. Harris is author of Black Box Voting, and the woman behind the BlackBoxVoting.com web site.

The rush to embrace computerized voting, of course, began with Florida. But, in fact, one of the Sunshine State's election-day disasters was the direct result of a malfunctioning computerized voting system; a system built by Diebold. The massive screwup in Volusia County was all but lost in all the furor over hanging chads and butterfly ballots in South Florida. In part that's because county election officials avoided a total disaster by quickly conducting a hand recount of the more than 184,000 paper ballots used to feed the computerized system. But the huge computer miscount led several networks to incorrectly call the race for Bush.

The first signs that the Diebold-made system in Volusia County was malfunctioning came early on election night, when the central ballot-counting computer showed a Socialist Party candidate receiving more than 9,000 votes and Vice President Al Gore getting minus 19,000. Another 4,000 votes poured into the plus column for Bush that didn't belong there. Taken together, the massive swing seemed to indicate that Bush, not Gore, had won Florida and thus the White House. Election officials restarted the machine, and expressed confidence in the eventual results, which showed Gore beating Bush by 97,063 votes to 82,214. After the recount, Gore picked up 250 votes, while Bush picked up 154. But the erroneous numbers had already been sent to the media.

Harris has posted a series of internal Diebold memos relating to the Volusia County miscount on her website, blackboxvoting.com. One memo from Lana Hires of Global Election Systems, now part of Diebold, complains, "I need some answers! Our department is being audited by the County. I have been waiting for someone to give me an explanation as to why Precinct 216 gave Al Gore a minus 16,022 [votes] when it was uploaded." Another, from Talbot Ireland, Senior VP of Research and Development for Diebold, refers to key "replacement" votes in Volusia County as "unauthorized."

Harris has also posted a post-mortem by CBS detailing how the network managed to call Volusia County for Bush early in the morning. The report states: "Had it not been for these [computer] errors, the CBS News call for Bush at 2:17:52 A.M. would not have been made." As Harris notes, the 20,000-vote error shifted the momentum of the news reporting and nearly led Gore to concede.

What's particularly troubling, Harris says, is that the errors were caught only because an alert poll monitor noticed Gore's vote count going *down* through the evening, which of course is impossible. Diebold blamed the bizarre swing on a "faulty memory chip," which Harris claims is simply not credible. The whole episode, she contends, could easily have been consciously programmed by someone with a partisan agenda. Such claims might seem far-fetched, were it not for the fact that a cadre of computer scientists showed a year ago that the software running Diebold's new machines can be hacked with relative ease.

The hackers posted some 13,000 pages of internal documents on various web sites—documents that were pounced on by Harris and others. A desperate Diebold went to court to stop this "wholesale reproduction" of company material. By November of last year, the Associated Press reported that Diebold had sent cease-and-desist letters to programmers and students at two dozen universities, including the University of California at Berkeley and the Massachusetts Institute of Technology. The letters were ignored by at least one group of students at Swarthmore College, who vowed an "electronic civil disobedience" campaign.

Equally troubling, of course, is the fact that the touchscreen systems Diebold, ES&S, and the other companies have on the market now aren't designed to generate a polling place paper trail. While ES&S says it is open to providing voter receipts, and has even designed a prototype machine that does so, the company isn't going to roll that prototype into production until state and federal elections officials make it mandatory.

Lawmakers in Congress and the Ohio legislature are scrambling to do just that. In Ohio, State Sen. Teresa Fedor of Toledo has proposed a bill requiring a "voter verified paper audit trail" for all elections in the state. Congressman Rush Holt of New Jersey is pushing a similar measure in Washington. But the efforts are being fought by Republicans in both places. In Ohio, Secretary of State Kenneth Blackwell has already signed $100 million in agreements to purchase voting machines. The bulk of the purchases would go to Diebold and ES&S, and Blackwell insists there is no need for paper receipts. Considering the political opposition and the companies' wait-and-see approach, it's almost certain that voters using touch-screen machines in November will walk away from their polling places without ever seeing a printed record of their choices.

At a trade fair held recently here in Columbus, a wide range of companies seeking to fill that void demonstrated technologies that could easily and cheaply provide paper receipts for ballots. One such product, called TruVote, provides two separate voting receipts. The first is shown under plexiglass, and displays the choices made by a vote on the touch screen. This copy falls into a lockbox after the voter approves it. The second is provided to the voter. TruVote is already attracting fans, among them Brooks Thomas, Tennessee's Coordinator of Elections. "I've not seen anything that compares to [the] TruVote validation system." Georgia's Assistant Secretary of State, Terrell L. Slayton, Jr., calls the device is the "perfect solution." But Blackwell argues the campaign for a paper ballot trail for Ohio is an attempt to "derail" reform. He says he'll comply with the demand only if Congress mandates it.

Meanwhile, in Upper Arlington, a 'lower profile' Wally O'Dell and his wife recently petitioned the city to get permission to serve liquor at future fundraisers and political gatherings.

Be afraid.

Intelligent, Amoral, Evolving: The Hazards of Persistent Dynamic Entities

from *Gangs of America* (2003)

Ted Nace

Freed, as such bodies are, from the sure bounds to the schemes of individuals—the grave—they are able to add field to field, and power to power, until they become entirely too strong for that society which is made up of those whose plans are limited by a single life.

—Supreme Court of Georgia,
Railroad Co. v. Collins, 1929

Early morning at the Dallas/Fort Worth Airport. As I step out to the taxi curb, I feel a coolness in the air that I suspect will not stick around once that big Texas sun reports for duty. I have arrived on a redeye flight, and as I take a taxi into the city I imagine the inhabitants waking up and drinking their breakfast coffee. I've never been to

Dallas before (*"The place where Kennedy got shot"* keeps sneaking into my thoughts), but the driver of my cab, a man full of stories and warm southern exuberance, quickly puts me at ease. Turning off his meter, he takes me the long way to my hotel, pointing out the local sights.

Far less welcoming is the darkened hall of grandiose proportions where I eventually find myself, in the midst of a hushed, submissive audience. In front is a podium raised to an unnatural height, where Lee Raymond, chairman and CEO of ExxonMobil Corporation, announces the company's recent triumphs and outlines its strategy going forward. Above the stage is the glowing logo of the corporation, and next to the logo, in a touch of exquisite irony, a glistening blue Image of Planet Earth hangs in midair as though floating through space.

It is a piece of choreography disguised as a democratic proceeding: the annual meeting of a Fortune 500 corporation. To the right of Raymond sits a group of seven men and three women. Their role appears to be the opposite of that of the chorus in a Greek play: to be seen, but not to make a sound. They are the nominees for the board of directors, each handpicked by management. Everything is preordained, except that there seems to be a small fly in the ointment. A party pooper.

In the aisle to my left a well-dressed woman approaches a freestanding microphone. This is the portion of the meeting during which stockholders are allowed to present statements for or against resolutions that have been proposed for a vote. The woman's voice is soft but firm, "Mr. Chairman, on behalf of the members of the Sisters of St. Dominic and the Capuchin Order of the Roman Catholic Church, I wish to argue in support of Resolution 8 tying the compensation of management to certain indices of environmental and social performance by the company—"

For a heartbeat, the lock-step march of the meeting seems in jeopardy.

"Whatever you have to say," cuts in the chairman, "the matter has already been decided in the negative by proxies received prior to this meeting. You have one minute forty seconds."

"Mr. Chairman, you have the power to restrict this debate, but your authority is not legitimate. I represent twenty thousand nuns and clergy who have an ownership stake in this company. Their pensions depend on its financial results, but at the same time they wish to see financial performance balanced against other factors including the urgent need to protect the environment and to safeguard human rights."

"You have fifty-five seconds remaining."

Speaker after speaker approaches the microphones to make statements on behalf of a variety of resolutions to reform the company. One asks for a policy forbidding discrimination against gays and lesbians. Another proposes that ExxonMobil alter its stance on global warming. Yet another opposes drilling in the Arctic National Wildlife Refuge.

The most startling of the proposals requests that Exxon-Mobil end its involvement in the Indonesian province of Aceh, where the company maintains a close relationship with military forces that have been ruthlessly suppressing a local separatist movement. According to a lawsuit filed in federal court by the International Labor Rights Fund, ExxonMobil provided buildings used by the Indonesian military to torture local activists, and its bulldozers dug the mass graves used to bury the victims. There will be no real debate on any of these matters. The atmosphere is oppressive, even intimidating. Security guards stand ready to forcibly eject from the hall any speaker who deliberately exceeds the meager time limits.

Of course, if this were a small family business, no one would expect nuns, environmentalists, and human rights activists to have any say over its dealings, nor would the public be interested. But according to the glossy materials in my hand, ExxonMobil represents the reunification of two of the thirty-four strands of John D. Rockefeller's Standard Oil empire: Standard Oil of New York (renamed Mobil in 1966) and Standard Oil of New Jersey (renamed Exxon in 1972). Its total revenues now exceed $200 billion annually. This is not a business, it is a world power. Its operations affect not only its tens of thousands of employees and millions of customers, but large areas of the planet. On a strictly dollar-for-dollar basis, the revenues of ExxonMobil exceed the governmental budgets of all but seven of the world's nations.

The man at the podium commands a private domain. That he conducts himself like a dictator is no accident. In fact, his power actually exceeds that of most dictators. Around the world, they are more likely to hurry to answer his phone calls than he would be to answer theirs.

As I watch this larger-than-life executive assert his power, I reflect on the notion that the corporation is a nobody—an entity divorced from human values or designs. That notion would seem to be belied by the very real somebody who is running this meeting, this human being named Lee Raymond, whose political views clearly drive this corporation and its policies. Thanks to Mr. Raymond, ExxonMobil has set itself apart. For example, on global warming, most of the other oil giants have taken a different stance. They have announced that they agree with the science that has forecast global warming and that they endorse the Kyoto Protocols on global warming. Competitors like British Petroleum (the largest maker of photovoltaic cells) and Royal Dutch/Shell (one of the biggest developers of wind farms) are racing to anticipate and ride the trend toward renewable sources of energy. Similarly, not every company opposes gay rights, as ExxonMobil does. Numerous corporations, seeking to retain talented staff, provide health benefits to domestic partners.

These policy differences among oil companies would seem to belie the notion of corporations as mindless, impersonal entities. Clearly, policy is in the hands of human beings, each free to adopt a wide scope in their tactics and strategies. Still, I would argue that this freedom is constrained. Let's imagine, for a moment, that the night before the meeting Lee Raymond had been visited by a series of Dickensian ghosts, who had rattled their chains and urged him for the sake of his grandchildren's lives and his own eternal soul to sacrifice a hefty share of ExxonMobil's profits in order to take the company on a radically divergent path toward social justice and environmental protection. At the annual meeting, Raymond—a young grandchild in each arm—had announced his intention of moving the company in the new direction, making a passionate speech about human rights and the fate of the planet.

What would have happened next? It is predictable enough. Either (a) Raymond's board of directors would have fired him posthaste, or (b) both Raymond and the board would soon have been staring down the barrel of a class-action shareholder lawsuit charging them with violating their legally mandated fiduciary responsibility toward the owners of the company.

In fact, that's exactly what happened to none other than Henry Ford, who wanted to plough his company's retained earnings into building more factories, in order to "employ still more men, to spread the benefits of this industrial system to the greatest possible number, to help them build up their lives and their homes." Unfortunately for Ford, his shareholders took him to court, demanding that the company's retained earnings be distributed as dividends. Even though Henry Ford had pioneered the assembly line, the Michigan Supreme Court ruled bluntly in 1919 in *Dodge v. Ford Motor Co.* that he could not devote the company he had created to his personal goal of creating as many factory jobs as possible, if doing so would reduce the profits of the company. Profits, said the court, were the only goal that Ford was allowed to pursue:

> A business corporation is organized and carried on primarily for the profit of the stockholders. The powers of the directors are to be employed for that end. The discretion of directors is to be exercised in the choice of means to attain that end, and does not extend to a change in the end itself, to reduction of profits, or to the nondistribution of profits among stockholders in order to devote them to other purposes.

Since Ford defended his plan of reinvestment in terms of social goals rather than in terms of maximizing shareholder returns, he lost the case.

Americans have always been fascinated by the personalities of business tycoons. But if we really want to understand what it would take to put corporations on a more socially healthy course, we have to look past the personalities and opinions of the human beings who manage these institutions. In truth, the power yielded by Lee Raymond has little to do with the man himself. CEOs will come and go, while ExxonMobil, this immense, morphing, shapeless entity, lives on. It is the company's power, not Raymond's intellect or force of will, that causes presidents and dictators to pick up the phone.

The purpose of this book has been to reveal the roots of that power. Corporate power may seem impregnable, a vast, looming shape. But when we pan in closer with our historical lens, tracing how the institution known as the corporation was constructed piece by piece, the looming shape comes into focus as a specific legal contraption, a thing made of nuts, bolts, wheels, belts, and wiring. The better we can diagram this device, the more easily we can change it

At one time, the institution known as the state seemed similarly impregnable. Prior to the late eighteenth century, virtually all cultures were organized as monolithic top-down power structures enforced by monopolies of overt violence and by ideologies such as "divine right of kings" that taught subservience and compliance. One way of thinking about the American Revolution is to see it as a reengineering of the state. Like a computer programmer debugging a piece of software, the framers of the American system rolled up their sleeves, tweaked this and that, and came up with a new design.

One can see this practical bent in *The Federalist Papers*, where Alexander Hamilton writes about society like a mechanic considering different bolts and screws:

> The science of politics, like most other sciences, has received great improvement. The efficacy of various principles is now well understood, which were either not known at all, or imperfectly known to the ancients. The regular distribution of power into distinct departments; the introduction of legislative balances and checks; the institution of courts composed of judges, holding their offices during good behavior; the representation of the people in the legislature, by deputies of their own election; these are either wholly new discoveries, or have made their principal progress towards perfection in modern times. They are means, and powerful means, by which the excellencies of republican government may be retained, and its imperfections lessened or avoided.

Social change, according to this vision of things, isn't just a matter of asserting values. It's also a matter of innovating and implementing specific ways for realizing those values, mechanisms like democratic selection of leaders, separation of powers, human rights, and judicial review.

For example, the concept of human rights can be seen as a safety feature—an organizational airbag that helps prevent large, powerful institutions from crushing vulnerable human beings. To make any such design feature work, it must be accompanied by legal systems to interpret it and police power to enforce it.

As new design ideas for the state were implemented in America and elsewhere, it became apparent that some worked better than others. For example, compare the American experience with that of the French in crafting a working system of human rights. Although France's Declaration of the Rights of Man and the Citizen is more extensive than America's Bill of Rights, the two countries diverged in mechanisms for enforcement. In France, enforcement was placed in the hands of the National Assembly and its representatives on the Committee for Public Safety. In America, Chief Justice Marshall's assertion of Supreme Court authority in *Marbury v. Madison* (1803) established judicial review in a separate branch of government. In France, the human rights system quickly broke down; in the United States it worked, however imperfectly. International human rights expert Geoffrey Robertson attributes the difference to the fact that *Marbury v. Madison* "provided human rights in the U.S. with a set of teeth, by endorsing courts rather than legislatures as their enforcement mechanism."

Just as it was necessary to innovate and implement specific new features in order to democratize and constrain state power, the same applies to corporate power. A short list of changes might include the following: (1) revoking the doctrine of corporate constitutional rights; (2) curbing corporate quasi-rights as appropriate—for example, requiring corporations to renew their charters every five years; (3) banning corporations from political activity; (4) shoring up the boundaries of "noncorporate" spaces in society—for example, prohibiting advertising aimed at children; (5) expanding the scope of worker and customer rights vis-à-vis corporations; (6) strengthening countervailing institutions, especially unions; and (7) promoting noncorporate institutions like public schools and economic forms like municipal utilities, family farms, consumer cooperatives, and employee-run enterprises.

Of course, the notion that we might simply decide on some design changes and then implement them, as though corporate power were a malfunctioning carburetor that needed some new seals and valves, is disingenuous. Unlike car parts, corporations are not passive objects. They're run by smart, resourceful people, who can be expected to defend their power. When you fix the carburetor on your car, the carburetor does not start thinking about how to undo the fix. This makes the problem of corporate power different from more routine problems. As the history of the late nineteenth century shows, corporations are veritable Houdinis in their capacity to slip out of legally imposed strictures. Corporate power is like a germ that develops a resistance to the newest antibiotic, like the mouse that learns to steal the cheese from the trap, like the recidivist who gets out of prison and then commits another crime. Corporations have a well-earned reputation for capturing regulatory agencies, undoing legal restrictions, and otherwise meddling in their own future.

It is the iterative, self-amplifying quality of corporate power that makes static metaphors inadequate. The corporation's ability to influence the shaping of its own legal framework—like a computer program capable of rewriting its own code—calls for a richer conception, one that captures the corporation's restless, dynamic qualities. The best strategy, perhaps, is to assume the role of naturalist and pretend we are looking at a new form of life, a previously unknown organism. We need to study it with fresh eyes. We might take as our model the discoverer of the microbe, Dutch dry-goods merchant, janitor, and amateur lens grinder Antoni van Leeuwenhoek. In 1672 van Leeuwenhoek sent a memo to the Royal Society of England, the main scientific body of the time, titled "A Specimen of some Observations made by a Microscope contrived by Mr. Leeuwenhoek, concerning Mould upon the Skin, Flesh, etc.; the Sting of a Bee, etc." In that document, van Leeuwenhoek reported his conclusion that many of the common substances we assume to be simple, uniform fluids or materials are actually vast, cavorting, tumbling herds of tiny "animalcules."

Outright derision and dismissal greeted the receipt of van Leeuwenhoek's letters by the Royal Society. If van Leeuwenhoek's outrageous notion was correct, then vast portions of the world previously labeled "scum" or "film" or "rot" would have to be reassigned into an entirely different ontological district—moved by a Dutchman's optical contraption from the static realms of the "dead" to the heavens of the "quick." It took years for the Royal Society to accept these findings. But the discovery of life at a very small scale proved to be a breakthrough of incalculable value, enabling phenomena that had previously been mysterious to become comprehensible, and opening the door to such advances as inoculation and antibiotics.

If we look at the corporation like a naturalist studying a new life form, we see that it has an evolutionary history, a characteristic structure, a set of behaviors. The genius of the corporation is the simplicity, flexibility, and modularity of its design. It scales to any size, serves virtually any function, adapts to any culture, and is robust—capable, at least in principle, of functioning indefinitely. It is programmed to survive, to maintain its structure and functional integrity, to grow, to avoid danger and recover from damage, to adapt, and to respond to the outside world.

There is nothing malicious or even conscious about the tendency of the corporation to seek power. The process is slow and incremental; the world is bent in tiny steps. But over time, such small acts result in the wholesale transformation of society.

Does that sound far-fetched? If so, consider the changes that propelled the conversion of the corporation from its legally restrained status prior to the Civil War to a liberated and empowered one at the end of the nineteenth century. Next, trace the trend of empowerment through the twentieth century, to nation-sized, politically aggressive corporations such as ExxonMobil. Finally, extrapolate the trend another century or two, as corporations continue to tinker with and alter the constraining web of laws that define their power, as they seek to overcome problems, eliminate threats, or achieve goals.

The notion of creating a technology so dynamic and lifelike that it becomes dangerous to ourselves has been a theme in the modern mind since 1818, when Mary Shelly's novel *Frankenstein* transposed the medieval legend of the golem—the creature composed of clay and animated by kabalistic incantations and procedures—to the industrial age. In general, such tales paint visions of horror and tragedy. The horror has to do with powerful life forces escaping the normalizing checks of nature. The tragedy has to do with the notion that in humans the talent for creating such trouble exceeds the capacity to prevent or manage it.

Because it is so adaptable, the corporation seems on an inexorable course toward permeating every aspect of life, not just the traditional economic spheres but increasingly such public spheres as schools and prisons, and such personal spheres as preparing meals and entertaining children. In many ways the corporation is coming to know us better than we know it. It involves itself with us intimately. It participates in our birthing, our education, even our sexuality; it tracks our personal habits, entertains us, imprisons us; it helps us fight off dread diseases, manufactures the food products that we eat, barters and trades with us in a common economic system, jostles us in the political arena, talks to us in a human voice, sues us if we threaten it.

In recent years, scientists have speculated about the potential of various existing or future technologies to veer out of human control. Nuclear power, genetic engineering, artificial intelligence, and the microscale engineering known as nanotechnology have all been the subject of such concerns, however theoretical. Writing in *Wired* magazine, computer scientist Bill Joy warned about the trajectory of research on nanotechnology, describing a nightmare scenario in which an artificially created microorganism, lacking any natural predators but capable of reproducing itself and metabolizing any sort of living substance, spreads out of control through the biosphere, reducing everything in its path to "grey goo."

It is time for those who worry about runaway technologies to include the corporation among the objects of their concern. In this case, the invention is not a new one or a futuristic one. The experiment is taking place all around us. The laboratory is the world. The scientists are

Tom Scott, Stephen Field, Lewis Powell, and many other legislators, businessmen, and jurists of yesterday and today. The chromosome of the creature is the legal system, the Constitution, the framework of global agreements. Innovations like the holding company, the SUN-PAC decision, and NAFTA are brilliant gene splicings.

So where is the grey goo? I just looked out my window, and I saw the sky, some trees, a rooftop. If our world is being chewed up by a swarm of organizational locusts, the process must be rather slow and quiet. Of course, that's exactly the point that the environmental movement has been making now for decades, and their concerns about global warming, species extinction, and general environmental degradation are based on fact, not speculation. The sky may not literally be falling, but it's filling up with greenhouse gases, and the rest of the biosphere is under continual assault. Again and again, when people organize to find political solutions to such problems, the chief obstacle blocking their way is the opposing political muscle of corporations like ExxonMobil.

There are two benefits to seeing the corporation as a technology, and a dynamic one at that. First, this recognition quickly reorganizes the question of whether corporations deserve rights. Rather than what *rights* corporations deserve, the question is reversed: What sort of *restraints* will prevent runaway corporate power? The basic approach is suggested by Isaac Asimov's "Three Laws of Robotics":

1. A robot may not injure a human being, or, through inaction, allow a human being to come to harm.

2. A robot must obey the orders given it by human beings except where such orders would conflict with the First Law.

3. A robot must protect its own existence as long as protection does not conflict with the First or Second Laws.

Obviously, a democratic society can't control corporate power by means of three simple rules. Nevertheless, Asimov's point is exactly right: either we control our creations, or they control us. There is no middle ground. Giving corporations constitutional rights does the exact opposite of what is needed. Rather than being prevented on constitutional grounds from implementing laws such as campaign finance reform, legislators need a free hand in creating a legal framework that can hold corporate power in check.

The second benefit to seeing the corporation as a dynamic technology—as a quasi-living thing—is that it allows us to place corporations into a familiar category of problem. Humans have a long and deep experience with the shaping and softening process known as "domestication," in which the useful qualities of a species are fostered while the dangerous ones are pruned away. The work of domesticating the corporation can't be accomplished with a single piece of legislation, and it's not even realistic to think it can happen in a single generation. It will involve a great deal of legislation, including constitutional change. It will involve the evolution of a clearer vision that *rights* are a human privilege, not an institutional one. It will involve the end of the notion that powerful organizations ought to enjoy indefinite terms of existence. It will require broadening the notion of human rights to incorporate the various forms of interaction between humans and corporations—as consumers, as workers, or in other contexts. It will require clear boundaries and firewalls that maintain politics as a "humans-only" space. It will require similarly clear definitions of other humans-only spaces: the family, education, and so on. Finally, and most importantly, it will require a deep change in attitude, an embedded skepticism. The corporation is a powerful tool, and that makes it a dangerous one. After we domesticate and democratize it—assuming we manage to do so—we'll still have to warn our kids: "Watch out. Keep an eye on this thing. And don't ever forget: it can bite."

THEY POLLUTE
OUR CULTURE

*with a quote by Ray Kroc;
cartoons by John McPherson and Wiley Miller;
and a Fact*

Corporations aren't content to take your money and steal your government. They want to control your neighborhood, your school, your town, your food, your medical care, your workplace, the very air you (try to) breathe. That's why you can't find a good diner or a cheap drugstore or a decent tomato in your town, let alone a good public school or a clean pond.

FACT

Number of the world's 100 largest economic
entities in 2000 that were corporations:
51
Number that were countries:
49[*]

*Max Alexander left a glamorous job in New York City to buy
a 150-acre farm in rural Maine; he figured he'd leave the
corporate nightmare behind. But big companies love rural communities; especially the ones that will let them dig 56-acre
gravel pits.*

from *Man Bites Log:*
The Unlikely Adventures
of a City Guy in the Woods

(2004)

Max Alexander

I f you should ever wake up on a fine spring morning
and discover that the eighth largest road-building company in America thinks your little town would be an excellent place for a 56-acre granite quarry with a rock crushing
operation and two manufacturing plants—one for concrete and one for asphalt—here is what you must do:

* Source: http://www.corporations.org/system/

First, you must listen carefully to the phoebes, vireos and grosbeaks in your oak tree. They won't tell you what to do, but you may never hear them again.

Then you must form a non-profit opposition group, and join it.

I am not a joiner by inclination, typically finding a way to distance myself even from causes that merit participation. I dropped out of the Maine Organic Farmers and Gardeners Association after learning they forbid coffee at their annual fair (oh, please). I'm not antisocial but I count only a few close friends, most of whom go back with me for decades. I'm perfectly happy working alone at home for days on end. I don't say any of this with pride; I strive to open more doors in my life—and opportunity just came knocking.

Here then is the backstage view of Maine's development woes: As coastal communities in the southern half of the state cope with suburban sprawl and Wal-Mart contagion, rural towns like mine are being raped for the raw materials to pave that sprawl. As Robert Kennedy Jr. points out in his book *The Riverkeepers*, poor communities are often victimized by a form of environmental red-lining: heavily polluting industries establish beachheads in such areas, where citizens have limited power of protest. The industry may well provide jobs but it also makes the community less desirable as a place to live; people who can afford to leave (generally those who pay the most taxes) move away, initiating a downward spiral that undermines the tax base and ultimately transforms the town into an industrial zone. Environmental redlining is not a problem in affluent communities, because property is too valuable for industry. But of course, the property is valuable precisely because there is no industry. It works out pretty well for affluent people.

When the dust settles—and strip mines make plenty of dust—it's all about gravel, a primary component of road-building. But this is not just another gravel pit. That's because natural gravel, like fossil fuel, seems to be running out. At any rate it's not uniform enough for today's more stringent engineering standards. The solution now is to blast schists of granite ledge out of the earth, then mechanically crush it into perfectly-sized gravel-like aggregate. Add limestone and sand, and you have concrete; add petroleum and you get asphalt.

Add one hundred trucks per hour on town roads where children wait for school buses. Add the Damariscotta Lake watershed, in which the site is located. Add the town's major aquifer, under or adjacent to the blasting zone. Add plummeting real estate values, which in fact are impossible to add because no one has been able to sell a house here since the proposal was announced. Add a zoning ordinance that prohibits manufacturing in the district. Add a town planning board with open contempt for the zoning ordinance they are charged to enforce.

Add the Lane Construction Corporation of Connecticut, which earns three hundred fifty million dollars a year—more than enough to lease fifty-six acres of granite from a farmer who needs money and is an easy target for exploitation.

Add torches and pitchforks on a starry night humming with blackflies, and you get a public hearing in my town in May.

At the hearing you must demand that the planning board, whose chairman is a used-car dealer, retain qualified experts to evaluate the complex proposal. You'll want to print up lawn signs that say "Lane, Lane, Go Away!" and put them all around town.

If you're lucky, you'll have a lawyer like Bo, who happens to live next door to the quarry site. Bo put his own practice on hold to secure a paper trail for the inevitable court challenges. The fight has exhausted but inspired him; when the dust settles, he may even decide to specialize in zoning law.

You may find in your town a bearded, old-school activist like Dave, who specializes in irony and also happens to be president of the North American Vexillological Association. Vexillology is the study of flags, which can come in handy; Dave once protested that an annual town meeting could not legally come to order without the presence of an American flag. He went on to observe that the solid green curtain draping the stage was in fact the flag of Libya, and did the town want to hold its annual meeting under the standard of Muammar al-Qaddafi? An American flag was quickly procured.

You might have a citizen like Vic, a polar bear of a man and a former U.S. Marshal from New York City. Vic is our unofficial investigator, spending hours quizzing citizens in other towns where Lane has operations, as well as poring over court and municipal records from Augusta to Belfast. Vic is the sort of fellow who knocks you over with a friendly backslap. He introduces himself at public meetings as "Big-mouth," except in his New-Yorkese it comes out "Bigmout."

Or you could turn to someone like Sandy, who raises Arabian horses just over the hill from the Lane site. Sandy is a gentle force who knocks on doors, gathers signatures and gets timid neighbors to speak up. She would make a good selectman, if not a governor.

Soon you might notice a new spirit in your town, and

in yourself. At that point you might step back and appreciate the higher wisdom that is behind even adversity like strip mines. If Lane was banking on bumpkins, they were in for a surprise. So was I. Until now I had no idea that my little town was home to so many people who, like us, had fled the Rest of America, and for similar reasons. And I met old-timers who were also shocked at the prospect of an asphalt plant, although most were reticent to speak up. But we were many and we had come far to this place, whether by ancestry or by design, and we were not ready to get redlined.

The first car to hit the skunk must have been small—not anything like a fully-loaded gravel truck, the primary form of vehicular transport along my country road. When *Mephitis mephitis* meets bituminous hot-top under the double-wheel of a dump truck, the evidence is pretty much destroyed. But this skunk was still a fully formed specimen, ready for the taxidermist. There he was, with V-shaped white markings identifying him clearly as the common striped skunk.

Skunks are members of the weasel family and are said to be quite tasty. Maine's Penobscot Indians used to eat them regularly. They were careful to remove the scent gland (located within the anus), and not just because it smells so noxious. The offending chemical, a sulfuric compound called butylmercaptan, is in fact a nerve poison that can be fatal if ingested. An angry skunk can squirt the stuff sixteen feet, but with pinpoint accuracy only up to nine feet. Either way, the stink travels as far as a half mile.

THEY POLLUTE OUR CULTURE

That's under laboratory conditions. Factor in a hot summer on a back road in Maine, with multiple tire encounters, and I believe you can double that distance. Every day for two weeks that skunk got flatter and flatter, and smellier and smellier, until finally he was découpaged into the pavement and the whole town could pick up the scent.

Dead skunks are supposed to get picked up long before they turn into folk art. But backcountry towns like mine are broke in summer; last winter's snowplowing bill has just been paid off, and the new tax bills don't get mailed out until August. High summer is when small Maine towns cut way back—which is in stark contrast to the citizens, who, reeling in cash from the summer people, are ready to tap a few keggers.

It makes for a strange tension around town, between ornery selectmen trying to pay the warrants and devil-may-care residents bent on a good time—especially when your town is trying to fend off a proposed asphalt plant that would spew fifty-five tons of sulfuric compounds into our air every year. That's more sulfur than several million skunks emit, but the plant would mean more dead skunks too, once its trucks start rumbling down our roads.

Concern about the Lane Construction plant heated up last week when the town's lawyer submitted a two thousand seven hundred dollar bill for his work on the hearings over the last two months. Our land use ordinance allows us to charge legal expenses to the applicant—a reasonable notion given that the plant is, after all, their idea. But some of our town officials can't see burdening a huge Connecticut corporation with legal bills that might have been avoided if a bunch of uppity citizens hadn't decided to protest the plant in the first place. If the taxpayers want to get all persnickety about a little sulfur dioxide pollution, let them pay the legal bill.

But this being July, the town has no money. Jim, a local accountant and former state legislator who's also on the town budget committee, gave a report to the planning board chairman that ended with stark reasoning: "It's like this, Bradley. The town has no money. If we don't get Lane to pay the lawyer, we can't have a lawyer anymore."

Taking a lead from Shakespeare, someone suggested that not having a lawyer might be a good thing. But given that the neighborly folks from Lane have two lawyers at every hearing, it was decided after much chin-rubbing that the town should probably have at least one.

Lane was ordered to pay, but some officials still grumbled about how a bunch of whining citizens were driving the town to financial ruin. Some even hinted darkly that the biggest complainers were "folks from away" although the accusers did not offer to eat skunk as a demonstration of their own native heritage. At any rate, the storm passed quickly because the summer people are up, the ice cream stand is crowded, and the locals are making money. Besides, it was time for the big summer opening at the Downtown Art Gallery.

The two things in my town of thirteen hundred that strangers are always surprised to see are its beautiful public library (staffed entirely by volunteers) and its very of-the-moment art gallery—actually a cooperative run by several local artists. Perhaps because it's off the coastal tourist beat, the Downtown Gallery doesn't traffic in lighthouse paintings; it puts on sophisticated exhibits by serious Maine artists. Its openings are festive affairs that draw a curious mix of locals in work boots and Soho refugees in black Nehru shirts and brocade vests. Last week we all came down to check out new landscapes by Lorna Crichton and Joan Freiman while sipping wine and engaging in our own novel brand of small-town summer chatter: comparing asphalt plant emission studies, and reminding each other to remove our "Lane, Lane Go Away!" road signs so the shoulder mower can get through.

"If he has to stop and move the signs, it'll cost the town money," someone warned. You see it's July, and the town is broke.

Sarah and I went out to round up our kids, who were climbing on the town's war memorial. Many of the names engraved in that cold stone are families that still work the land here, reminding us that freedom comes at a particularly heavy price for small towns. I decided we should thank God when the bill for democracy comes from the lawyer— as opposed to the stonecutter and the undertaker.

I can't say what made Madison, Lincoln or even Hoover turn to politics, but it was probably something larger than a fifty-six-acre strip mine. (Maybe not in the case of Hoover, who was a mining engineer.) At any rate the strip mine in the woods is where it all began for me.

Almost two years have passed since Lane came to town with its quarry application. To no one's surprise, the planning board finally approved a version of the mine last summer (without the concrete and asphalt plants), and now we are appealing, to the town's appeals board. So is Lane; the company brazenly wants to win back its plants, even though it voluntarily "withdrew" them from the application in order to get the quarry passed. The company's duplicity shocked no one; as its lawyer said from the very beginning, "We're not here to make friends."

In the meantime, this naïve back-to-the-lander, who wanted nothing more than a heap of dung to call his own, has been transformed into an unlikely activist, defender of community rights, and, most recently, candidate for third selectman.

As I write these words it happens to be snowing while the sun is shining, which is pretty much how I feel about the whole thing. I'm not sure what will make me happier on March 28, 2003—winning or losing. Either way, I'll come out of it a better, if exhausted, man.

Which is not to say I'm kicking back and waiting to see what happens. My town has roughly 1,100 registered voters, about half of whom actually vote. You need about 250 of those votes to become a selectman. It would be hard to imagine people in my town voting for a local candidate they've never met, so if you don't know 250 people, you need to get out and knock on doors.

After living here four years, I figured I personally knew about a hundred people—not enough. So every Saturday I drive around town, visiting voters and handing out flyers that spell out my platform: "A progressive candidate who favors thoughtful planning that allows for traditional land use while protecting the community and the environment from unrestrained development." It sounds straightforward enough, but people have plenty of questions, only some of which can be predicted. "If you're elected, who will you put on the planning board?" (I had an answer for that one.) "If I vote for you, can I get a sidewalk?" (I hadn't thought about that.)

Some folks invite me in and want to talk for an hour. One older woman kept firing rhetorical questions at me ("Don't we want a town where people can feel safe walking down the street?"), and every time I answered correctly (which is pretty easy with rhetorical questions) she said "Bingo!"

"Bingo!" I made a mental note to go down to the VFW hall on bingo night.

Other voters open their door a crack and clearly don't want to be bothered. Some seem lonely, others angry, but most are grateful that a candidate cares enough to call on them. Everybody has dogs, and they all bark at you, especially by the end of the day when you smell like every other dog in town. Your car gets stuck in lots of icy driveways, which is where you learn spin control.

I think I have a good chance of winning, but it won't be easy. Unlike many small New England towns that have a hard time mustering any volunteers for local government, my town has seven candidates in the running for three selectman seats, including all the incumbents. The current third selectman, Donnie, is a native son and a career National Guard officer. His family is one of the oldest and most respected in town; he is an honest, intelligent and conservative man who governs only when necessary. I don't think of this race as anything personal against him— I tell people I'm simply running *for* selectman, not *against* Donnie—but he becomes noticeably cool to me after I announce my candidacy. At any rate his re-election seems inevitable to many, and I doubt if he campaigns any more actively than he governs.

Even more conservative is my third opponent Christine, a sincere and pleasant young woman who is running, as far as I can tell, on a get-government-off-our-backs platform. She has been endorsed by the rubble rousers. Without a doubt she will draw votes away from the incumbent, and I have encouraged her candidacy.

With all these competing factions and interests, I decided it wouldn't make sense to knock on every door; some people are simply never going to vote for me. I needed a plan. I needed a database. I needed Dave.

I spent two days in the town office with Dave, who's running for second selectman. Dave lost by eleven votes last year, and he's determined to win this time. So the two of us put the whole voter registration roll into a Listmaker data program. We identified who votes and who doesn't, who's likely to support us and who won't, who's gone, who's Green, who's dead and who's Republican. At home later, I took the list and cross-checked it with the town's 911 road list. I drew a yellow highlight through every household I wanted to visit. Then I grabbed my flyers and hit the road.

A lot of voters wanted to know where I came from, and they didn't mean which side of Davis Stream. I haven't tried to hide the fact that I'm from away, or anything else about who I am. When I was designing my flyer on the computer, I noticed I could manipulate the photo of myself to make me look thinner. I played around with it, briefly admiring the thinner me, then put it back to normal. If I'm going to win, it'll be the real me.

When I showed up at the town office on Friday night to watch the vote count, one of the more vocal rubble rousers glared at my muddy boots. I'd been working in my greenhouse all day, and I hadn't taken off my Tingleys with the steel toes. "If you get elected," he said, "you can't wear them boots in here."

He wasn't worried about mud on the floor. No, his meaning was clear: I was a college boy, a Topsider faker who hadn't earned the right to wear real farm boots around town. I wanted to tell him how my grandfather arrived in this country with just one pair of shoes. I wanted to knock the manure off my boots into his lap, and tell him what he could grow in it. I wanted to ask him if I could wear these boots when I danced on his grave. But I was a politician, so I bit my tongue and smiled. "I didn't know there was a dress code."

The hand count of paper ballots took six women several hours, but I knew I had lost after ten minutes. Some of the women were mouthing the names of the candidates under their breath as they counted, and I didn't hear my name nearly enough times. I lost my first political race to Donnie, the incumbent colonel, during wartime. No surprises there, and Donnie was beaming. I saluted him (figuratively) at the town office when the count ended around eleven o'clock, and I offered him my support in the coming year.

In our three-way race of five hundred nineteen votes, Donnie scored two hundred thirty-nine, winning by a plurality; oddly, my other opponent Christine and myself each got exactly one hundred forty votes, which we laughed about. So I lost by ninety-nine votes, roughly the same as Al Gore. (Unfortunately Dave also lost in his run for second selectman, by an even wider margin than the previous year.)

One hundred forty votes might not seem like many, but out here in the backcountry, people don't vote for you unless they know you—and despite the influx of retirees and the organic crowd, it's a rare flatlander who wins public office. When uppity newcomers do cast fate to the wind and run for office here, they typically round up a few dozen votes—close friends and family. That generally embarrasses them enough that they go into hiding for twenty years. For a relative newcomer like myself to get twenty-seven percent of the vote was regarded as quite an accomplishment. My strong showing, way beyond my immediate support base, was directly due to my diligent door-to-door campaigning (five Saturdays from nine to five), and (I believe) my inclusive but progressive stance.

I was peppered with praise at Saturday's open town meeting, and was surprised to find myself enjoying new-found status as a town statesman. Even some of the rubble rousers (some of whom I'd come to appreciate during the campaign) were respectful.

I also slept well Friday night, in part because Sarah and I were both getting cold feet about the whole thing, although she was looking forward to becoming Third Lady. When I decided to run I didn't have a lot of work (as in paid work), but in the cyclical nature of these things, I'm now pretty busy, and I was getting nervous about finding the time to help run a town and do my work. (The office of third selectman pays three thousand dollars a year, which I was planning to donate to local charities.) In that sense, my respectable loss was a relief.

There's an old gospel song that says, "Every road goes higher and higher." Win or lose, I found running for public office, even in my tiny town, to be an amazingly positive experience. It made me feel proud about citizenship and democracy, and not in an empty, flag-waving way. On a personal (okay, egotistical) level, just walking into the voting booth and seeing my own name on the ballot made it worthwhile. But the real value was in gaining a deeper appreciation of the people who live here (especially the people I don't agree with)—knowledge I hope I can carry forward in community service. Best of all, it wasn't about money. (I spent $15.75 on copying and $83.25 on stamps.)

Presidents used to come from similarly small towns, and get their start on similarly modest campaigns. I wish it still worked that way, because small-town politics teaches you to listen, and not just to voters: during my door-to-door campaign, I became an expert at telling which barking dogs were likely to bite, and which were just glad to see you. Listening is a virtue that seems lost on a lot of today's leaders, who spend most of their time talking into the lens of a TV camera. Maybe that's the way it has to be, but I suspect we'd feel our Presidents and prime ministers were more human if they had spent some time in dairy boots, banging on trailer doors.

For anyone seeking a do-it-yourself life, away from the experts in New York and Hollywood who think they know better than you how to make money and have fun, I urge you to point your VW van (the one you painted yourself, with the underwear elastic for a carburetor spring and the two-by-four thingy that keeps the clutch from popping) straight in the direction of rural Maine.

The backcountry around me is Mecca for those who

would do just about anything themselves rather than ask a pro. From local government to barn building, rural Mainers prefer their own version, no matter the result. It's the doing that counts, danger aside. For a state that recently turned down casinos, it's amazing how many rural Mainers with no masonry experience will gamble on constructing their own chimneys. The most commonly heard phrase out here is "How hard could it be?" (Followed later by the famous last line: "She's not goin' anywhere.")

It's a lifestyle I essentially endorse. Still and all, there are times when the experts are needed. I was thinking about this the other day as I stood, knife in hand, before two dead pigs, which were hanging from a tree and bleeding into the snow around my boots.

I was staring at the pigs, but what made me think of the need for experts was a recent special town meeting called by our selectmen. It seems that our town spent more than was budgeted for legal costs last year—about ten thousand dollars more, quite a large sum in my town. Everybody knew why. A series of local land use decisions, most significantly the ongoing Lane case, meant lots of work for the town's attorney, whom we call the Eggman. Whenever an angry citizen stood up at a Lane hearing to gripe, the Eggman dipped into his suit jacket pocket and whipped out an egg timer. "You have three minutes!" he intoned, cranking the dial.

But this being rural Maine, not too many folks take kindly to experts bearing egg timers. Just about everybody keeps on talking till the hard-boiled stage, while the Eggman scowls and his ears turn red. Meetings in our town can get unruly, and the latest was a corker.

The meeting was required by law, which says that

whenever selectmen spend beyond the approved town budget, they need to go back to voters and get permission. Statute aside, the vote is obviously pro forma; bills must be paid. Should voters elect not to pay the bill, the selectmen would simply take the money out of reserve funds, and there would be an asterisk on the town report.

But that was beside the point to the rubble rousers— including Bradley, whom the selectmen did not reappoint to the planning board when his term was up. By then, the Lane case had moved on—through our appeals board (which upheld the planning board's decision to grant the rock quarry but turned down the rock crusher) and up to state Superior Court. Of course, Lane isn't happy about losing its processing plants and rock crusher; it doesn't do them a lot of good to blast out car-sized pieces of granite if they can't crush them into stone and make a product. And we at the Land Association still maintain that the quarry itself is illegal under our zoning rules. The result is that both Lane and the Land Association are in court challenging different aspects of the town's decisions. It's an expensive mess that might have been avoided had Bradley handled things better from the beginning.

That's probably what the selectmen were thinking when they bounced him from the board. So for Bradley, it was personal. He showed up with his friends from the Rights Association at the town meeting, where they hoped they could make the selectmen squirm by voting down the payment to the lawyer. It was a classic small-town grudge match.

But we saw it coming, and we got out our own vote. In total about sixty people squeezed into our little community room, and the mood was as hard and cold as the metal folding chairs. The moderator asked for comments, and things got off to a bad start. "How do we know all these people live here?" asked a swarthy crew-cut guy in the back. "Are you checking them off on the voter rolls?"

Cheryl, our very able town clerk, tried to suppress a *gimme-a-break* glare and said "I know everyone in this room, Jim. We've never checked voter rolls for these meetings, and I don't believe it's a problem."

It went downhill from there, with lots of interruptions and accusations, until Janet got into it with Arlene. Arlene, who works down at Bradley's garage and also tends some of the cemeteries around town, is an outspoken member of the Rights Association. Janet is the outspoken wife of Dave, a member of the Land Association's executive board.

Arlene's family is one of the oldest in town, going back to the original, unruly band of settlers that squatted here in the colonial days and thumbed their noses at the English proprietors who owned the land; Janet is from the Bronx, where making rude noises is called cheering. It is neither a compliment nor an insult to suggest that from a pugilistic standpoint they are evenly matched.

After interrupting each other a few times, Arlene finally said "Janet, I'm sorry, I know you been sick, but if you wanna step outside and settle this right now, let's go!" And she jabbed a grease-stained thumb toward the door.

To say Janet had been sick was an understatement. A week earlier, doctors at Mass General had removed her cancerous kidney. So when Arlene challenged her to a fight, everyone gasped—except Janet, who jumped up and said "Let's go!"

"Sit down, Janet," said Dave, tugging her arm. To the relief of the selectmen, Janet sat down and the meeting went on. No blows were exchanged, and *yeas* outweighed *nays* by about a dozen votes.

Governor Baldacci believes we pay a steep price for those votes. He wants to consolidate local government, and in many ways he's right; the legal bills in my town—and a lot of anger—could be reduced if land use decisions were made by professional, regional planners, not volunteer townsfolk whose eyes glaze over at two hundred fifty-page mining applications and environmental impact studies. The applicants show up with three hundred dollar an hour lawyers and hydro-geologists, against boards consisting of goat farmers and snow-plow drivers. No wonder we get into trouble. No wonder we get socked with legal bills. It's not a fair fight.

But so long as we insist on do-it-yourself government (how hard could it be?), we will keep getting creamed by other people's experts. Baldacci is hopeful for change, but I'm not sure. As they say around here, she's not goin' anywhere.

More on McDonald's from the man who wrote Fast Food Nation.

Slow Food
from TheEcologist.com (3/22/04)
Eric Schlosser

When the fast food industry is made to bear the costs it is now imposing on the rest of society, it will collapse. The alternative to fast food now seems obvious—slow food.

In February a report by George W. Bush's Council of Economic Advisers (CEA) suggested that fast food workers might in the future be classified as manufacturing workers. A CEA report asked: "When a fast-food restaurant sells a hamburger, for example, is it providing a 'service', or is it combining inputs to 'manufacture' a product?"

Reclassifying fast-food restaurants as "factories" would have a number of benefits for the Bush administration. It would, in a single stroke, add about 3.5 million manufacturing jobs to the U.S. economy, at a time when such jobs are rapidly being exported overseas. From a statistical point of view, it would make the U.S. seem like an industrial powerhouse once again, instead of an ageing superpower threatened by low-cost competitors. And it would allow the fast-food industry, a strong backer of the Republican Party, to enjoy the tax breaks provided to U.S. manufacturers.

The CEA's chairman N. Gregory Mankiw was derided and ridiculed in the press for making the proposal, and his plan is likely to go nowhere. Yet there was an underlying logic to it. Fast food is indeed factory food, perhaps the most heavily processed food on the planet, and the low-paid workers who defrost, reheat and reconstitute it have jobs as boring, highly regimented and strictly supervised as the workers in a 19th century textile mill would have had. Moreover, the founding fathers of the industry probably wouldn't have minded the manufacturing label at all. Bringing the philosophy of the assembly line to the commercial restaurant kitchen was the simple innovation responsible for Ronald McDonald's global conquest.

The fast-food industry began in 1948. Richard and

Maurice McDonald were growing tired of running their successful drive-in restaurant in San Bernardino, California. They were tired of constantly hiring new car-hops, the teenaged girls who took food to customers waiting in parked automobiles. They were tired of replacing the dishes and glasses broken by their adolescent customers. But most of all, they were tired of paying the high wages demanded by skilled short-order cooks.

So the McDonalds decided to shut down their drive-in and replace it with a revolutionary new form of restaurant. The McDonald brothers started by firing all their car-hops and short-order cooks. They simplified the menu, hired unskilled workers and made each worker perform the same task again and again. One person only made French fries. Another only made shakes. Another only flipped burgers. By ending getting rid of skilled workers, by serving food and drinks in paper cups and plates, by demanding that customers wait on line for their own meals, the new "Speedee Service System" allowed the brothers to serve fast, cheap food.

The new restaurant was an instant success. It fitted perfectly with the new culture emerging in post-war southern California—a car culture that worshipped speed, convenience and the latest technology. Ray Kroc, the milk shake machine salesman who bought out the McDonald brothers in the early 1960s and later exported their Speedee system around the world, embraced a blind faith in science: a Disneyesque vision of society transformed through chemistry and families living happily in plastic homes and travelling in sleek, nuclear-powered cars.

Kroc also believed fervently in the ethic of mass production. A philosophy of uniformity, conformity and total control that had long dictated the manufacture of steel wire was now applied not only to food, but to the people who prepared the food. "We have found out . . . that we cannot trust some people who are non-conformists," Kroc declared. "We will make conformists out of them in a hurry . . . The organisation cannot trust the individual; the individual must trust the organisation."

For the first two decades of its existence, the McDonald's operating system had little impact on the way people lived and ate. In 1968 there were only 1,000 McDonald's restaurants, all of them in the U.S. The chain bought fresh ground beef and potatoes from hundreds of local suppliers. But the desire for rapid growth—and the desire for everything to taste exactly the same at thousands of different locations—transformed not only the McDonald's supply system, but also the agricultural economy of the entire U.S.

McDonald's switched entirely to frozen hamburger patties and frozen fries, relying on a handful of large companies to manufacture them. Other fast food chains spread nationwide at the same time, helping to drive local restaurants, small suppliers, independent ranchers and farmers out of business. And by the 1970s McDonald's began to expand overseas, taking with it a mentality perfectly expressed years later in one of the company's slogans—"one taste worldwide."

Half a century after Richard and Maurice McDonald decided to fire their car-hops, the world's food supply is dominated by an agro-industrial complex in which the fast-food chains occupy the highest rung. Monsanto developed genetically-modified potatoes to supply McDonald's with perfectly uniform French fries—and then halted production of the "New Leaf" GM potato when McDonald's decided, for publicity reasons, not to buy it. When the fast-food industry wants something, the major food processors rush to supply it.

Although many of the foods we eat look the same as the ones we ate a generation ago, they have been fundamentally changed. They have become industrial commodities, with various components (flavour, colour, fats) manufactured and assembled at different facilities. If you bought a hamburger in the U.S. 30 years ago, it would most probably have contained meat from one steer or cow, which would have been processed at a local butcher shop or small meat-packing plant.

Today a typical fast-food hamburger patty contains meat from more than 1,000 different cattle, raised in as many as five different countries. It looks like an old-fashioned hamburger, but is a fundamentally different thing.

Here is a partial list of what fast food and the fast-food mentality have recently brought us: the homogenisation of culture, both regionally and worldwide; the malling and sprawling of the landscape; the feeling that everywhere looks and feels the same; a low-wage, alienated service-sector workforce; a low-wage, terribly exploited meat-packing workforce; a widening gap between rich and poor; concentration of economic power; the control of local and national governments by agribusiness; an eagerness to aim sophisticated mass marketing at children; a view of farm animals as industrial commodities; unspeakable cruelty toward those animals; the spread of factory farms; extraordinary air and water pollution; the rise of food-borne illnesses; antibiotic resistance; BSE; soaring obesity rates that have caused soaring rates of asthma, heart disease and early-onset diabetes; reduced life-expectancy; a cloying, fake, manipulative, disposable, plastic worldview, the sole aim of which is to make a buck.

None of this was inevitable. The triumph of the fast-food system was aided at almost every step by government subsidies, lack of proper regulation, misleading advertisements, and a widespread ignorance of how fast, cheap food is actually produced. This system is not sustainable. In less than three decades it has already done extraordinary harm. When the fast-food industry is made to bear the costs it is now imposing on the rest of society, it will collapse. The alternative to fast food now seems obvious: slow food.

By "slow food" I do not mean precious, gourmet food, sold by celebrity chefs and prepared according to recipes in glossy cookbooks. I mean food that is authentic, that has been grown and prepared using methods that are local, organic and sustainable. Most slow foods are peasant foods. Somehow mankind existed for thousands of years without Chicken McNuggets. And I'd argue that our future survival depends on living without them.

McDonald's, which makes its money selling bad food to children (check out the clown!), owns thousands of "restaurants"; it also "owns" 131 words and phrases—including "McDonald's Means Opportunity" (a bald-faced lie, of course; see the story on page 297).

Serving Up the McDictionary

Las Vegas Weekly (5/22/01)

Kate Silver

The Golden Arches are said to be more widely recognized than a Christian cross. All thanks to Ronald McDonald.

McDonald's represents capitalistic imperialism at its best, pushing hamburglars and cheeseburglars into countries where people used to value things like kosher products, low-fat foods and vegetarianism. And the xenophobic clown won't be stopped.

Still, with more than 26,000 restaurants worldwide, they're obviously doing something right. Besides stepping on toes in other countries, they also create items adapted to different cultures. In Hong Kong, they have things called the Curry Potato Pie, Shake Shake Fries and a Red Bean Sunday. In Italy, they have four salads: Marinara, with shrimp and salmon; Vegetariana; Mediterranea; and Fiordiriso, with rice, tuna, ham and mushrooms. In Japan, they have the Teriyaki McBurger, which is sausage on a bun with teriyaki sauce. In the Netherlands, they have the McKroket, a burger made of beef ragout with a crispy layer around it, topped with a mustard/mayonnaise sauce. Switzerland serves a Vegi Mac.

Yes, that redheaded clown has bought and sold his way into the hearts of billions.

But to some, McDonalds is an evil empire. They market unhealthy, fat-packed, fiber-filled food to small children through their grease-painted spokesman and toy-strewn happy meals. They produce ungodly amounts of waste. And more cows die for your Big Mac attacks than for any other company.

McDonalds has restaurants in 120 different countries and serves a whopping 29 million people a day. But here's something you may not have known: They also own 131 different words and phrases—including such surprises as "Black History Makers of tomorrow" and "Healthy Growing Up." They've trademarked them so no one else can use them. We've copied them off the McDonalds Web site to show you that if we're not careful, McDonalds may someday own the McWorld. Literally.

According to the Web site, "(t)he following trademarks used herein are owned by the McDonald's Corporation and its affiliates:

1-800-MC1-STCK; Always Quality. Always Fun; America's Favorite Fries; Arch Deluxe; Automac; Big Mac; Big N' Tasty; Big Xtra!; Birdie, the Early Bird and Design; Bolshoi Mac; Boston Market; Cajita Feliz; Changing The Face of The World; Chicken McGrill; Chicken McNuggets; Chipolte Mexican Grill; Cuarto De Libra; Did Somebody Say; Donatos Pizza; emac digital; Egg McMuffin; Extra Value Meal; Filet-O-Fish; French Fry Box Design; Gep Op Mac; Golden Arches; Golden Arches Logo; Good Jobs For Good People; Good Times. Great Taste; Gospelfest; Great Breaks; Grimace and Design; Groenteburger; HACER; Hamburglar and Design; Hamburger University;

Happy Meal; Happy Meal Box Design; Have You Had Your Break Today?;

Helping Hands Logo; Hey, It Could Happen!; Iam Hungry and Design; Immunize for Healthy Lives; Lifting Kids To A Better Tomorrow; Mac Attack; Mac Tonight and Design; McDonald's Racing Team Design; Made For You; McBaby; McBacon; McBurger; McBus; McCafe; McChicken; McDia Feliz; MCDirect Shares; McDonald-land; McDonald's; McDonald's Earth Effort; McDonald's Earth Effort Logo; McDonald's Express; McDonald's Express Logo; McDonald's Is Your Kind of Place; McDonald's Means Opportunity; McDouble; McDrive; McExpress; McFamily; McFlurry; McFranchise; McGrilled Chicken; McHappy Day; McHero; McJobs; McKids; McK-roket; McMaco; McMemories; McMenu; McMusic; McNifica; McNuggets; McNuggets Kip; McOz; McPlane; McPollo; McPrep; McRecycle USA; McRib; McRoyal; Mc Scholar; McScholar of the Year; McSwing; McWorld;

Mighty Wings; Millennium Dreamers; Morning Mac; Quarter Pounder; Ronald McDonald and Design; Ronald McDonald House; Ronald McDonald House Charities; Ronald McDonald House Charities Logo; Ronald McDonald House Logo; Ronald Scholars; Sausage McMuffin; Single Arch Logo; Speedee Logo; Super Size; The House That Love Built; The House That Love Built Design; twoallbeefpattiesspecialsaucelettucecheesepick-lesoniononasesameseedbun; We Love to See You Smile; What's On Your Place; When the U.S. Wins You Win; World Famous Fries; You Deserve a Break Today."

He Said It . . .

"We have found out that we cannot trust some people who are non-conformists. We will make conformists out of them in a hurry. The organization cannot trust the individual; the individual must trust the organization."

—Ray Kroc, founder of McDonald's

"For heaven's sake, Ed! I'm sure the Wilsons have heard the story of how you refused to sell out to corporate America at least 10 times!"

Enron was only the tip of the tip of the tip of the iceberg. Its screw-up made headlines (for a while, anyway) mostly because its victims included some rich people.

It's the Corporate Economy, Stupid

from TheEcologist.com (6/22/02)

Steve Gorelick

Why has everyone in the media and government made such a fuss about Enron and the like when there are far worse corporate abuses that never make the front page?

Here in the U.S., the collapse of energy giant Enron has been like a tune you can't get out of your head. It has plenty of hooks—crestfallen employees, disgraced stock analysts, shredded documents and red-faced politicians. But a more important reason why it has colonised our minds is that the media has played it constantly, like a number-one song on a top-40 radio station. (Even its B-side, The Ballad of Arthur Andersen, might eventually top the news charts.)

However, at the same time as the public was being bombarded by stories about bad auditing and inflated share values, it was being kept in the dark about far more serious crimes. Take GM giant Monsanto, for example. It has recently been tried in Alabama for dumping tonnes of deadly PCBs in the poor community of Anniston and then trying to cover its tracks.

In March a jury found the company guilty of every count levelled against it. Monsanto's crimes included negligence, suppression of the truth, and conduct "so outrageous in character and extreme in degree as to go beyond all possible bounds of decency;" conduct, in fact, that is "atrocious and utterly intolerable in civilised society." By comparison, Enron's book-juggling is the moral equivalent of shoplifting.

Perhaps there was a brief article about the Anniston case buried in the *New York Times*. There may have been some 20-second sound bite on the nightly news. If so, I missed them both. There was certainly nothing to match the wall-to-wall coverage of Enron. The government easily matched this bias: a dozen different congressional committees have been investigating the Enron collapse, but not one is looking into Monsanto's actions.

How to account for this singular focus? Simple. While Monsanto's crimes were directed at the environment and people (poor people at that), Enron's undermined confidence in the stock market—thereby threatening the economy. The media's choice of what to cover merely reflected the sad truth that absolutely nothing in this country is more sacred than the economy. When push comes to shove—people and the environment be damned—it's the economy, stupid, that matters.

And not just any economy. The economy that counts is the one that is run by and for huge corporations. There is no particular concern about the fate of local economies that support small farmers, locally-owned businesses, local craftspeople and artisans.

Like people and the environment, those local economies can be—and systematically are—sacrificed for the good of the corporate-led economy.

The fact is, it wasn't Enron's criminal behaviour that attracted so much attention. It was the destabilising effect those crimes had on the stock market and the economy.

Corporations and the people who run them can do just about anything with impunity, so long as they don't rock the economic boat. Just look at Jack Welch, departing CEO of General Electric. Over the years Welch laid off so many workers that he was given the nickname "Neutron Jack" after the bomb that kills people but leaves buildings intact. His final days at GE were spent trying to evade responsibility for the 1.3 million pounds of PCBs the company dumped into the Hudson River.

Is Welch vilified? Hardly. His company was immensely profitable and its stock soared with Welch at the helm. He is widely regarded as a hero, the "model CEO." His self-congratulatory memoir topped the business best-seller lists for months.

Given the primacy of the corporate economy, it isn't surprising that every post-Enron reform floated so far has been designed to do little more than raise people's comfort levels about their stock market investments. But one of the proposals, if fully enacted, might actually do some good. It would require "truth in accounting" and "full disclosure" from corporations—an idea I fully support.

But by "full disclosure" I don't just mean revealing money laundering and shady partnerships. I mean:

- Annual reports from agribusinesses like Cargill would explain the connection between their booming profits and the rapidly declining fortunes of small farmers;

- Pesticide manufacturers would be required to calculate the costs of their toxic agrochemicals on human health, with tables cross-referencing exposure categories (production worker, farmworker, consumer) with types of illness (cancers, reproductive disorders, birth defects, and so on);

• All polluting companies would be required to indicate how many billions of dollars in environmental costs they shift from their expense sheets onto that of the public and future generations;

• The oil, coal, and auto industries should reveal how much they spend each year to keep the U.S. from doing anything about global warming; calculations should include separate figures not just for campaign contributions and lobbying expenses, but also for funding of flimsy "scientific studies," greenwashing campaigns and phoney grassroots organisations; annual reports might include a graph of rising sea levels; allowing investors to determine whether company resources are being allocated efficiently;

• Mega-stores like Wal-Mart would have to disclose how many small, locally-owned businesses they destroy during the year (charts might compare this year's toll with last year's performance); and the fair-market value of "free trade" agreements, which enable their stores to carry goods produced by the lowest-paid, least-protected workers in the world, would also be reported.

But don't hold your breath.

THEY USE OUR CHILDREN

*with quotes by Joel Babbit, Procter & Gamble;
and a Fact*

Nothing is sacred to a corporation—not life, not liberty, not happiness. So why should childhood be an exception?

Students for Sale

from *The Nation* (9/27/99)

Steven Manning

When Susan Crockett walked Amy, her 8-year-old daughter, to her school bus stop last September, she was in for a surprise. The school bus that rolled up was covered with advertisements for Burger King, Wendy's and other brand-name products. A few weeks later, Amy, a third grader, and Crockett's three older children arrived home toting free book covers and school planners covered with ads for Kellogg's Pop-Tarts and Fox TV personalities. Then, in November, came news that local school officials were pushing a year-old contract giving Coca-Cola exclusive permission to sell its products in district schools. That was the last straw for Crockett.

"It really angers me that the school is actively promoting and pushing a product that's not good for kids," says Crockett, whose oldest child was a senior last year in the Colorado Springs, Colorado, school system. "What's next: Will kids be required to wear Nikes before they are allowed to go to school?"

These days, lots of parents are asking that question.

Eager to attract a captive audience of young customers, almost every large corporation sponsors some type of in-school marketing program. Many also sponsor curriculum materials salted with brand names and corporate logos. Throughout the nation, nearly 40 percent of schools begin their day with current events and commercials transmitted by Channel One, the in-school TV news program for teens. Started in 1989 by controversial entrepreneur Chris

Whittle, Channel One is probably the best-known in-school marketing program, but more recent examples are even more alarming:

- An exercise book that purports to teach third graders math by having them count Tootsie Rolls.

- A classroom business course that teaches students the value of work by showing them how McDonald's restaurants are run.

- Multimillion-dollar contracts that have turned some schools into virtual sales agents for Coke and Pepsi.

Why the stampede into the classroom? "That's where the kids are," says Alex Molnar, director of the Center for the Analysis of Commercialism in Education at the University of Wisconsin, Milwaukee. "Companies like to say they are promoting education and school-business partnerships, but what they're really doing is going after the kids' market anywhere they can." Ira Mayer, publisher of *Youth Markets Alert*, an industry newsletter, notes that companies "want to get them started young—and hopefully keep them for life—that's what brand loyalty is all about." In 1997, children 4 to 12 spent an estimated $24.4 billion, according to *American Demographics*. Last year, kids 12 to 19 spent an estimated $141 billion, according to Teenage Research Unlimited. Meanwhile, many cash-strapped public schools find it difficult to resist corporate-sponsored advertising and handouts, especially when they come with free computers or new football stadiums and scoreboards.

Nowhere is the convergence of schoolhouse need and corporate greed more apparent than in Colorado Springs. At Palmer High School, students walk through hallways dotted with signs for national brands and local companies, eat in a snack bar sporting brand-new vending machines, use computers with ad-bearing mouse pads and play basketball in a gym decorated with banners of corporate sponsors.

"This was the first school district in the nation to offer advertising opportunities, and the results have been great for our students," said Kenneth Burnley, superintendent of Colorado Springs School District 11. Burnley dreamed up the district's advertising and corporate-partnership programs in 1993, after years of coping with harsh budget cuts. When Burnley took over in 1989, the school district was $12 million in the red. Although Colorado Springs, located about sixty miles south of Denver, is best known for its beautiful weather and tourist attractions like Pike's Peak, it's also the state's second-largest city, and its schools suffer from ills common to urban school districts: overcrowded classes, lack of extracurricular programs and crumbling school buildings. There's also the problem that until 1996, city voters had not approved a tax increase for education in more than two decades. (In a 1999 survey by *Education Week*, Colorado was ranked forty-ninth in the nation in the adequacy of resources devoted to education.)

"Our taxpayers have challenged us to be more creative and businesslike in how we finance the schools, so we decided to take a page out of business's book," says Burnley. "I realized we could sell for cash something we always had, but never knew we had"—access to students. So far, some fifty companies have signed up as corporate partners, at a cost ranging from $1,500 to $12,000. Top dollar buys advertising rights on school buses, in all schools and four public-address announcements at every basketball and football game, among other benefits. A $1,500 check buys a 2 feet x 5 feet sign in one school and tickets to attend school athletic events. District 11 officials say the advertising packages bring in about $100,000 in revenue annually.

But the district's biggest and most lucrative deal is with Coke. Under a contract signed nearly two years ago, the district will receive $8.4 million over ten years—and more if it exceeds its requirement of selling 70,000 cases of Coke products a year. Along with the contract come other Coke-sponsored sweeteners, like a contest in which a Chevrolet Cavalier was awarded to a senior with perfect attendance.

Last fall, a top District 11 official sent a letter to administrators urging them to increase sales of Coke products in their schools in order to meet their sales goal. In the letter, John Bushey, the official who oversees the contract, instructed principals to allow students virtually unlimited access to Coke machines and to move the machines to where they would be "accessible to the students all day." Wrote Bushey: "Research shows that vendor purchases are closely linked to availability," adding, "location, location, location is the key." The confidential letter, which was first published by the Colorado Springs *Independent,* also urged teachers to allow students to drink Coke in the classroom: "If soda is not allowed in classes, consider allowing juices, water, and teas." Bushey signed the letter "The Coke Dude."

The letter, and the district's policy of establishing school sales quotas—including in elementary schools— has alarmed critics of school commercialism. "This is the first concrete evidence we've had that the soft-drink companies are turning schools into virtual sales agents for their products," says Andrew Hagelshaw, senior program director of the Center for Commercial-free Public Education, a nonprofit group based in Oakland, California. "These kinds of contracts are going to change the priorities from education to soda consumption."

Bushey and other officials deny that the letter was meant to encourage kids to guzzle more Coke. "Our only purpose was to inform people about how the contract works, its incentives and disincentives," said Bob Moore, the district's chief financial officer. A spokesperson for Coca-Cola in Atlanta insisted that the company doesn't have a set quota policy. "It's up to the individual school district," said Coke's Scott Jacobson. "If they want to make more money by selling more product, we'll work with them."

Most teachers in Colorado Springs are apparently willing to work with Coke as well. "We haven't had a single complaint," says Kathy Glasmann, the president of the Colorado Springs Education Association, the local teachers' union. Superintendent Burnley agrees, attributing lack of protest against the corporate-sponsorship program to the "mores" of a community that is heavily Republican, fiscally conservative and strongly opposed to taxes. Plus, says Nancy Haley, a seventh-grade science teacher at a Colorado Springs middle school, "You just don't turn down a deal that will bring $20,000 a year to your school."

Still, there are pockets of furtive dissent. "Many teachers are quietly opposed to the advertising," says Ed Bailey, a fifth-grade math teacher at Steele Elementary School. "We feel we are being forced into the position of telling students, 'We approve of Coke, we approve of Burger King;

we, the school, approve of these products, so they must be good for you.'" Some teachers have taken to hiding ads they've been asked to post in hallways, Bailey says. Others, like John Hawk, a twenty-five-year veteran of Colorado Springs schools, uses them for lessons on propaganda in his social studies classes at Mitchell High School. "Students and teachers need basic training on how to deal with the corporate invasion of every aspect of life," Hawk says. "Schools used to be the one safe haven where kids weren't exposed to a constant barrage of advertising. Now even that's gone."

Yet few students at Mitchell or other area schools seem to know or care what schools used to be like. This doesn't surprise John Crockett, Susan Crockett's oldest child. "Commercials, ads, videos, that's all my generation has known," says Crockett. "The ads [at Doherty High School] are no big topic of hallway conversation, that's for sure. They just seem to fade into the background."

Meanwhile, District 11 is determined not only to attract more corporate sponsors but to spread the Colorado Springs model nationwide. "We get dozens of calls every day from school districts wanting to replicate what we've done," says Bob Moore. "Can they visit here? Can they talk to us? We say, 'Sure, we want to spread the word.'" Already, the Denver, Houston, Newark and Jefferson County, Colorado, school districts have set up soft-drink or marketing programs. Jefferson County even got Pepsi to kick in $1.5 million to help build a new sports stadium, and some county schools tested a new science course, developed in part by Pepsi, titled "The Carbonated Beverage Company," in which students taste-test colas, analyze cola samples, take a video tour of a Pepsi bottling plant and visit a local Pepsi plant.

In its publicity efforts, District 11 has its own high-pow-
ered corporate partner, Dan DeRose, an entrepreneur who
has single-handedly invented a brand-new mini-industry:
the school-marketing broker. DeRose is the founder and
president of DD Marketing, a firm that specializes in putting together exclusive marketing contracts for public
schools and colleges. DeRose brought not only Coke to
District 11 but also U.S. West—in the first exclusive partnership between a telecommunications company and a
school district. (Sign up for phone service or call waiting
with U.S. West, and a commission is paid to one's school
of choice.) But DeRose has bigger ambitions.

A 37-year-old former professional football player and
college athletic director, DeRose is evangelical in his belief
that advertising deals are good not only for schools and
education but also help level an unfair playing field:
"Schools have been opening their doors to corporate
America for years," DeRose says, noting that many school
districts cut their own marketing deals with big companies, only to wind up with "peanuts" in exchange. "Our
philosophy is if you're going to allow corporate America
into your schools, maximize your return."

DeRose claims that he and his staff have visited more
than 800 school districts nationwide during the past
year, of which about 150 have signed exclusive soft-
drink contracts, while 600 more are in the negotiating
stage. According to published accounts, DD Marketing
gets a 25-40 percent cut of each deal. DeRose is known
for his imaginative pitches to interested schools and companies. During negotiations for a $3.5 million, ten-year
exclusive contract for the Grapevine-Colleyville Independent School District in Texas with Dr. Pepper/7-Up, some

school board members expressed unease with having advertisements in classrooms. As an alternative, DeRose helped arrange for Dr. Pepper logos to be painted on the rooftops of two high schools that lie directly under the flight path for Dallas-Fort Worth International Airport.

Critics like Andrew Hagelshaw say the cash being paid out to schools isn't all that impressive. In Colorado Springs, for example, the annual school budget is $165 million. Broken down, the ten-year, $8.4 million Coke contract works out to be a payment of $840,000 per year, or 0.5 percent of the total yearly budget. "On a per pupil basis, that's nothing," says Hagelshaw. "They're selling their kids out cheap."

Indeed, while school officials claim that their main motivation for seeking corporate contracts is money, there is some evidence that in the long run the deals may undermine their ability to obtain more state funds and may reinforce classic financial distinctions between poor and wealthy school districts. Low-income school districts that are desperate for school supplies often are the first and most eager clients of companies that provide free equipment to schools, such as Channel One and ZapMe! The result: Poor schools get their ten or fifteen free televisions or computers (and the advertising that goes along with them), while district and state officials feel less motivated to provide the schools with adequate equipment or an in-school technology plan. Wealthier school districts often turn to corporate cash after being squeezed by local and state funding cutbacks, as was the case with both the Colorado Springs and Grapevine-Colleyville districts. The danger is that school administrators will become dependent on corporate handouts and forget that it was the failure to provide schools with adequate public funding that brought them to the begging bowl in the first place. As Colorado Springs social studies teacher John Hawk notes, "It says something about our country's social priorities when we have to resort to corporate contracts to fund our schools."

DeRose brushes aside such criticisms. "Every school district of any size in the country wants in on this," he says. Unfortunately, that seems to be the case. Except for the occasional renegade school officials—like the Rhode Island administrator who recently physically removed all the soda machines from his school—most schools seem eager to get on the corporate gravy train. Although a number of educational organizations, including the national PTA and the National Education Association, have endorsed voluntary guidelines to help schools determine which, if any, in-school commercial activities have merit, most educators are unaware of them.

There are a few school districts, however, where parents and students are fighting back. At Berkeley High School last year, the Pepsi-Cola Company offered the school $90,000 and a fancy new electronic scoreboard for the football stadium in exchange for an exclusive vending deal. Meanwhile, Nike approached the school's athletic director with a proposal to provide athletic equipment and uniforms—as long as all student-athletes wore a Nike swoosh on their back. The deals were ultimately scuttled, in large part because of the efforts of a determined 15-year-old sophomore, Sarah Church. Church organized a student-led forum on whether the school should accept the deals, then inspired her classmates to testify against them at school board meetings. "We took a strong stand against selling out students to advertisers," Church says. Today, she is trying to launch a national student movement against in-school advertising.

In June, in neighboring San Francisco, the school board approved the Commercial Free Schools Act, the first measure of its kind in the country. The act bars the district from signing exclusive beverage contracts or adopting educational materials that contain brand names.

But perhaps the most ambitious and successful anticommercialism campaign has been in Seattle. Three years ago, the Seattle school board proposed a far-reaching corporate-sponsorship program that officials predicted would bring in $1 million a year. The proposal caught the attention of Brita Butler-Wall, a teacher-trainer at the University of Seattle and the mother of two children in Seattle schools. "I thought the idea was wacky, since it seems counter to everything schools are supposed to stand for," she says. Butler-Wall contacted a few other parents, and they decided to "go to the mat on the issue." The group, calling itself the Seattle Citizens' Campaign for Commercial-free Schools (CCC), sponsored a series of public meetings on the issue that drew statewide attention. Then they organized a series of "commercialism walk-throughs" of the city's schools, collecting as many examples of already existing commercial material as they could, sending a copy of their findings to the school board.

The CCC also won support from a group not usually involved in educational battles: organized labor. Mike Miller, a local Teamsters activist and father with a son in the public schools, and David Yao, head of the local postal workers' union, presented a resolution condemning the school board's plan to the King County Labor Council, and to their surprise it passed unanimously. "We are opposed to exposing schoolchildren to corporate values in an educational environment where they assume that whatever is presented to them carries the approval of the educational establishment," the resolution read in part. While the city's teachers' union declined to take a position on the commercialism issue, other local unions played an important role in galvanizing opposition.

In March 1997 the school board rescinded the advertising sponsorship policy. Instead, it appointed a school-community task force—members of the CCC—to study the issue and make policy recommendations. Those recommendations, issued last September, call for sharp restrictions on most forms of commercial activities. The task force's final report, though, is still waiting for official approval. In the meantime, the Seattle school board signed its own exclusive soft-drink contract with Coca-Cola, over the strenuous objections of the CCC and others.

Which raises the question: Are opponents of school-house commercialism fighting a losing battle? For now at least, it seems that the corporations have the upper hand. Unless more parents, teachers and legislators start paying attention, consumerism may replace learning as the predominant value in American public education.

They Said It . . .

"The advertiser gets a group of kids who cannot go to the bathroom, who cannot change the station, who cannot listen to their mother yell in the background, who cannot be playing Nintendo, who cannot have their headsets on."
—Joel Babbit, former president of Channel One

"It mimics nature's way of getting rid of trees."
from "Decision: Earth," a Procter & Gamble "educational" handout for schoolchildren, explaining why clear-cutting is good for the environment

Branding Kids for Life

from *The Nation* (11/20/00)

Steven Manning

If you are the parent of a newborn, beware. Fourteen to eighteen months from now your child will be programmed to nag for a new toy or snack every four hours, "branded for life" as a Cheerios eater or a Coca-Cola guzzler and placed in the loving care of a market researcher at the local daycare center.

That, at least, was the view of early childhood development presented by the 400 children's-market honchos at the third annual Advertising & Promoting to Kids Conference, held in New York City on September 13–14. Conferencegoers attended sessions on topics like Building Brand Recognition, Marketing in the Classroom and The Fine Art of Nagging ("40% of sales of jeans, burgers and other products occur because a child asks for the product"). They cheered winners of the Golden Marble Awards for best breakfast-food and video-game commercials.

The marketing confab was held as the government released a report documenting the growing commercialization of public schools and also as the Federal Trade Commission blasted media companies and the advertising industry for deliberately marketing violent films and products to children. Although kids have been targets of marketing for decades, the sheer amount of advertising they are exposed to today is "staggering and emotionally harmful," says Susan Linn, a Harvard Medical School psychologist who studies media at the Judge Baker Children's Center in Boston. Linn and other child psychologists, educators and healthcare professionals led a protest outside the Golden Marble Awards to draw attention to the effects of the $12-billion-a-year kid-ad industry, including the epidemic of obesity in children and increasing violence in schools. "It's appalling that creativity is being rewarded in the service of manipulating children," Linn says. "We hope this is the beginning of a national movement to challenge this."

In fact, this fall has been a good one for grassroots opponents of corporate commercialism. The Madison, Wisconsin, school board voted in August to terminate its exclusive beverage contract with Coca-Cola, making it the first school district in the country to cancel an existing marketing deal [see Manning, "Students for Sale: How Corporations Are Buying Their Way Into America's Class-rooms," September 27, 1999]. The board cited "over-whelming public opposition" as the reason for its decision. That action came hard on the heels of successful campaigns to stop proposed school-marketing deals in Oakland and Sacramento, California; Philadelphia; and the state of Michigan, where a cola contract involving 110 school districts was shot down. In October the American Dental Association passed a resolution urging its members to oppose the marketing of soft drinks and junk food in schools, and the American Psychological Association, under pressure from many of its members, agreed to form a task force to examine whether it is unethical for psy-chologists to advise companies that market to children. Meanwhile, ZapMe!, the in-school marketing company, abandoned its educational business after failing to con-vince enough schools to accept its offer of free computers in exchange for delivering student eyeballs to advertisers.

"We're seeing a dramatic increase in local resistance to

all forms of corporate marketing to kids," says Andrew Hagelshaw, executive director of the Center for Commercial-Free Public Education, in Oakland. "The issue has finally hit critical mass with the public." Hillary Rodham Clinton has jumped on the bandwagon. Citing a "barrage of materialistic marketing" aimed at young children, the Democratic candidate for senator from New York wants the government to ban commercials aimed at preschool children and to prohibit advertising inside public elementary schools. Anticorporate activists welcomed Clinton's proposals but said they don't go far enough. Opponents of a New York City school board plan to finance free laptop computers for students through in-school advertising say her proposals won't protect millions of high school students. Nor would the proposals apparently affect the commercial in-school TV program Channel One, whose market is primarily middle school students.

Corporate lobbyists are already putting the heat on members of Congress who might support legislation reining in children's advertising. Hagelshaw believes the real battles will take place in local school boards and state legislatures, which may be more receptive to anticommercial arguments. There's never been a better, or more important, time for local activists to step up the pressure on corporate exploiters of children.

FACT

Percentage of corporate-sponsored academic
materials that contain biased or incomplete
information and promote the consumption of the
sponsor's product or service:
80*

The New Product Placement

from *The Nation* (2/24/03)

Rebecca Segall

L ast fall, a half-dozen child psychologists lurked
around New York's Yale Club at a convention called
"Advertising & Promoting to Kids" in search of new, higher-
paying clients. They were hoping to sell their smarts to marketers and advertisers attending lectures on "Emotional
Branding" and on the troubled post-September 11
economy. As marketer David Bryla put it, today's advertisers must employ a "full frontal attack" on children. Over
the past decade more and more psychologists have been
helping corporations win their war, successfully preying on
kids' developmental stages, anxieties and vulnerabilities.

In the crowd sat Susan Linn, an idealistic, old-fashioned
therapist, gasping and sighing in disgust as the guest
speaker declared, "Remember folks, all kids want to do is

* source: Consumers Union

fit in!" and "Brand them when they're babies!" In disbelief, Linn exclaimed loud enough for her fellow attendees to hear, "These are the only people I know who talk about kids incessantly without asking: 'But is it good for them?'" Linn has been mortified over the fact that psychologists are using their training, as she sees it, to exploit rather than to help kids.

Linn was at the conference not as a participant but as a spy. As an organizer of another conference, held at the same time one floor below, called "Consumer Kids: Marketers' Impact on Children's Health," she wanted to hear the rhetoric firsthand. The Harvard-affiliated group she works for, Stop Commercial Exploitation of Children (SCEC), had intentionally planned the conference, along with a demonstration outside the club, to fall at the same time and place as the advertising one.

Linn has a few major concerns. She believes it is unfair to market to kids under 8 because they don't understand that commercials are supposed to make them want what they see. And worse, she says, the commercials are bad for their health. "Most food ads targeted to kids are high in fat, sugar and calories," says Linn. Preschoolers' risk of obesity increases by 6 percent for every hour of television watched per average day, she adds. She contends that sloppy political changes have only deepened the problem. Budget cuts to the Education Department, along with a call to corporate America to do something about education, paved the way for programs like Channel One (mandatory sponsored newscasts and marketing in schools, which Consumers Union calls "Captive Kids"), which broadcasts to 12,000 middle, junior and high schools a day. She is concerned about

how kids' health has been affected since desperate officials, in need of funds for textbooks and teachers, gave
Coca-Cola and McDonald's entree into their schools. She
laments the day children's television was deregulated—
when psychologically savvy marketers were given free rein
to use kids' entertainment as a marketing tool for toys,
exploiting kids' vulnerabilities in the comfort of their own
home. "The negative impact of marketing to children
depends on each child's weaknesses or predilections," she
says. Researchers who presented at Linn's anticonference
linked marketing to youth to childhood obesity, poor
body image, eating disorders and violent behavior.

As advertising to kids becomes a bigger and bigger
industry—children spent more than $28 billion of their
own money in 1999 and directly influenced the spending
of more than $600 billion of their parents' money by
2000—advertisers turn to psychologists to learn how to
"brand" children more efficiently. There is at least one psychologist on almost every advertising team that promotes
to children. And spending on marketing and advertising to
kids hit $12 billion in 1999, leaving kids bombarded with
more than 40,000 manipulative ads a year on TV alone.

Linn's associates, Allen Kanner and Tim Kasser, co-editors
of *Psychology and Consumer Culture* (to be published by
the American Psychological Association in October), are
trying to convince the leaders of the APA to declare that
helping child marketers appeal to children is unethical.
The APA has set up a task force to review their proposal,
signed by sixty psychologists, which also asks that the
organization issue a public statement denouncing the use
of psychological techniques to assist corporate advertising to children and that it launch a campaign to

review and research the negative effects of advertising on kids and teens.

Kasser explains that young children don't have the cognitive capacity to understand persuasive intent, and that the actor on the screen is paid to seem happy. "Teens have a more finely tuned sense of these things," he says, "but they are entering another vulnerable period. They are starting to leave the family group and enter the world of peers. They are becoming self-conscious and very aware of being looked on by others. And marketers prey on that."

These activists make a strong case suggesting that children and teens don't have such a developed sense of the world, which leaves them—in the minds of marketers—defined by and valued for their plasticity. In *Branded: The Buying and Selling of Teenagers*, Alissa Quart systematically shows us how far toy, fast-food and clothes companies, plastic surgeons and their marketers, together with their partners in television, film, public education and politics, and even parents, have gone to make sure that kids are well branded despite the potential consequences for self-esteem and physical health. Quart, who focuses mostly on middle-class white kids, eerily demonstrates how the relentless marketing to kids has insidiously permeated what used to be, not even fifteen years ago, youth's sacred spaces: the teen movie and magazine, youth literature, school social events, video games, extreme sports, the dressing room and worst of all, their inner lives.

Take, for example, the 2001 documentary *Dogtown and Z-Boys*, on the history of skateboarding. According to Quart the film was funded by Vans sneakers, and it's Vans shoes that are seen flashing and dashing throughout every scene, leaving behind their emotional stamp of cool. She quotes Jay Wilson, vice president for marketing at Vans: "We really try to connect emotionally with the kids and find new ways of doing things. We're getting more public relations on this thing than we ever imagined."

Quart also compares teen movies of the 1980s with those of today. *The Breakfast Club* and *Heathers* depicted freaks and losers as heroes and ultimately united youth against self-interested adults and mainstream authority, observes Quart, in contrast to movies such as *Clueless, Bring It On* and *Legally Blonde*, which celebrate popularity and status quo. Quart's explanation of the change subtly lies with the new marketing technique of placing products throughout films: Losers don't sell Clairol, Clinique, Tiffany bracelets and Prada. And clearly, the goal of the day is to sell.

"Teens suffer more than any other sector of society for this wall-to-wall selling," Quart argues in the introduction of her book: They are at least as anxious as their parents about having enough money and maintaining their social class, a fear that they have been taught is best allayed by more branded gear. And they have taken to branding themselves, believing that the only way to participate in the world is to turn oneself into a corporate product or corporate spy to help promote products to other kids.

Marketers and advertisers seek to appeal to adult psychology as well, but clearly the playing field is not as skewed. Emotional branding guru Marc Gobé just published *Citizen Brand: 10 Commandments for Transforming Brands in a Consumer Democracy,* a book that seeks to help companies develop socially responsible brand strategies in order to "earn buyers' loyalty." Gobé is the executive creative director of Desgrippes Gobé Group, which is responsible for emotion-driven brand design for Coca-Cola, IBM, Reebok, Starbucks, Gillette and Victoria's Secret. In adult-targeted campaigns, rather than focusing on anxieties such as kids' desire to fit in, Gobé suggests, marketers indulge buyers' healthy desires, such as women's tendency to bond with one another, the bohemian middle class's urge for adventure and thrill-seeking, gay and lesbians' desire to be accepted and openly depicted in the copy and images of ads, and Generation X's celebration of racial diversity. When it comes to sports, Gobé points out, women are more interested in the "experiential and personal perspective and less interested in the external achievement." A Nike ad that targets "everyday women" shows a female runner sprinting through the city and says "I am not Marion Jones." Nike's website explains, "It's not about perfection and not about winning or losing. It's about human potential. It's the feeling you get when you finish your first marathon, 10K race or walk around the block . . . It's small, personal victories as well as large public ones." Rather than take advantage of us, these ads appeal to adult sensibilities.

Most parents don't have the time and energy it requires to fight the ubiquitous and overwhelming influence the media have on their children's inner lives. Many are even grateful to television for keeping kids occupied. But some older kids maintain a critical perspective and can detect when they are being manipulated, and are trying to fight back in their own way. Quart's book takes surprisingly uplifting turns as the author includes many examples of teens leading the fight to remain "unbranded" in this era of unregulated marketing to kids. She brings her readers to the precocious youth magazine *New Moon*, where young teen reviewers and activists—privy to and intolerant of a society that desperately relies on exploiting kids and teens in order to drive an unstable economy—vent. She quotes 16-year-old Lynn Grochowski critically analyzing *She's All That:* "When Laney makes the move to 'normal' it is only because of her new wardrobe, haircut, addition of makeup, and loss of glasses." A 15-year-old adds, "This movie would be much less shallow if Zach were to be interested in Laney for who she really is, not because she turns out to be beautiful after a makeover." And as an 11-year-old put it in a review of *The Princess Diaries,* "I wonder how many young girls, after seeing this movie, wanted to throw out their glasses, straighten their hair, pluck their eyebrows, or cover their freckles."

But movie plots and product placement are only one form of attack that kids' self-esteem is up against. According to Quart, a 1970s antitrust court decision that deregulated medical advertising and ads for learned professional service laid the foundation for ads in *Teen Vogue* and *Seventeen* for an herbal breast-enhancement tablet. Perhaps it is no coincidence, Quart points out, that a *Seventeen* poll of readers recently found that 25 percent had considered liposuction, a tummy tuck or breast augmentation. The magazine in effect exploited its loyal (and impressionable) readers' anxieties rather than helping to diminish them through articles and analyses. The freedom of the Internet hasn't helped protect youth either: Doctors who, as Quart puts it, may have once "tried to maintain a special dignity in their marketing" now offer online inspirational profiles of young teens who have rid themselves of their "hook noses" or "weak chins."

But, according to Quart, when public education sells out

to the marketing-obsessed culture, the whole system seems finally to turn on its head. She closes her book with a refreshing—and quite rare—respectful depiction of teenagers as enlightened young people who will do what it takes to place much-needed boundaries on the misguided adults in their midst. In the chapter "Schools for Sale," Quart draws an inspiring picture of teens from a severely underfunded public school in Philadelphia demonstrating consistently against the privatization of their school by Edison Schools Inc., a publicly traded, New York-based company that operates more than 133 public schools in twenty-two states and Washington, D.C. Chris Whittle, founder of Channel One—the advertising-laden station that blasts into classrooms—is Edison's CEO.

"Edison is like Channel One," says 17-year-old Max Goodman. "It will have an unconscious effect on all the students just like advertising in the schools. And The Gap has money [invested in] Edison, so maybe one day they'll say, 'This lesson is brought to you by the Gap.'" Another student chimes in, "My education shouldn't be for profit. Do I want to learn that one plus one equals Pepsi?" Edison eventually became the subject of a Securities and Exchange Commission investigation centering on improper accounting and classification of revenue. The investigation resulted in the company restating its revenues. Quart surmises that the ongoing student protests, compounded with the scandal, finally put Edison on the defensive and ultimately led the board of education to cease relinquishing additional schools to Edison's control.

Quart, a product of academic parents and lefty summer camps, is more than a journalist. She has profound activist assumptions and intentions that surfaced even in the initial stages of writing, as she aggressively insured the preservation of her chapter called "Unbranding," which—unlike most literature that focuses on the vulnerability and victimization of youth—highlights kids' fighting their exploitation in a variety of small and large ways. Quart seamlessly weaves within her cultural criticism and warnings an extremely insightful analysis of the transformation of youth social movements:

When I was a teenager in the late 1980s, teen activists directed their energies to the battle to end apartheid and in honor of abstractions like world peace. . . . Now, the youth movement is very much directed at issues of youth and against the forces that oppress them in their schools and at home. Kids may well consider youth itself something of an embattled minority—and that in turn informs their politics, the area of focus being the retention of civil rights in their classrooms. . . . The Philly activists are more evidence that some among Generation Y have not taken the merchandizing of their minds, bodies, and subjectivities lightly. They are willing to fight back.

In her profound and pivotal work *No Logo*, Naomi Klein included an important story of adult activists working hard to enlighten resistant teens, arduously setting the theoretical and logistical groundwork for such a youth movement. Quart in *Branded* fused philosophy and structure with the passion and fury of fully aware and fed-up real-life adolescents. German philosopher Hannah Arendt believed that only a tiny percentage of humanity is capable of transcending the "human condition" to think critically about social norms. If she were alive today, I wonder if she would suggest that American culture's apathy toward corporate manipulation of children is an example of the "banality of evil." If so, activists such as Linn, Kanner, Kasser and Quart are making extraordinary strides in fighting it, considering what they are up against. Quart's work hasn't been embraced by seemingly pro-branding reviewers but was called "brilliant" in, of all places, the Sunday Business section of the *New York Times*. And Linn, for her part, is making some child marketers stop and think, at least for a moment. As the marketers' conference ended and a speaker rapped joyously about "kids as essential consumers," one twentysomething, dolled-up attendee turned to me and whispered: "You know, now that I'm thinking about it, the way they're talking about children *is* pretty creepy."

THEY THINK
WE'RE SLAVES

*with cartoons by Tom Toles
and Facts*

*Companies ranging from Wal-Mart to Tyson
Foods refuse to pay a living wage, provide
decent benefits or offer safe working conditions
to employees. This refusal undermines our
culture, our democracy—our very civilization.
Workers unite!*

Wal-Mart treats all of its rank-and-file employees badly—but it treats women even worse than men.

Wal-Mart Values

from *The Nation* (12/16/02)

Liza Featherstone

Wal-Mart is an unadorned eyesore surrounded by a parking lot, even its logo aggressively devoid of flourish. Proving that looks don't matter, however, the retail giant has a way with women: Four out of ten American women visit one of Wal-Mart's stores weekly. They like the low prices, convenience and overall ease of the shopping experience. Even snobbish elites are discovering its delights: A few months ago, *New York Times* fashion writer Cathy Horyn revealed, to the astonishment of fellow urban fashionistas, that much of her wardrobe comes from Wal-Mart ("Marc Jacobs?" "No, it's Wal-Mart"). Retail consultant Wendy Liebmann ecstatically dubs Wal-Mart the "benchmark by which American women rate all shopping."

Would that $15 runway knockoffs were Wal-Mart's primary contribution to women's lives. But Wal-Mart is not only America's favorite shopping destination; it's also the nation's largest private employer. The majority of Wal-Mart's "associates" (the company's treacly euphemism for employees) are women. Their average wage is $7.50 an hour, out of which they must pay for their own health insurance, which is so costly that only two in five workers buy it.

Yet Wal-Mart is not only a horrifyingly stingy employer:

Many workers say it is also a sexist one. From the Third World factories in which its cheap products are made, to the floor of your local Wal-Mart, where they're displayed and sold, it is women who bear the brunt of the company's relentless cost-cutting. Ellen Rosen, a resident scholar in Brandeis University's Women's Studies Research Program, recently observed that around the world, Wal-Mart's business practices "may be leading to a new kind of globally sanctioned gender discrimination."

Gretchen Adams worked for Wal-Mart for ten years, in five different states. As a co-manager, she opened twenty-seven "Supercenters" (gargantuan, twenty-four-hour grocery/general merchandise hybrids). "There were so many inequities," she sighs with amazement, reflecting on her time at Wal-Mart. She saw men with little to no relevant experience earning starting salaries of $3,500 a year more than her own. "I had the title but not the pay," she says. "They take us for idiots."

Adams is now a witness in *Dukes v. Wal-Mart*, in which seven California women—current and former Wal-Mart employees—are charging the company with systematic sex discrimination in promotions, assignments, training and pay. Betty Dukes, for whom the suit is named, is a 52-year-old African-American woman who still works at Wal-Mart. First hired by the company in 1994 as a part-time cashier in Pittsburg, California, she was an eager employee with a sincere admiration for founder Sam Walton's "visionary spirit." A year later, with excellent performance reviews, she was given a merit pay raise and a full-time job. Two years later, after being promoted to the position of customer service manager, she began encountering harsh discrimination from her superiors; she says she was denied the training she needed in order to advance further, while that same training was given to male employees. She was also denied the opportunity to work in "male" departments like hardware, and was made to sell baby clothes instead. "I can mix a can of paint," she told reporters just after filing the suit. "I want the chance to do it."

When Dukes complained about the discrimination, managers got back at her by writing her up for minor offenses like returning late from breaks, offenses routinely committed by her white and male co-workers, who were never punished, she says. When she kept complaining, she was denied a promotion and finally demoted back to her cashier job. She went to the Wal-Mart district office to complain, but the company did nothing. Being demoted was not just humiliating: It deprived Dukes of other promotions, and her cashier job offered fewer hours and a lower hourly wage. When she was once again eligible for promotion, four new management positions, none of which had even been posted, were filled by men.

Along with more than seventy witnesses, the other named plaintiffs in *Dukes v. Wal-Mart* tell similar stories:

- In August 1997, Patricia Surgeson, then a single mother of two, began working evenings as a part-time cashier in a Wal-Mart tire and lube department while attending community college. Within two weeks, while she was stocking shelves, she says, a male co-worker began grabbing and propositioning her. He was allowed to remain in his job, while she was transferred to the health and beauty aids department. Over the next four years, Surgeson held more responsible jobs at Wal-Mart, but these promotions weren't accompanied by raises. Many of her male co-workers were paid better than she was, she charges, even though they had less responsibility and were newer to the company.

• Hired to work in the returns department in the Livermore, California, store in fall 1998, Cleo Page, who had already worked in two other Wal-Mart stores, was quickly promoted to a customer service manager position. Interviewing a little over a year later for a promotion, she charges, she was told that it was a man's world, and that men controlled management positions at Wal-Mart. She was repeatedly passed over for promotions, which were given to male employees, and to white women. (Page, who is African-American, also has a race discrimination claim against Wal-Mart, as does Betty Dukes, but these charges are not part of the class-action suit.) At one point, her store manager discouraged her from applying for the sporting-goods department manager position, she says, because "customers would feel comfortable" buying sporting goods from a man. She heard male co-workers complain that "women were taking over" the store, and she heard them ask each other if they knew other men who would be interested in working at Wal-Mart.

• Christine Kwapnoski, who is still employed in a Concord, California, Sam's Club (a division of Wal-Mart), has worked for the company since 1986. She charges that management positions were never posted, though when she heard one was opening up she'd tell supervisors she was interested. Still, the jobs were given to men less qualified than herself, whom she then had to train. A store manager suggested that she "needed to blow the cobwebs off" her makeup and "doll up." She says she saw men getting paid at higher rates than she was, and getting raises more often; in one instance, Kwapnoski, a divorced mother of two, questioned a male co-worker's raise, and was told he had a family to support.

• After thirty years of retail experience, Deborah Gunter began working at a Riverside, California, Wal-Mart in 1996 as a photo lab clerk. She says she applied for management positions and was passed over for less experienced men. She requested further training and never got it. When she was transferred to the Tire Lube Express department, she did the work of a support manager but never got the title or the pay. Her supervisor sexually harassed her, and when she complained, her hours were reduced, she says. After she trained a man to fill the support manager job, he got the title and salary, and her hours were reduced. When she complained about her reduced hours and requested a meeting with the district manager to protest the discriminatory treatment, she was fired.

And on and on. Women make up 72 percent of Wal-Mart's sales work force but only 33 percent of its managers. A study conducted for the *Dukes* plaintiffs by economist Marc Bendick found such discrepancies to be far less pronounced among Wal-Mart's competitors, which could boast of more than 50 percent female management. Even more striking, comparing Wal-Mart stores to competitors in the same location, Bendick's study found little geographic variation in these ratios, and little change over time. In fact, the percentage of women among Wal-Mart's 1999 management lagged behind that of its competitors in 1975. (Wal-Mart spokesman Bill Wertz says it's "too soon" to say how the company will defend itself against these charges.)

Depending on the outcome of a class-certification hearing next July before a San Francisco federal judge, *Dukes v. Wal-Mart* could be the largest civil rights class-action suit in history, affecting more than 700,000 women. Though a California judge ruled recently that the case must be limited to California plaintiffs, discovery is nationwide, as is the proposed class. If the plaintiffs have their way, any woman employed by the company from 1999 on would win damages. But even more important, says Brad Seligman, Betty Dukes's lawyer, "The idea is to change Wal-Mart. We will not have done our job unless we transform the personnel system at Wal-Mart and make sure there are additional opportunities for women."

Dukes is the culmination of a long history of individual sex-discrimination suits—including sexual harassment and pregnancy discrimination—against Wal-Mart, going back at least to 1981. Courts have often, though of course not always, ruled for the plaintiffs in these cases; in several sexual-harassment suits juries have awarded employees millions of dollars in punitive damages. Wal-Mart recently settled an EEOC sexual-harassment suit on behalf of a group of Wal-Mart employees in Mobile, Alabama, and several women unconnected to *Dukes* have discrimination suits under way.

Some of the lawsuits against Wal-Mart reflect common grievances cited by working women, inequities hardly unique to Wal-Mart, but that women's advocates rightly find particularly outrageous in the world's largest corporation. For example, a suit filed in Georgia by Lisa Smith Mauldin, a Wal-Mart customer service manager and a 22-year-old divorced mother of two, charges the company with sex discrimination because its health plan does not cover prescription contraceptives (it does cover other prescription drugs, but as the complaint spells out in painstaking legalese, only women get pregnant). Mauldin works thirty-two hours a week and makes $12.14 an hour, so the $30 monthly cost of the Pill is a significant burden for her (and certainly a prohibitive one for many fellow employees, who earn significantly lower wages). In September Mauldin's suit was certified as a class action, demanding reimbursement for all female Wal-Mart employees who have been paying for birth control out of pocket since March 2001, and demanding that Wal-Mart's insurance cover FDA-approved prescription contraceptives in the future.

Wal-Mart is also criticized for indifference to the workers, mostly young women, who make the products sold in its stores. While most major-clothing stores traffic in sweated labor, Wal-Mart's record on this issue is unusually bad. Much of the clothing sold at Wal-Mart is made in China, where workers have no freedom of association. Unlike many companies, Wal-Mart has adamantly refused to tell labor rights advocates where its factories are, rejecting even the pretense of transparency. Last year, Wal-Mart was removed from the Domini 400 Social Index, an influential socially responsible investment fund, for its failure to make sufficient efforts to uphold labor rights and for its "unresponsiveness to calls for change." Other than Nike, Wal-Mart is the only company that has been booted from the fund for this reason.

Last June, citing all of the above issues, the National Organization for Women named Wal-Mart its fifth "Merchant of Shame" and launched a public education campaign against the retailer. "It's part of our emphasis on economic justice. We don't think Wal-Mart is a woman-friendly workplace," says Olga Vives, NOW's vice president for action. NOW has asked Wal-Mart for a meeting to discuss its complaints, but since the company has not responded, Vives says, "we are getting their attention in other ways." On September 28, 600 NOW chapters demonstrated at Wal-Mart stores across the country, from Tallahassee to Salt Lake City.

NOW has been cooperating closely with the United Food and Commercial Workers, who have been trying for several years to organize Wal-Mart workers [see John Dicker, "Union Blues at Wal-Mart," July 8], an effort ruthlessly resisted by the company. Gretchen Adams, who quit Wal-Mart in December 2001, now works as an organizer with the UFCW. She's angry, not only about the way she was treated, but also about the plight of the hourly workers she supervised. "They were not paid enough to live on. There were a whole lot of single mothers," she says. "They would come in crying because they had hard decisions: whether to take their child to the doctor or pay their rent." Many hourly workers were on public assistance because their pay was so low, she recalls.

Not a single Wal-Mart store is unionized yet, but there's

substantial evidence that many of the problems suffered by Wal-Mart's female employees would be alleviated by a union. A study on women in the retail food industry, published in February by the Institute for Women's Policy Research and funded by the UFCW, found that women workers in unions faced smaller gender and racial wage gaps, and earned 31 percent higher wages than women who were not in unions. In addition, the study showed that two-thirds of women in unionized retail jobs had health insurance, while only one-third of their nonunion counterparts did. Such advantages were even more dramatic for part-time workers, who are even more likely to be women.

At a November 18 press conference in Washington, D.C., to announce a UFCW-initiated National Day of Action on November 21—rallies were held in more than 100 cities and towns, supported by a broad coalition of religious, environmental, student and labor groups—NOW president Kim Gandy said Wal-Mart should know that "continuing their greedy, abusive ways will cost them the business of thinking consumers." This seems unlikely, though it's probably important to make the threat. In any case, the UFCW is not calling for a nationwide Wal-Mart boycott. "We are calling for a boycott in Las Vegas," says Doug Dority, president of the UFCW. In Las Vegas, where a vigorous organizing campaign is under way, Wal-Mart has committed numerous violations of the right to organize. Las Vegas is also the most heavily unionized city in the United States. Elsewhere, however, the UFCW is not ready to take that step. "It's hard to boycott and organize at the same time," says Dority. "Because Wal-Mart uses that against you: 'Hey, the union is trying to take away your job.'"

THEY THINK WE'RE SLAVES

Still, it makes sense for activists to appeal to the possible solidarity between Wal-Mart's female customers and its female work force. UFCW vice president Susan Phillips said in a recent speech, "As women, we have tremendous power. We control both sides of the cash register. We are the cashiers on one side and we are the customers on the other side. If we join hands across the cash register, we can change the economic future for women in America." Far from telling consumers not to shop at the "Big Box," on the November 21 Day of Action many UFCW locals dramatized consumer power through "shop-ins," urging protesters to go into the store, buy something while wearing a T-shirt with the UFCW's phone number on it, and tell employees they supported their right to join a union. In Seekonk, Massachusetts, a UFCW local even gave each November 21 protester a $20 bill to spend at Wal-Mart, donating the purchases to a nearby women's shelter.

In fact, Wal-Mart customers and workers have much in common: They are increasingly likely to be anybody in America. The working poor are even more likely than other Americans to shop at Wal-Mart, not necessarily because they find it a shopper's paradise—though of course some do—but because they need the discounts, or live in a remote area with few other options. (Many Wal-Mart workers say they began working at their local Wal-Mart because they shopped there; when they needed a job, they filled out its application, because Wal-Mart was already such a familiar part of their lives.) Through shoppers and "associates" alike, Wal-Mart is making billions from female poverty.

In addition to court mandates and worker organizing, changing Wal-Mart is going to take massive pressure from many constituencies; union locals will need an approach to coalition-building that is highly community-specific, yet networked nationwide, similar to that used by the progressive labor organization Jobs With Justice. The range of groups that turned out on November 21 was promising, and they have vowed to stay committed to a "People's Campaign for Justice at Wal-Mart."

Asked how long it will take to unionize Wal-Mart, Gretchen Adams, who is 56, answers without hesitation: "The rest of my life." But she's determined. As a manager opening a new store in Las Vegas, Adams says, "I was not allowed to hire any experienced help, because they might be union." Now, she deadpans, "I'm trying to get Wal-Mart the help it needs."

Union Blues at Wal-Mart

from *The Nation* (7/8/02)

John Dicker

"GOT ANY NACHOS READY?"

That's what Joe Hendrix said to the folks at the Radio Grill, his employer's in-house snack bar. Hendrix was on his way to punch out from his shift in the meat-cutting department at the Wal-Mart Supercenter in Jacksonville, Texas; eight months earlier, in February 2000, he'd voted yes in the first successful election for union representation at a U.S. Wal-Mart store. For failing to pay when placing his nacho order, he was fired.

Seventy-two-year-old Sidney Smith also voted yes; he

got axed for eating a pre-weighed banana on the checkout line. Such were the excuses offered by management as union supporters were systematically routed from their jobs. But this was well after the real damage had been done, when Wal-Mart announced two weeks after the Jacksonville vote that it was switching to case-ready, or pre-cut, beef and would be eliminating meat-cutting operations in 180 stores. Wal-Mart claimed its decision had nothing to do with the organizing drive, but the union filed a complaint with the National Labor Relations Board. Although the board ruled in the union's favor, the timing of the news contained a chillingly clear message to Wal-Mart workers nationwide: This is what you can expect if you try to organize.

Wal-Mart's legendary ferocity in such situations has, until recently, kept unions from trying to make inroads in its million-strong work force. But after more than a decade of pussyfooting, the United Food and Commercial Workers union and the Teamsters are gearing up to take on Wal-Mart Stores, Inc., with the former taking the retail stores and the latter handling 100-plus distribution centers. For the UFCW, this undertaking is less the result of newfound militancy than it is about mere survival. Seventy percent of the union's 1.4 million members work for national groceries like Kroger and Safeway, as well as smaller, regional chains. With a strong presence in the top 100, mostly urban, markets, the big chains can hold steady in the face of Wal-Mart encroachment. The regional chains, however, are getting walloped. And with Wal-Mart circling on the fringes of larger markets, its lower wages and benefits will likely erode those enjoyed by UFCW members.

In its forty-year reign Wal-Mart has amassed a jaw-dropping trophy rack of titles—"world's largest retailer," "world's largest private employer" and the recently acquired "world's largest corporation," edging out Exxon-Mobil for the top spot in this year's Fortune 500. The chain accounts for a staggering 6.4 percent of the nation's retail sales and, as reported in *The Economist*, 7–8 percent of U.S. consumer spending (excluding cars and "white goods" like refrigerators, washers and dryers). With KMart, until recently its closest rival, now in bankruptcy, the path is clear to ever greater domination.

The only Wal-Mart store to unionize successfully was in Ontario, Canada, abetted in no small measure by the province's once-progressive labor laws. But the fledgling union was broken by the company's flat-out refusal to recognize the contract. While a climber at Mount Everest base camp can point to the many individuals who have summited and lived, a Wal-Mart worker trying to join a union knows no such consolation. Two unions, neither a paragon of union democracy or member mobilization, face an employer that has been growing by 15 percent each year, recession and all: In the context of a labor movement that has not been weaker since the 1920s, with a legal system seemingly rigged against it, this is an Everest ascent with no Sherpas in sight.

Wal-Mart manifests itself in three main forms: The traditional Wal-Mart retail store, which peddles everything from panties to Pennzoil and averages about 90,000 square feet; SAM's Club, a warehouse club store where "members" pay an annual fee to receive greater discounts on dry goods and groceries; and Supercenters, the company's biggest growth vehicle, a combination retail and grocery store clocking in at 190,000 square feet. This year, Wal-Mart plans to open a new one every other day.

"Wal-Mart's strategy is very similar to Mao Zedong's," says retail analyst Burt Flickinger. "Conquer the country-side first and take the cities second." If this sounds alarmist, consider the Neighborhood Market. It's a proto-type grocery store roughly the size of three 7-Elevens. In the past few years Wal-Mart has deployed them for greater market saturation in its urban strongholds like Oklahoma City and Dallas. While zoning laws and real estate costs impede the development of most forms of Wal-Mart in the larger metro areas, the trim Neighborhood Market might squeeze into places a Supercenter could neverdream of occupying.

Sam Walton built his empire on a belief that rural America saw more business than anyone in the corporate world was recognizing. This vision—combined with a zealot's dedication to low overhead, undercutting the competition through lower profit margins and higher sales volumes, investment in technology and aggressive growth—blazed a trail for an imperial corporation that now operates in nine countries.

Walton has been dead for a decade, but he lives on as a deity, the customer-service superego of Wal-Martians nationwide. So entrenched is the myth of "Mr. Sam" as a benign patriarch that rather than contradict it, the UFCW plays along, with campaign messages about "restoring Sam's vision." Unfortunately, Walton's vision never included unions. As *Wall Street Journal* reporter Bob Ortega chronicles in his book *In Sam We Trust*, Walton was bent on maintaining low labor costs, paying workers sub-minimum wages when he could get away with it and showing no qualms about threatening store and warehouse closures to beat back union campaigns. The company's trumpeted profit-sharing plan and "open door policy" for addressing grievances were all born out of the pleading of Walton's unionbusting consigliere, John Tate. Tate believed that Walton could circumvent labor problems by convincing his workers that he was on their side. For Walton, this turned out to be a winning strategy—a full-time union-prevention program.

Sam drove a pickup truck, shot quail and probably spent more time studying KMart than KMart's own executives. He embodied a peculiarly American paradigm that endures at company headquarters in Bentonville, Arkansas, to this day. He was a self-made, rock-em-sock-em, capitalist cowboy in an industry devoted to peddling every fathomable consumer good, and yet he remained puritanically frugal in his personal and corporate expenditures. Unlike the Gap or Starbucks, Wal-Mart is not selling brand lifestyle. Its aesthetics in architecture and advertising are decidedly no-frills, its corporate offices stark. Executives pay for their own coffee, and even CEO Lee Scott has been known to share a hotel room on business trips. Wal-Mart's subordination to the bottom line permeates all levels. For instance, to curtail frivolous energy consumption, lights, heat and air conditioning at all 3,289 U.S. Wal-Marts are controlled from Bentonville. Not surprisingly, this ethos hits those at the bottom of the food chain the hardest.

Managers are under considerable pressure to keep profits up, and one of the few ways they can achieve this is by cutting operational costs, of which labor comprises about 50 percent. Former managers and employees attest to an unofficial policy of putting experienced "associates"—as the Wal-Martian wage slave is eloquently titled—out to pasture through firing for minor infractions or pushing them to quit by other means. Why pay $10.50 an hour when a new hire can be culled from the street for $7?

A perpetually churning work force offers the added benefit, from management's perspective, of keeping the union out. By its own admission, Wal-Mart burns through 70 percent of all new hires each year, a considerable number in a work force of over a million. As Bernie Hesse of UFCW Local 789 in the Twin Cities explains it, the paradox of retail organizing is "I'm working retail, this job sucks. If I don't like it I'll go get another job that pays $6.50 an hour." While many retail workers don't see their jobs as being worth a long, arduous battle for representation, they also cower at the real consequences of supporting a union: demotions, reduction in hours and "got any nachos ready"-style firings.

Although the union faces skepticism and fear among workers, it has discovered a few potent organizing issues—most notably, healthcare. Effective January 1, a full-time associate with two children and no spouse would pay $36 a week for basic coverage and $3.50 for dental, in addition to a $350 deductible for each individual on the plan. This tallies out to more than $3,000 a year for someone earning less than $16,000. Should it be any surprise that only 38 percent of Wal-Mart associates elect to have coverage? When the company announced a 30 percent hike in premiums this fall, it gleefully noted that associates had a "CHOICE to elect what will be done with 1/2 of the Wal-Mart contribution to our 401(k) account." One of these so-called choices was to "direct it toward paying health care rates." This change was illuminated in a video so slick that SAM's Club cashier Alan Peto said, "If I didn't know any better I really would have thought they had done me a big favor."

Just for shits and giggles, dial (501) 273-8300. That's Wal-Mart's twenty-four-hour "Union Hotline," designed for store managers to call on the first whiff of union activity. Your kind message will activate the beeper of an associate in Wal-Mart's "People Division." Assuming you are a store manager (and not a pinko prankster), your call will be promptly returned. If your associates are talking union, a flying column of unionbusters will be quickly dispatched to put out the fire.

Since the UFCW began talking to meat-cutters en masse in 1999, the People Division has increased from twelve employees to nearly seventy. In terms of preparedness, though, Wal-Mart has always trumped the unions. Before any national campaign was afoot, Wal-Mart was publishing and distributing manuals like "A Manager's Toolbox To Remaining Unionfree," producing videos and running two-day workshops for store managers stressing their role as the "first line of defense" against a union campaign.

On paper Wal-Mart stays within the bounds of how an employer can legally respond to a union drive. "They're cosmetics," says unionbuster-turned-union-adviser Martin Levitt. "The company will wave them like a flag to show that they know the law, but once management and supervisors have been pulled into one-on-one meetings with the unionbusting forces, they are carefully programmed on how to break the law and told clearly that their very job depends on doing so." While a store manager has likely been briefed on extralegal maneuvers, the dirty work is often delegated to nonsalaried department managers with no knowledge of labor law. Gretchen Adams, a co-manager at a Las Vegas Supercenter, was instructed by her district manager not to hire anyone with union experience, while Stan Fortune, a former department manager and security guard, was told to solicit grievances from union supporters, implementing raises and promotions to buy their loyalty. "I never knew I was breaking the law," he says. Wal-Mart spokeswoman Jessica Moser Eldred said the company follows all state, federal and local labor laws. "In no circumstance do we deviate from them."

Part of Wal-Mart's strategy is to deny contact between workers and the union. When it owns the land on which its store sits, it will invoke trespassing laws. "It got to the point where as soon as the organizers got out of their cars, the security guards would be in the parking lots telling them to leave," says Alan Peto. In other cases, managers or security guards shadow organizers throughout the store, making it impossible for them to speak to workers. Organizers from the UFCW international staff are currently barred from all Wal-Marts under an injunction that forbids solicitation. The company has infuriated shoppers suspected of being union organizers by ejecting them; they've even booted Girl Scouts and Salvation Army bell ringers for fear that contradicting its no-solicitation policy will give the union an inroad.

Faced with the inevitable litany of unfair-labor-practice charges from the union in response to its illegal maneuverings, Wal-Mart can count on the glacial pace of the labor board to stall the campaign. If the board rules in the union's favor, the company suffers a slap on the wrist, posting a notice of company malfeasance in the break room. This is union organizing still haunted by the ghost of the 1947 Taft-Hartley Act.

The UFCW is now attempting to build a case before the NLRB arguing that Wal-Mart's violations are not the result of a few rogue store managers but part of a systematic policy of illegal intimidation, surveillance and terminations, all designed to keep workers from organizing. The union has filed forty complaints against Wal-Mart in twenty-four states, resulting in forty complaints issued by the NLRB against the company. The UFCW hopes ultimately to attain remedies like "affirmative workplace access," a corrective ruling from the board that allows organizers to talk to workers in break rooms and to rebut management's captive-audience meetings, where workers are deluged with anti-union speeches and videos. Rulings for affirmative access are rare, and they typically take many years to attain. But they have been delivered with great success to UNITE at Fieldcrest Cannon and SEIU at Beverly NursingHomes. Given a labor board stacked with Bush appointees and Wal-Mart's legal motto of WDWDW (What did we do wrong?), however, chances of an imminent victory are remote.

In the fourteen years since Wal-Mart opened its first Supercenter, the UFCW has run a damage-control campaign bent on stemming the tide of expansion and sullying the company's image. The union has helped call attention to Wal-Mart's use of sweatshops and child labor overseas, as well as its bogus "Buy American" program, where the company wrapped itself in a "made in the U.S.A." flag until it was revealed that most of its apparel was made in overseas sweatshops. The union also forged coalitions with anti-sprawl activists to stem Wal-Mart's growth.

All of these are noble pastimes, but without a strategy to organize workers, about as effective as pummeling the Taliban with passages from The Betty Friedan Reader. Until recently, it was hard to tell if the UFCW was boycotting Wal-Mart, organizing it or simply functioning as a thorn in its side. The mixed messages provide the People Division an opportunity to inoculate its associates with videos like "Wal-Mart Under Attack," which shows footage of UFCW rallies with members chanting "Wal-Mart: Not in My Neighborhood" and highlights various local efforts to get union members to sign pledges not to shop at Wal-Mart. When many associates openly identify with the company, the message that the union is against Wal-Mart packs a punch.

In the past year, however, the UFCW seems to have developed a more focused approach. Their line in the sand is Las Vegas, a city with a strong union presence in the service sector. While unionized groceries enjoy 90 percent of Vegas's market share, Wal-Mart is making headway with five Supercenters, five retail stores and four SAM's Clubs. Since March of last year, the union has been organizing in Las Vegas, with some activity in northeast Ohio and Texas. In Vegas, the UFCW hosts a radio show and maintains a website, www.walmartworkerslv.com, which chronicles Wal-Mart's anti-union campaign and offers a needed arena for counterarguments and open communication among workers. (However, 12 percent of the website's hits come from Bentonville.)

This past November, workers at Las Vegas SAM's Club Store 6382 were set to vote in the third storewide election at a U.S. Wal-Mart. But as the election approached, the company went into a hiring frenzy, disrupting the laboratory conditions required by the NLRB. Watching its support ebb as the company packed the unit with new hires—all of whom were subjected to anti-union videos and meetings—the union filed charges, which resulted in the board's decision to block the election; on March 28, the NLRB issued a complaint against the company, but the best the union is likely to get is another election with little to guarantee that Wal-Mart won't do the same thing again.

And what of the Teamsters? So far, their activity has been limited to two locals in California and Missouri. At a San Bernardino distribution center, a recent election was lost by a swing margin of twenty-eight votes—an impressive result considering management was promising $3 raises in the week preceding the election and that the campaign was the work of a single organizer. Since Wal-Mart's distribution systems are models of efficiency and integral to the company's success, the Teamsters and UFCW might give Bentonville a run for its money if they coordinated their efforts, applying simultaneous pressure by engaging both truckers and retail workers, thus stretching the capacity of the People Division. But in light of Teamsters organizing director John Murphy's stated goal of transforming his department into "a desk and a telephone," and the union's overall stagnation under Jimmy Hoffa, it's hard to imagine they're going to attempt such a conquest anytime soon.

The UFCW, for its part, has taken a largely top-down approach to the campaign, which has been guided by pressure tactics coming from union HQ in Washington—with some exceptions. "I get members asking me how it's going, how many people have signed cards, and I say what's the point? Why go through a regular election just to get knocked down?" says UFCW organizer Bernie Hesse.

"I'm not trying to go store by store; I'm trying to build a social movement." Hesse's Local 789 has launched a campaign called "You Are Worth More" (www.youare worthmore.org) for retail workers in the Twin Cities. Rather than home in on one particular company, Hesse's local is planting roots in the community, establishing itself as a presence among a multiracial work force at metro-area Targets, KMarts and Wal-Marts.

There's no single war-winning strategy for bringing the union to Wal-Mart workers. Given the UFCW's history of bowing to hostile employers and suppressing its own dissidents, it remains to be seen whether the union is movement building or just circling wagons around its most endangered markets. At risk of excessive parade pissing, consider that even if SAM's Club 6382 wins an election, there are still 3,288 more to go. Wal-Mart is likely to be a decades-long struggle, fought by a largely female work force with no union experience. The struggle is now being waged by a vanguard of union lawyers. Ultimately they will have to take a back seat to shop-floor workers, member organizers and, most significant, the communities where workers live. When the lines between union and community collapse, an employer's traditional mode of attack—labeling the union an alien third party—disintegrates, and the campaign becomes less dependent on legal wrangling. Then, when Wal-Mart denies workers access to the union, wrecks an election or fires activist workers, the outrage does not come from a lone UFCW mouthpiece but from a movement.

Given this campaign's stakes—both real and symbolic— a movement is what Wal-Mart workers need. "If these retailers are going to be the jobs of the future, if we've really switched from a production to a service economy, than what is so revolutionary about insisting that they pay a living wage?" asks Bernie Hesse. Millions of associates and citizens may have to ask this question a million more times before a movement becomes something tangible, and not just a feel-good progressive mirage.

America's Epidemic of Too Little Sleep
–how it works

ALARM GOES OFF, JOE GETS UP EARLY.

...GOES TO WORK WHERE HE DOES TWICE WHAT HE USED TO DO.

CORPORATION HE WORKS FOR CHALKS UP RECORD PROFITS.

JOE TRIES TO FOLLOW WHAT THEY'RE DOING IN WASHINGTON.

CORPORATION DONATES RECORD AMOUNT TO POLITICIANS.

WASHINGTON PRETENDS TO REFORM CAMPAIGN FINANCING.

SO JOE HAS TO GET A SECOND JOB, COMPLAINS.

WASHINGTON REPEALS A FEW MORE WORKER PROTECTIONS.

PRICE OF COFFEE— JUST WENT UP.

TOLES

UNIVERSAL PRESS SYND.
2 ©1997 THE BUFFALO NEWS

2/16/97

FACTS

Ratio of the income of the average CEO to that of the average worker in 1980, 1990 and 2000, respectively:
42:1; 85:1; 531:1 *

Ratio of the income of Wal-Mart CEO Lee Scott to the income of the average Wal-Mart worker:
897:1 **

The people who serve us fast food should be paid a decent wage for their work—even if that means paying a few more cents for a bad hamburger.

The Burger International
from LeftBusinessObserver.com (11/98)
Liza Featherstone

Diners may complain about the dry burgers and the soggy rolls, and Wall Street may complain about sagging market share, but McDonald's has done a fine job at what it does best—taking over the world. It's the largest retail property owner in the United States, and with 23,500

* Source: http://www.corporations.org/system/
** Source: "Reform at Wal-Mart?" by Nico Pitney, CommonDreams.org

restaurants in 113 countries, also the world's largest food-service corporation. The Golden Arches are the second most recognized symbol in the world (topping the Christian cross, though lagging behind Olympic rings).

McDonald's is also very good at union-busting. It may be one of the most doggedly antiunion companies on earth: In the 1994–7 McLibel trial, McDonald's executives acknowledged quashing some 400 serious unionization efforts worldwide in the early 1970s alone. Nonetheless, this July, when Tessa Lowinger and Jennifer Wiebe, both now 17, were fed up with working conditions in a Squamish, British Columbia (BC), McDonald's, they decided to join a union. "It seemed like the only way," Lowinger says. "We'd tried rap sessions with managers, everything else."

To the two young women, management's disrespect was the primary problem. "If we spilled a drink or forgot a cheeseburger," says Lowinger, "we'd be yelled at in front of the public and our peers." Scheduling was also unfair—seniority was no guarantee of more or better shifts—and sick workers were responsible for finding their own replacements. Their equipment was dangerous, too. "One light switch had no panel," says Lowinger. "You'd actually get a shock when you touched it." Huge toasters—plugged in—were precariously balanced on a muffin cart, which, says Lowinger, always had to be moved out of the way—no easy task, since it "weighed maybe a hundred pounds—it was really hard to move." (At least one person—Mark Hopkins, of Manchester, England, in 1992—has died of electrocution working at McDonald's.) Lowinger has talked to McDonald's workers in Montreal, Ontario, and Ohio, and found "we all have the same problems, with management, with unsafe working conditions. Do they go to some sort of course?"

Wiebe and Lowinger called Canadian Auto Workers Local 3000, and two days later, met with 24-year-old Ryan Krell, the CAW's youth organizer (and former fast-food worker). After four days, they had signed up more than the 55% of their co-workers required by the BC labor code for certification.

ARCH ADVERSARY

The day after Wiebe and Lowinger began their sign-up campaign, the McDonald's franchise hired 28 new employees, and challenged the certification on the grounds that the newcomers should be allowed to vote. A local lawyer, Randy Kaardal, also challenged the certification bid, representing a group of workers who had signed up for the union but claimed to have changed their minds. Kaardal claimed that under the province's Infants Act, they couldn't join a union without their parents' permission. (He normally charges some C$260 an hour, while the kids he represented make C$7—just who was paying his fee?) But the CAW's unfair labor practices complaint against the Squamish McDonald's outlet for the timing of its new hires was strong enough that after two days of hearings, both Kaardal and McDonald's withdrew their challenges. Then, on August 19, the Squamish franchise became the first unionized McDonald's in Canada. (None of the nearly 13,000 U.S. stores are unionized.) Neither Jennifer Wiebe nor Tessa Lowinger realized that their victory would be such a historic first. "They told us after we had won," says Lowinger. "Jen and I just looked at each other and went, 'Whoa.' Kind of puts Squamish on the map, doesn't it?"

Bargaining for the first contract has begun and organizers expect it to be a long, tough process; the McDonald's lawyer is already practicing the timeworn strategy of delaying negotiations. But the shop is strong; Lowinger says: "people who were initially against the union are now on the bargaining committee." When they started the campaign, Lowinger and Wiebe didn't plan to make an issue of their wages—"Des Peanuts," as their colleagues say up in Montreal, where a much shakier campaign is underway—but their co-workers have since voted to do so at the bargaining table. (They can't say what else is on the agenda.) In September, the CAW applied to represent workers at a second McDonald's—this one in Rutland, BC—but subsequently withdrew the application because of a lack of worker support.

The CAW successes have been watched with intense interest by fast-food workers and unionists throughout North America, among them a group of McDonald's employees in Macedonia, Ohio. Last April the workers, mostly high school and college students, shed their visors and hairnets and organized a five-day strike—the first strike ever against a U.S. McDonald's. The strikers succeeded in getting management to sign a contract agreeing to some of their demands, including "people skills" classes for rude supervisors, paid vacation for full-time workers, some salary hikes, and "no repercussions" for employees who participated in the strike. But the aftermath was disappointing; managers did improve their manners, but for some workers, per-hour starting wages declined by 25 cents an hour.

The workers then began a campaign to join the Teamsters Local 416, which ground to a standstill in June after two pro-union workers, Bryan Drapp, 19, and Jamal Nickens, 20, showed up to work with "Go Union" painted on their faces and got into a fight with a manager who tried to photograph them. (The manager alleges that Drapp—the fry cook who had organized the strike—threatened to break the camera over his head; Drapp, who isn't giving interviews, has admitted that he threatened to break the camera but has denied any threat of physical violence.) Drapp and Nickens were fired—and, surreally, banned from eating at any of the franchise's outlets. The two have filed an unfair dismissal complaint with the National Labor Relations Board; the hearing is scheduled for December 8. Dominic Tocco, president of Teamsters Local 416, says the campaign is on hold for now. "But if the Labor Board rules in their favor," he says, "the kids will start up again." Workers at more than a dozen local McDonald's, Taco Bell and Burger King outlets, galvanized by the strike and subsequent union drive, have contacted Tocco about joining the Teamsters.

McDonald's sheer might—and barely legal tactics—have proved the biggest obstacles to organizing. The $130 billion-dollar fast-food behemoth has the resources to beat unions into the ground; last year, McDonald's hired fifteen lawyers to fight workers at just one restaurant in Quebec. The company has quashed union efforts in Chicago, Detroit, Ann Arbor, East Lansing (Mich.), San Francisco and worldwide. Several Canadian attempts have also been defeated.

McDonald's strategy in Squamish—sudden and unnecessary new hires, odd challenges from expensive lawyers mysteriously hired by near-minimum wage workers—was typical of what CAW organizer Roger Crowther calls "the

Big Mac Counter-Attack" to a union campaign. In the CAW's push to organize the Rutland, BC, McDonald's, one vocally pro-union employee was fired, and ten new workers were hired. Last year, in St. Hubert, Quebec, after 51 out of the 62 McDonald's workers signed a request for Teamsters' certification, franchise owners closed the restaurant. (They first, unsuccessfully, tried a number of other ways to break the union, including an "employee challenge" similar to the one in Squamish.) Workers seeking to join the Teamsters in a Montreal McDonald's have enough signatures for certification—but McDonald's has delayed Labor Board hearings till early December (a year after the union filed its application). With the typically high turnover, only one of the union's original supporters is still working at the restaurant.

It would be tough for anyone to fight a corporate giant with that much economic force at its fingertips. McDonald's workers have long been cited as the classic unorganizable group, at least in North America. As in most of the retail sector, turnover is high; the mostly-young (at the Squamish outlet, 80% of the workers are under 19) employees have preferred, quite understand-ably, to see their jobs as short-term, and to leave as soon as something better—school, better-paying job—came along. Young workers' inexperience is also a huge obstacle. As Lowinger points out, McDonald's is a first job for many people—indeed, more than 10% of Americans are esti-mated to have worked their first job at McDonald's—"so they don't know they have rights."

This summer, a Teamsters effort to unionize one McDonald's in every major city in Quebec failed miser-ably. Management consistently outsmarted the union. If unionists were waiting in the parking lot to talk to employees, managers would give the kids a ride home. On one such occasion, says Teamsters organizer Rejean Levigne, "they took all the kids to see 'Titanic'! What can you do?"

DID SOMEBODY SAY RESISTANCE?

But CAW Local 3000 has a history of successes in this sector. Over the past two years, the local has unionized 12 Vancouver Starbucks stores, and secured a contract—a global first for the chain. Local 3000 has represented Kentucky Fried Chicken workers in its area for decades—and has also applied to represent a Denny's restaurant, which if successful will be another global first.

Part of the CAW's unusual success with fast-food workers can be attributed to its willingness to treat young people as a serious constituency, even hiring a special youth organizer—Ryan Krell. Local 3000 is working overtime to overcome the generation and class gap that often turns these workers away from unions, the perception—easily, and often, exploited by management—that they can only serve the interests of aging, well-paid white men.

CAW's triumphs with young workers are unprecedented, but more and more young North American workers are braving the chains. Last year, concession employees at a Cineplex Odeon in Montreal and at a Windsor, Ontario, Wal-Mart negotiated union contracts—the first ever for both chains. Although Canadian laws are much more favorable to union organizing than those in the United States, the victories have given U.S. union organizers—and workers—new hope. Inspired by the Ontario Wal-Mart victory, a number of U.S. Wal-Mart campaigns are currently underway. Meanwhile, employees at Borders Books & Music, in Des Moines, Chicago, and New York, as well as at West Coast chain Noah's Bagels, joined the United Food and Commercial Workers last year, and (mostly young) booksellers are organizing at Barnes & Noble stores around the country.

There is considerable desperation behind this youthful organizing fever. Too much of the economy's endlessly vaunted "growth" is in McJobs. Most Gen-Xers aren't educated for the much-hyped explosion of chic infotech jobs—which isn't all that much of a gusher anyway: as UFCW vice president Beth Shulman pointed out in the November/December 1996 *American Prospect*, "Wal-Mart is the largest creator of jobs in the United States—not Intel, not Boeing, not Microsoft." Young workers as a group are earning much less relative to national averages than earlier generations.

Younger workers used to see retail jobs as transitional, but now many have to stick with them indefinitely. Hoping for better wages, benefits, and work conditions, they're turning, increasingly, not to other industries, but to unions. It still remains to be seen just how well unions will accommodate the new activists. Unions have historically shunned the young, low-wage workers that staff the retail sector, but that may be changing. "[Unions] are starting to realize this is where the jobs of the future are, that this is where all those young people attending university are going to end up," says John Henson, a United Steelworkers organizer who worked on Ontario's recent Wal-Mart negotiations. "And this is the sector that needs unions the most."

The CAW's Roger Crowther points out that his local has cultivated these workers partly as a matter of its own survival; the region has had a fast-food-dependent economy for years. Increasingly, that model is dominating the North American labor market. Kids like Tessa Lowinger and Bryan Drapp—once the antithesis of organizable labor—now look like organized labor's future.

Some smart organizers are starting to think like the chains: big. That means spending money, and coordinating efforts. Taking on a multibillion-dollar, multinational chain is a tough job for a small union local; Patsy Shafer, an organizer working on several Wal-Mart campaigns in northern Wisconsin, says "What I'd like to see is a unified, national Wal-Mart campaign, maybe through the AFL-CIO. That would be a big strain on the company— they couldn't be everywhere all the time."

But don't ask Tessa Lowinger about organizing any more McDonald's franchises. "We've still got to get through bargaining with this one," she says, sounding tired. A negotiating meeting has just been canceled. McDonald's canceled it? She says again: "It got canceled."

Unions aren't perfect—but if you want to see the alternative, read on.

Tyson's Moral Anchor
from *The Nation* (7/12/04)
Eric Schlosser

One of America's finest union leaders and her supporters are now under assault by one of the nation's meanest, toughest corporations. For years Maria Martinez, head of Teamsters Local 556 in Walla Walla, Washington, has been battling IBP, the meatpacking giant now owned by Tyson Foods. In 1999 Martinez helped launch a wildcat strike at IBP's beef slaughterhouse in Wallula, Washington, protesting safety hazards and excessive line speeds. In 2001 she helped workers there win a lawsuit against IBP for violations of the Fair Labor Standards Act, gaining as much as $7.3 million in back wages that the company still refuses to pay. She has fought not only for higher wages and better working conditions but also for food safety and animal welfare. With support from Teamsters for a Democratic Union (the progressive, reform-minded wing of the Teamsters), Martinez energized Local 556, reaching out to immigrant workers and linking them with college students, consumer activists and animal rights groups. In response, Tyson Foods has worked hard to get her kicked out of the plant, at one point prohibiting her from even setting foot on the premises. The type of immigrant/activist coalition that Martinez has built is crucial to the future success of the U.S. labor movement—and that is one of the reasons Tyson is so eager to crush it.

A generation ago, meatpacking workers earned some of the highest wages of any industrial workers in the United States. Working in a slaughterhouse was a hard, dirty job, but it provided a stable middle-class income. Today meatpacking is one of the lowest-paid industrial jobs, with one of the highest turnover rates. It is also the nation's most dangerous job, measured by the rate of serious injury. During the 1970s IBP was largely responsible for changing the industry's labor policies, breaking unions, slashing wages and recruiting an immigrant work force. In a very tough business, IBP gained the reputation of being by far the toughest. In 1974 IBP was convicted for collaborating with organized-crime figures in New York City to bribe meat wholesalers and union leaders. Any meatpacking company that hoped to compete with IBP had to cut wages and benefits, too. Over the past twenty-five years some wages in the meatpacking industry, adjusted for inflation, have declined by more than 50 percent.

When Tyson Foods bought IBP in 2001, many workers feared that the company would try to make wages in the beef industry similar to those in the poultry industry, where the pay is even lower. Those fears now seem to be justified. Tyson Foods is the largest meatpacking company the world has ever seen, supplying supermarkets and fast-food chains with beef, chicken and pork. The company's size and scale give it a tremendous advantage when trying to break a local union. In February 2003 members of the United Food and Commercial Workers at the Tyson plant in Jefferson, Wisconsin, went on strike to prevent cutbacks in wages, benefits and vacation time. Tyson promptly hired replacement workers and kept the plant running. After eleven months on the picket line, UFCW members voted to end the strike—but Tyson wouldn't rehire most of them. The National Labor Relations Board has ruled that the scabs can be considered permanent replacements, paving the way for Tyson to get the UFCW out of the plant completely. Workers at the Tyson plant in Cherokee, Iowa, now face similar demands for wage and benefit cuts. At a Tyson slaughterhouse in Brooks, Canada, sixty "team members" (Tyson's term for its employees) were recently fired after a protest against poor working conditions. The plant has no union, and "team members" are expected to work six days a week.

The turnover rate at the Tyson slaughterhouse in Wallula is high, and about 90 percent of the workers are immigrants, mainly from Latin America and Bosnia, who do not speak English. It isn't easy to maintain union solidarity among such a work force. In April Martinez narrowly defeated an attempt, sponsored by Tyson, to decertify her union in advance of contract negotiations. Local 556's contract expired on May 31. Workers are still employed under the terms of the old contract, but Tyson has stopped deducting union dues from their paychecks. Among other things, Martinez is demanding a safer workplace, a slower line speed, and much more careful handling of cattle, so that none are dismembered while still alive. Local 556 has also forged ties with consumer groups in Mexico, Korea and Japan, demanding that Tyson test all of its cattle for mad cow disease. The worldwide ban on American beef, imposed in December after the discovery of a heifer with mad cow disease in Washington State, threatens the livelihood of workers at the Tyson plant in Wallula, which used to ship as much as 40 percent of its meat to Asia.

Although mad cow disease has reduced Tyson's overseas sales, the company is hardly on the verge of bankruptcy. Tyson Foods' second-quarter revenue in 2004 was up 6.9 percent from the previous year, while profits increased by more than 65 percent. Some executive compensation has gone up as well. In 2003 the company chairman, John Tyson, was paid $20.9 million. At a time when the company was demanding wage and benefit cuts from impoverished meatpacking workers, John Tyson's annual compensation nearly tripled. His corporate perks attracted the attention of the Securities and Exchange Commission, which has launched a formal investigation. During an interview with Deborah Norville on May 26, Tyson outlined his personal theory of labor management. "One must have a moral compassion or a moral anchor," Tyson said. "You have to serve the people that work for you . . . and in effect become a servant to the people that work for you." He said it with a straight face.

The problem of worker exploitation is bad in this country, and far worse overseas. We don't have to witness it, but we know it's happening—and we're complicit unless we object in ways that can bring about change.

Global Agenda
from *The Nation* (1/31/00)
William Greider

The promise of [the 1999 anti-globalization protests in] Seattle was captured in an antic moment observed by one young environmental activist. Amid broad ranks of protesters, he saw that a squad of activists dressed as sea turtles was marching alongside members of the Teamsters union. "Turtles love Teamsters," the turtles began to chant. "Teamsters love turtles," the truck drivers replied. Their call-and-response suggests the flavor of this loose-jointed new movement—people of disparate purposes setting aside old differences, united by the spirit of smart, playful optimism.

The corporate-political establishment doesn't get it yet, but sea turtles and Teamsters (with their myriad friends) can change the world. This popular mobilization, disparaged as "Luddite wackos" by the prestige press, is still inventing itself, still vulnerable to the usual forces that can derail new social movements. But its moment is here, a rare opportunity to educate and agitate on behalf of common human values. Among its tasks, this new movement can excavate the human spirit, buried by a generation of arrogant power and a brittle-minded economic orthodoxy.

So what's next for turtles and Teamsters? The World Trade Organization's failure at Seattle (gridlocked on commercial disputes, oblivious to the reform agenda from the streets) has inspired a new organizing slogan: "Fix it or nix it." The WTO is the visible symbol of globalization, and the network of forty country-based campaigns that produced Seattle is working now on when to stage another international day of action.

The U.S. coalition is, meanwhile, gearing up for another crucial fight: blocking Congressional action that would give China a permanent "good housekeeping seal"—instead of annual approval of most-favored-nation status—as it joins the WTO. Any genuine reform of the global system becomes far more difficult if China is to be treated as a "normal" trading partner—one reason business is so anxious to win this one.

Beyond immediate battles, this new movement will sustain itself and grow powerful only if it goes on the offensive—that is, if it can tell a positive story about how the world will look if its values prevail. It can do this with hard facts about the present realities, facts that blow away the establishment's smug abstractions. It should propose concrete legislation—reform laws to be endorsed at the community or state level and enacted by Congress. Not after years of diplomacy, but right now.

What follows is a rough draft of what this national legislation might look like (based on conversations with some leading activists and my own reflections). The central principle is that Americans have the sovereign power to impose rules on the behavior of their own American-based multinational corporations (notwithstanding the WTO's pretensions). Congress did so in 1977 with the Foreign Corrupt Practices Act, which prohibits corporate bribery in overseas projects. That law was passed in response to public outrage over repeated scandals revealing that major U.S. companies were buying foreign governments. Human abuses present in the global system are far more grave than business bribes.

Since it's obvious that the WTO and other international forums have no intention of acting, Americans really have no moral choice but to assert responsibility. After all, random brutalities in the production system are done in our name and to our benefit as consumers, shareholders, company managers. As the United Students Against Sweatshops has demonstrated, when people learn the facts, moral revulsion follows. Famous brand names find themselves confronted by what they have long denied.

In addition to holding U.S. companies accountable, this first round of legislation should focus on empowering voiceless peoples on the other end of the global system—workers, civic activists, communities—mainly by providing them with the industrial information that will help them speak and act in their own behalf. That means collecting hard data from American companies on where and how they produce overseas. Why would the business cheerleaders object, since they claim globalization itself fosters free-flowing information and democratic values?

These initial proposals are deliberately modest in scope because reformers from the wealthy nations, especially the United States, must first establish their bona fide intentions. The objective is not to stymie industrial development in low-wage economies or to rewrite laws for other societies. Poorer countries are naturally skeptical of our high-minded motives, since they've had long experience with the power of American self-righteousness. If this movement is truly international, it will begin by convincing distant others (the citizens, if not their governments) that our commitment to common humanity is genuine.

If these modest measures succeed, however, they will draw a new map of the world—delineating factory-by-factory which multinational companies are actively subverting shared human values, which nations are truly trying to improve conditions for their people and which are merely participating in the exploitation. The map separates sheep from goats, culprits from victims.

The information is essential because it can set the stage for subsequent legislation that eventually establishes minimum standards for corporate behavior on environmental protection, labor issues and human rights. Then penalty tariffs or other measures could be aimed at the firms or nations that systematically pursue the low road, profiteering on human suffering and ecological despoliation. Trade reform can likewise reward and nurture those nations struggling to break free of the "race to the bottom."

Business will howl that these new measures would put it at a competitive disadvantage, just as they opposed the antibribery law as an intrusion on quaint customs in foreign lands. The impact will be quite marginal if one believes the companies' own lofty claims about their offshore production. In any case, as the world's main buyer of last resort, the United States has the market power to lead on these reform issues. Our trade diplomats should start lobbying Europe and Japan to join this effort because eventually public opinion will turn on any multinational producer that attempts to reap short-term profit by ignoring standards for humane conduct.

Obviously, this is politics for the long haul and difficult at every stage. But none of the barriers are insurmountable if we have our values straight. The action can begin with simple, straightforward matters like fire prevention.

THE PRO-LIFE FACTORY

In 1993 the worst industrial fire in the history of capitalism occurred at a mammoth toy factory outside Bangkok—188 workers killed, 469 seriously injured. All but a handful were women, some as young as 13. They were assembling toys for American children—Sesame Street dolls, Bart Simpson and the Muppets, Playskool "Water Pets" and many other popular items.

The most macabre fact about this historic tragedy was that hardly anyone in America noticed, though the Kader Industrial Toy Company's production supplied famous U.S. brands like Fisher-Price, Hasbro, Tyco and Kenner, and retailers like Wal-Mart and Toys 'R' Us. Indeed, the Thai death toll surpassed the most scandalous calamity in America's own industrial history—the Triangle Shirtwaist

Factory fire of 1911—and resembled it in haunting detail. Fire exits were blocked or inadequate, doors were locked to prevent pilfering, flammable materials were stacked randomly on the shop floors. Not even the most rudimentary fire precautions were provided for this factory with 3,000 workers. Desperate women jumped from upper-story windows by the score, just as young American women had done eighty-two years before in New York City.

Nor was this event unique in industrializing Asia. In 1994 ninety-three were killed and 160 injured in a Zhuhai textile factory when a fire led to the collapse of the building. In 1993 eighty-seven women died in the Zhili toy factory fire in Shenzhen, China. At Dongguan, a raincoat factory burned in 1991 and killed seventy-two people. Also in 1993, a textile plant fire killed sixty-one women in Fuzhou province. "Why must these tragedies repeat themselves again and again?" the *People's Daily* in Beijing asked. China's *Economic Daily* blamed "the way some of these foreign investors ignore international practice, ignore our own national rules, act completely lawlessly and immorally and lust after wealth."

The factory fires continue to this day in Asia, though they haven't been quite as horrendous. These routine human tragedies provoke local protests and official investigations but somehow escape the attention of the U.S. media. One obvious cause of the fires is the so-called three-in-one factory design—peasant workers sleep in a dormitory on the top floor, with the factory and warehouse beneath them. When a fire starts, the women are trapped, often suffocated by noxious fumes. This arrangement is officially illegal in China but still widely used.

Last June the Zhimao Electronics plant fire at Shenzhen

left twenty-four dead and forty injured; the *China Labor Bulletin* described it as "a copycat of at least six similar fires in south China." Nineteen people, including five children, died in a furniture factory fire last spring at Nanyang. In August the largest apparel factory in Dhaka, Bangladesh's industrial zone burned to the ground on a Sunday night in August (evidently without casualties). Firefighters reported the absence of any fire-safety system. In October factory fires in Guangzhou's Baiyun district and Zengcheng's Shitan county killed thirty-one women, according to the *South China Morning Post*. A year ago, five workers were killed and twenty-three injured at a toy factory in Shenzhen when two of the dorm's balconies collapsed.

We begin with this mundane subject because there is absolutely no mystery about how to build and operate a safe industrial factory protected against this ancient hazard. It costs a bit more, that's all. What's missing in the global system is the political will to punish those who are scoring easy profits by ignoring such long-established industrial standards.

Congress can start here. It should enact a law that prohibits entry for any goods made in a factory that is not independently certified as employing standard fire-prevention design and equipment. The target is not mom-and-pop sweatshops operating in back alleys but the vast industrial plants producing for major global companies. They can afford to do this. Because the safety issue is so clear-cut and the human losses so dramatic, the law should permit zero tolerance for firms that ignore prudent precautions.

Does that sound too burdensome for business or too intrusive on foreign sovereignty? Consider this: The Federal Aviation Administration routinely performs similar safety tasks for aircraft, both at home and abroad. The FAA inspects production of foreign-made components that go into Boeing airplanes, certifies the airworthiness of foreign-made airliners and examines the work done offshore at overseas repair centers. Would you fly on a jetliner that was not certified by the FAA?

In fact, there are numerous other matters in which the U.S. and other governments demand the right to inspect foreign production or the content and origins of imported goods before trade is permitted. If America has the power to protect U.S. patents and copyrights by investigating knockoff CD factories in Southeast Asia, it is surely capable of protecting the lives of low-wage workers who make the toys, shirts, shoes and electronics we buy. If other nations don't wish to accept those terms, we can buy shirts and shoes somewhere else.

This issue, simple as it sounds, goes right to the heart of how globalization is organized because it challenges the irresponsibility of the "virtual corporation," that model of efficiency widely praised by management experts. "Virtual" firms operate like the central brain of a nervous system, connected to far-flung networks of suppliers and capable of shifting contracts regularly from one subcontractor to another, with no fixed accountability. One can blame the foreign-owned suppliers who scrimp on fire safety or blame local governments that do not enforce their own laws. But the moral culpability ultimately resides with the multinationals that run this arrangement (and, by extension, with the people who buy their products).

Subcontractors cut corners recklessly because they are compelled to compete on price for the next contract—a continuing cost-cutting contest that drives standards downward and ensnares poor nations as a whole. If Thailand enforces its laws too vigorously, the factories pick up and move somewhere else—Vietnam or China or Bangladesh—where workers are even cheaper and officials more compliant. This flexible system describes the treadmill that frustrates progress in poorer economies. Pioneered in low-end sectors (apparel, toys), it is increasingly evident in high-end production (autos, aircraft, advanced electronics).

Simple morality requires that we throw a little sand in the treadmill. Elementary rules, set in law, would reverse the incentives for corporate managers. Otherwise, as price-conscious consumers, we are all responsible for what happens to those young people.

Eco-Justice Goes Global

In federal district court in New York City, 30,000 residents of Ecuador are suing Texaco for class-action damages to their health and local environment. The oil company's executives are accused of making a conscious decision to dump more than 16 million gallons of oil and toxic wastewater into the Amazon River over two decades—three times the size of the Exxon Valdez oil spill in Alaska. The plaintiffs include three indigenous tribes and are represented by a Philadelphia law firm [see Eyal Press, "Texaco on Trial," May 31, 1999].

Stay tuned—this is a fast-developing new front in the globalization of law enforcement. In recent years, inventive lawyers have revived a 200-year-old federal law (the postrevolutionary Alien Tort Claims Act) as the legal basis for foreign citizens to sue U.S. multinationals in U.S. courts for their environmental or human rights abuses overseas. Unocal is being sued by Burmese workers for alleged collaboration with forced labor and torture by SLORC, the hideously repressive government of Burma. Royal Dutch/Shell announced a new code of conduct on human rights hours before the family of Ken Saro-Wiwa filed a lawsuit alleging Shell's role in the Nigerian military's execution of Saro-Wiwa.

This doctrine of legal standing is a long way from being established in the courts, but these and other suits are attempting to hold companies liable for malpractices abroad and the deception of American consumers at home. Obviously, this is not what American business had in mind as "tort reform." But the legal risks are quite real for U.S. multinationals, according to Stanford's Armin Rosencranz, an authority on international environmental law. It also opens a promising new field for trial lawyers, who took on big tobacco and showed that significant reform is still possible, despite America's stalemated politics.

Reform legislation, both at the state and national level, can advance the cause by ratifying in law that foreign citizens have clear standing to sue U.S. companies in U.S. courts, thus pre-empting the Supreme Court's business-friendly conservatives.

At the same time, Congress could require the companies to provide hard, precise data on environmental damage to those foreign communities and citizens who are usually kept in the dark about what's being done to their surroundings. Information *is* powerful. That's why companies don't often volunteer it. Daniel Seligman, head of the Sierra Club's responsible-trade campaign, suggests a preliminary outline: Congress could enact legal requirements that U.S. multinationals disclose toxic releases at overseas production facilities that would parallel the existing laws for industry at home. When an oil or mining company plans to open a new project in a foreign country, it would have to prepare the equivalent of an "environmental impact" assessment and share it with the affected community. The company would be required to engage in open discussions on potential consequences, not just with the national government but with the people whose health and habitat are threatened.

Furthermore, multinationals and their affiliated producers would have to disclose an annual inventory of what exactly is being dumped in the river or ground, what emissions are released into the air and, of course, what toxics are inside the factory. This does not intrude on any country's pollution standards, but it does equip citizens to act for themselves.

As U.S. environmentalists have learned from long experience, the process of enforcing pollution standards can be torturously slow and incomplete if it relies solely on government agencies. Enactment of U.S. toxic "right to know" laws in the eighties was a crucial turning point. The information unleashed grassroots energies and compelled many companies to accelerate compliance. No one should imagine that poor people in Asia, Latin America or elsewhere are indifferent to what's happening to their local environment. The problem is that they usually have no voice in the matter.

Thus, a new law would embody two fundamental reforms: First, companies would be compelled to make full disclosure of their pollution, and, second, affected foreign citizens would have the right to sue them for damages in American courts.

"This has nothing to do with eco-imperialism," Seligman emphasized. "It simply holds our own firms accountable to our values. It's not dictating the levels of pollution, but it's giving communities, not just governments, the information they need to decide their own destiny."

This reform should further stimulate the development of international civil society and the rule of law, both of which the business establishment claims to want. Local citizens, alarmed by the despoliation, could seek expert help from established environmental groups elsewhere in the world. If the facts are truly alarming, they could hire a lawyer to represent them in American courts.

WHERE ARE THE WORKERS OF THE WORLD?

When consumer activists targeted the wages and working conditions associated with Nike and other famous brands, Mattel decided to act on its own, before Barbie dolls got caught in the same cross-hairs. Half of the Barbies are now made in China, where labor conditions are notorious and Mattel uses 300 subcontractors, according to the Asian Monitor Resource Center. Mattel developed a detailed industrial code for its producers, prescribing standards for everything from injury rates to the number of bathrooms per 100 workers.

The three-member Independent Monitoring Council chosen by the company to oversee compliance includes economist Murray Weidenbaum, an antiregulation conservative and well-known apologist for business practices. PricewaterhouseCoopers, the global accounting firm, was hired to audit. No one should be surprised that their first report, in November, covering three major factories in China and some others in three other nations, gave Mattel high marks. It describes the local managers as enthusiastic about correcting certain deficiencies.

Still, even Mattel's own handpicked inspectors were baffled by the payroll records at two Chinese plants—the accounting system for wages, hours worked, overtime paid. The monitoring committee admitted that it "experienced difficulty in verifying certain elements of the pay structure. . . . A large majority of workers . . . expressed a lack of understanding of their pay stubs."

The workers, likewise, seemed unfamiliar with Mattel's "Global Manufacturing Principles," though the new standards were supposedly explained to them. The council noted that when some workers responded to questions, "it appeared that these were memorized answers." Nor were workers able to say much about free expression or complaints to managers. "Most of them were either not conscious or were reluctant to talk about the freedom of association or unionization issues," the report noted.

A less charitable explanation of the wage-and-hour confusion was provided by the Asian Monitor Resource Center in a March 1999 report on what its citizen investigators found at twelve Chinese toy factories, including several where Mattel is active. "During the peak season, not a single worker can leave the workplace after eight hours' work," the center reported. "Most workers in these toy factories work ten to sixteen hours a day, six or seven days a week . . . . Since most toy workers are paid by piece rate, they never receive overtime pay."

Corporate codes of conduct have led to some improvements, the center noted, including on fire safety. "However," the report added, "we still found numerous blatant violations of workers' basic labor and human rights—including flagrant violations of China's own Labor Law, even though many of the factories we investigated are subcontractors for [multinationals] having codes of conduct on paper."

The Asian center, for instance, found that the Tri-S factory in Dongguan, which it identified as a Mattel and Tyco supplier, was still operating a "three in one" factory that is ostensibly illegal. Three hundred workers slept on the third floor; the second floor was full of raw materials.

The issue is not Mattel's sincerity. The question is whether Americans will allow enforcement of labor rights to be "privatized"—left to the moral judgments of individual companies—or whether these complex matters must be codified in law as clearly stated benchmarks, so that corporate claims can be tested by independent verification and, if necessary, challenged in courts of law. Even if one accepted any individual company's good intentions, that still leaves millions of peasant workers subject to low-road practices by thousands of other companies and their contractors, responding to fierce market pressures that cut costs at human expense.

The first weapon is disclosure. One can collect countless horror stories on several continents, but the lack of reliable, comprehensive information remains a central problem. The codes of conduct, of course, further confuse the picture, since brand-name firms develop PR campaigns around them, while still refusing access to independent investigators.

In fact, until quite recently, companies would typically not even reveal where their goods were made—much less how their workers were treated. Under pressure from student activists and universities, Nike folded last October. It disclosed the locations of forty-two of its 365 factories.

Once again, national legislation should start with simple stuff—requiring firms to disclose information that enables citizens here and abroad to check out corporate behavior, and giving private citizens and organizations the legal standing to sue for damages if companies falsify their reports to the U.S. government. Given the overbearing political influence of the multinationals, legal standing for private lawsuits is crucial.

This much we do know: The U.S. government cannot be trusted to enforce labor standards, since it has repeatedly failed to do so under already existing laws. One especially sickening example occurred in 1994 when Suharto still ruled Indonesia. The Clinton Administration certified the regime's improving labor policies—thus keeping Indonesia eligible for trade preferences—at the very moment Suharto was smashing a promising new labor federation, imprisoning scores of its brave leaders and charging them with subversion.

An initial labor code should, obviously, require all U.S. multinationals to identify the names and addresses of offshore factories and their subcontractor plants, the owners and principal investors. Next, the corporations would answer some fairly simple questions about each factory: the number of workers and what they make, the base pay for production workers, the factory's labor costs as a percentage of its value-added output.

Finally, for every production site, the company would be required to certify the existence of well-accepted labor standards or to explain why its factory ought to be granted an exemption. Does the workplace comply with the host country's own labor laws? Does it comply with the International Labor Organization's "core labor standards," guaranteeing the right to organize, forbidding child labor and forced labor? If not, why not?

A more controversial suggestion would require each company to attest that its industrial workers do at least receive a "living wage," that is, income sufficient to provide for basic subsistence in terms of their own country and culture—food, housing, clothing, health and education. If not, these powerful companies would have to explain why such a minimal benchmark for modern industrial life is too expensive for them.

No one can demand that American companies alter another society's laws and customs, but once again we are separating bad guys from innocent players. It is not always the foreign government that suppresses labor rights but sometimes American companies who insist on it. My favorite example is the U.S. semiconductor industry's production platform in Malaysia—famous names like Intel, Motorola, Texas Instruments, Hewlett-Packard. At their insistence, the electronics sector operates union-free, though Malaysia has vigorous, independent unions everywhere else.

A typical reaction is: Do these foreign workers really want or need our help? Despite sometimes harsh conditions, aren't they better off with the jobs and grateful? It is true that many of the young people in poor countries, entering industrial life for the first time, are quite bewildered by their new circumstances. They have migrated from the desperate poverty of rural villages, eager for wage incomes. Many of them do not even grasp what a union is, much less understand the broader rights accorded to workers elsewhere in the global system.

What many of them do understand, however, is that

they are being exploited. They don't have to be told this by do-gooders from America. They know it from the sordid working conditions or from meager wages and their own disappointed hopes. That's why there are so many wildcat strikes—thousands of spontaneous strikes that occur regularly across developing nations, not organized by any unions but by workers themselves. Angry workers even strike in China, despite the real risk of imprisonment.

These sporadic, local protests are seldom mentioned in the U.S. press, but together they constitute an optimistic statement about our common humanity.

FREEDOM AND UNFREEDOM

Nobel economist Amartya Sen begins his new book, *Development as Freedom*, with a provocative comparison: "The battle against the unfreedom of bound labor is important in many third world countries today for some of the same reasons the American Civil War was momentous." Is it possible that Americans are once again participating in an economic system that is half free, half unfree?

The question does not seem farfetched when one examines more closely the predicament of the young women in many Chinese factories. Typically, they are recruited from remote villages by a government agency that collects a fee from them for the job. They must pay for their own travel, then place a "deposit" with factory managers, who will withhold their wages for the first month or two and frequently also take away the workers' official ID cards. Hired under three-year contracts, they cannot leave or jump to better jobs without losing their money and perhaps identity papers too. Their factory dorms are fenced and guarded, the workers cannot come and go freely, the stories of brutality by security guards are commonplace.

This is not slavery, to be sure, but it does resemble a sly form of indentured servitude, imposed on people who are powerless to resist its terms. What can be done to stop it? For starters, a serious Congressional investigation that digs into the ugly facts and calls corporate CEOs to explain themselves would do more than embarrass industry. The American people, I believe, cannot bear the guilty knowledge of how their consumer trifles are produced, any more than they could live with knowledge of the racial caste system in America once the civil rights movement compelled them to confront it. This new movement has the same task of teaching and confronting.

The "enhancement of human freedom," Sen argues, "is both the main object and the primary means of development." Democracy and civil rights are thus central to economic progress, but the "unfreedoms" Sen describes involve much more than legal guarantees of free speech and religion or standards for powerful corporations. Poverty also enslaves lives. So do the still-existing, precapitalist feudal systems that deny individual aspirations in some countries. So do the social hierarchies that send adolescent girls to work in the factories while the boys go to school. These confining forces and others interact with the marketplace, which sometimes liberates people and sometimes uses unfreedoms for its own ends.

Human rights, in other words, pose the most profound challenge for reform because the issues go to the core nature of every society, and legislation alone cannot resolve them. Americans, above all, must remember to bring humility to this struggle. The promise of life expectancy, as Sen observes, is greater for people in some very poor nations than it is for African-American males in the United States. Our luxurious wealth, not just our values, is sometimes implicated in the unfreedom of others. As this new movement educates us about global realities, we shall see ourselves more clearly.

THEY POISON
OUR FOOD

Corporations see our food supply as a profit center—nothing more. After all, corporations don't have to eat.

Thomas Jefferson believed that small farmers were the backbone of our democracy—so it's no surprise that big corporations are doing all they can to destroy the small farm. One side effect: so-called food that tastes like we bought it at Home Depot.

The Last Farm Crisis
from *The Nation* (11/20/00)
William Greider

THE NEW POLITICS OF FOOD

The contemporary triumph of free-market capitalism has revealed to farmers, if not to other Americans, the bitter last act in this drama. Farmers can see themselves being reduced from their mythological status as independent producers to a subservient and vulnerable role as share-croppers or franchisees. The control of food production, both livestock and crops, is being consolidated not by the government but by a handful of giant corporations. While farmers and ranchers suffered three years of severely depressed prices at the close of the 1990s, the corporations enjoyed soaring profits from the same line of goods. Growers are surrounded now on both sides—facing con-centrated market power not only from the companies that buy their crops and animals but also from the firms that sell them essential inputs like seeds and fertilizer. In the final act of unfettered capitalism, the free market itself is destroyed.

In farm country these developments are often described, with irony, as America's top-down version of collectivization. "It's interesting," said James Horne, who leads an Oklahoma center for sustainable agriculture.

"Our system of support payments for the farmers survived about as long as the Soviet system did, around seventy years. Now, here in the United States we're doing exactly what the Russians are undoing in their agriculture. They're decentralizing and we're centralizing."

Farmers tend to express the point more pungently. "We're in a death struggle out here, and we're getting our butts kicked," said Fred Stokes, a former career Army officer who retired to raise cattle in his home state of Mississippi. Stokes calls himself a Reagan Republican, but frequently begins a statement by saying, "Now, I'm not a socialist but . . ."

"The thing that bothers me most is the Big Brother aspect of this deal," he said. "It's clear the government is more concerned with mining big profits for these corporations than it is with food security or family farmers. It's all about more money for a handful of guys who will be the elites. The rest of us wind up swinging machetes. You talk about feudalism. This thing makes farmers indentured on their own land; they're going to be the new serfs."

The media's usual take on this new farm crisis is a tear-jerk feature story that begins with a worried farm couple poring over bills at the kitchen table, children crying in the background; and it closes with a romantic elegy for Jefferson's doomed yeomanry. Too bad, but that's the price of progress, end of story. I intend to skip over the pathos of farm families, widespread though it is, and focus instead on the intricate economics of monopoly power and why collectivized agriculture promises ruinous social consequences for the rest of us. Farming, as an industry, is inescapably different from other sectors—since weather is always a big wild card in production—but the patterns of concentration and control in food production provide a visible primer for what's also been under way in the larger economy. The same great shifts in structure and market domination are fast forming in finance and banking, telecommunications, media and other sectors. The much-celebrated entrepreneurial spirit is steadily neutered—"rationalized," the players would say—by the same rush of mergers, acquisitions and "strategic alliances" among supposed rivals. (See Adam Smith on how businessmen always yearn to escape from price competition through collusion.)

Some farmers and ranchers are mobilizing for a last stand—those at least who haven't been thoroughly demoralized by recurring crises during the past twenty years. But this time, they recognize that farm rebellion is bound to fail unless they can persuade city folks—consumers, environmentalists, church activists and humanists, even animal rights advocates—that this political struggle involves much more than saving the family farm. Its purpose is also restoring the promise of safe and wholesome food, protecting consumers from monopoly pricing and stopping techno-agriculture's harsh new methods for abusing the environment as well as animals. "To win this thing—and we're way behind—we've got to connect with the general public and let them know they've got a dog in this fight," Stokes explained.

Toward that end, the Organization for Competitive Markets (OCM), an interstate group of farmers, ranchers, political leaders and professionals that Stokes heads, assembled an unusual cross-section of kindred spirits at a church retreat center in Parkville, Missouri, a few months ago. Around the conference table for three days, sharing

expertise and background papers, were agricultural economists from major land-grant universities in the Midwest
and South, antitrust experts from law school faculties, rural
sociologists and community advocates, environmentalists
and leading critics of such notorious practices and products
as hog factories and genetically manipulated seeds. They
produced a comprehensive "vision statement" on how
Americans might seek to replace industrialized agriculture
with a "whole-food system" that incorporates humane
values and quality, that moves farm economics away from
high-tech, capital-intensive bigness and toward the diversity
that is possible if smaller farms survive. Their report and
papers (available at www.competitivemarkets.com) provide
an intellectual starting point for serious conversation
about food between city and countryside—the threads
that might become fabric for a political alliance that could
have far more strength than embattled farmers alone. The
warm, serious spirit of the Parkville gathering reminded
one of Seattle, where the turtles and Teamsters discovered
their mutual self-interest.

This political initiative, however, raises an ironic banner
for left-liberal social reformers because it calls them to
rally on behalf of "competitive markets." That may seem a
wrenching twist for many who have devoted their political
energies in recent decades to holding back the market ideology's relentless encroachment on public space and
public values, and to fighting the many battles over deregulation and privatization. Nevertheless, if people's social
values are to prevail in this fight, it has to begin by
defending the marketplace against the collusive power of
emerging monopolies. Aroused citizens must likewise
reawaken government and push it to confront this new

landscape of concentrated economic power. The legal doctrine called antitrust got its name from oil, banking and many other "trusts" 100 years ago—combines that pursued the same brazen impulse to strangle free markets and control prices to the injury of smaller competitors and the public. A century ago, the Populists and Progressive reformers understood the centrality of free exchange of goods, honest pricing and markets free of collusion to the vitality of democracy and individual freedom. This generation has to relearn the economics. Then it must invent a robust new vision that challenges the present circumstances of globalizing market power.

In fact, a feisty new politics is already bubbling up around the nation, based on this same understanding. In Wyoming and the northern plains, citizen activists are forcing passage of laws to control the megafarms. The Western Organization of Resource Councils includes six state councils, from Idaho to the Dakotas, that unite independent ranchers with environmentalists against the big guys. In North Carolina angry citizens were already confronting the hog factories that pollute coastal rivers and estuaries before Hurricane Floyd came along and unleashed ruinous tides of manure overflowing from the hog-farm lagoons. In dozens of states the activists are also organizing direct-marketing devices that will sustain smaller farmers: open-air produce markets, cattle ranchers selling grass-fed beef to consumers by subscription orders and other conduits that boost farm incomes by cutting out agribusiness. These efforts seem frail alongside the corporations, but the big guys are no longer dismissing organic-food marketing, as they did a generation ago.

Rita Wilhelm, a graphic designer and mother of three

from Annville, Pennsylvania, seems typical of the grass-roots action. She was alarmed when a hog factory was built down the road—9,200 animals clustered in barns on 120 acres, with manure lagoons and an overpowering stench. "I grew up in the country," Wilhelm said, "but this is far beyond making a living—this is making a killing." She and neighbors—after discovering that Republican Governor Tom Ridge was already on the other side, weakening environmental regulation to attract these strange new factories—organized Pennsylvanians for Responsible Agriculture, which now connects similar activists in thirty-nine groups across seventeen counties. Her local colleagues include farmers, an environmental engineer, even two township supervisors.

Their primary issues are not only the destruction of water supplies and clean air but also unsafe food. "If you're going to eat synthetically produced food with all the chemicals and everything, you're going to get that out of it, and now that's showing up in health problems," Wilhelm said. The group's new website (www.pfra.org), she hopes, will help local farmers to find direct customers for their free-range beef, pork and poultry. With help from a young environmental lawyer, Thomas Linzey from Shippensburg, Pennsylvania, the group has lobbied county and township boards to enact an anti-corporate farming ordinance—legislation Linzey borrowed from nine states in the West and Midwest. As president of the Community Environmental Legal Defense Fund, he has promised to defend, for free, the first corporate challenge to these legal barriers that local governments are erecting.

This same story pops up regularly across the nation. The home-grown activists have come to this realization: If there is any hope of liberating the food system from corporate control, they must first help rescue smaller producers from their fate, so they can endure to develop the alternative modes of farming (actually, old farming methods, in many instances) that will deliver food in ways that are both nature-friendly and humane. "I think the conversation changed when we started talking about markets," Linzey observed. "Then you could bring together a much larger group of interests." He added, "We are literally in a war with the agricultural extension offices, because their regulatory system is set up simply to support large, concentrated production."

THE VANISHING MARKET

Let's name some names. The dominating leaders in grain trade and processing: Cargill (which swallowed Continental, the second-largest grain trader), Archer Daniels Midland (ADM), ConAgra. Beefpacking: IBP, ConAgra, Cargill (as owner of Excel). Cattle feedlots: Cargill, Cactus Feeders, ConAgra. Pork processing: Smithfield, IBP, ConAgra, Cargill. Hog growers: Smithfield (the largest pork processor has bought the largest and second-largest hog producers, Murphy Family Farms and Carroll's Foods), Cargill, Seaboard. Biotech and seeds: Monsanto, DuPont/Pioneer, Novartis, Aventis. Supermarkets: Kroger, Albertson's, Safeway, AHOLD (Giant), Winn-Dixie, Wal-Mart.

As the repeated names suggest, a few far-flung firms are positioned on many sides of the market at once and, indeed, are incestuously connected through a dizzying galaxy of "strategic alliances" and cross-ownership. Smithfield, the world's largest hog producer and pork processor, recently bought a 6.3 percent stake in its putative rival, IBP, the second-largest pork processor. ADM already owned a 12.2 percent share of IBP. This cross-ownership will continue, as IBP itself is to be acquired in a friendly takeover by the Wall Street brokerage firm Donaldson, Lufkin & Jenrette (which was recently bought by Credit Suisse First Boston). Some analysts are watching to see if Smithfield makes a rival bid for the meatpacking giant. Cargill and Monsanto have fashioned a labyrinth of joint ventures that runs from fertilizer and seeds to grain and raising cattle, hogs, turkeys and chickens, then on to the slaughterhouses.

Sector by sector, four firms control 82 percent of beef-packing, 75 percent of hogs and sheep, and half of chickens. Major supermarket chains are now concentrated regionally, though not nationally. Four firms hold 74 percent of market control in ninety-four large cities; experts anticipate a new merger wave that could swiftly increase that percentage while doubling the four firms' overall national concentration up to 60 percent. And so on. As antitrust theory would predict, this kind of market leverage ought to give companies a pricing advantage over farmers and ranchers, and it has, according to Wisconsin law professor Peter Carstensen. The spread between prices paid for livestock and the wholesale price of meat has widened in the past few years by 52 percent for pork and 24 percent for beef, he reported.

Yet these extraordinary levels of concentration unfolded without government opposition. The consolidation quickened after Ronald Reagan's antitrust division at the Justice Department swept away the old rules and thresholds for opposing mergers and takeovers. Reagan's lawyers effectively gutted the theory with a narrow laissez-faire interpretation that declared bigness no longer a problem if it could not be proven, in advance, to distort consumer prices. Cheap food was consecrated as the only issue that matters to the public. The Clinton Administration, notwithstanding its activism against Microsoft, has been generally passive on big mergers of all kinds and nearly as pliant as the Reaganites were (among leading seed companies, sixty-eight acquisitions occurred between 1995 and 1998). Consumers may judge for themselves whether they have benefited at the checkout counter.

The disadvantage for farmers was compounded greatly as the companies moved aggressively into vertical integration—acquiring top-to-bottom elements in the chain of production. Owning feedlots or signing output contracts with individual farmers for poultry, hogs, cattle and, in some instances, grain and soybeans has given the processing companies their own "captive supplies." Their privately held stores of livestock mean giants like IBP no longer have to rely on auction-price purchases in the open market for most of their supply. In fact, according to farmers, the companies regularly deploy this leverage to depress market prices for the independent producers.

Such practices are ostensibly illegal, and the Agriculture Department has belatedly promised to look into them. Mike Callicrate, a feedlot owner in St. Francis, Kansas, has filed a class-action damage suit against IBP on behalf of cattlemen, one of a number of promising legal challenges under way. "Captive supplies are just devastating to the cash market," Callicrate explained. "IBP would come to your feedyard and bid you a very low price—a bid not to buy, we call it—because they are just searching around for the weakest cattleman. Who needs to sell today? Of course, they intimidate him too, by saying, 'If you don't take this price today, we're not going to buy your cattle three weeks from now.' When he does take the low price, the word goes out instantly and everyone else gets nervous. Then IBP takes the price down further because they don't need the cattle right now; they've already got their own supply [in feedlots or under contract]. What's their motivation? They just want cattle to be available at lower prices when they do want to buy. You've got a very well organized buyer dealing with very disorganized sellers."

The final blow to small producers came in 1996, with enactment of the Freedom to Farm Act, the law intended to phase out the federal government's price-support payments and production-restraint mechanisms (better known among farmers now as the "Freedom to Fail" Act). The Clinton Administration, much as it did in welfare reform, made common cause with Republican ideologues to repeal a New Deal landmark. The premise was that market forces, once liberated from the Feds, would gradually reconcile supply and demand in farm output, mainly by persuading many marginal farmers to get out of the business, thereby insuring decent prices for those who survive. The law failed utterly to do either. As surpluses and collapsing prices engulfed farm states, politicians from both parties blinked. Instead of gradually reducing the federal support payments (supposedly to zero after seven years), the public's subsidy for farmers has doubled and tripled in size—$16 billion in 1998, $23 billion last year—as Congress repeatedly enacted "emergency" relief measures. With that great trauma, the last act for agriculture began to unfold.

Among the consequences, the capital-intensive tread-mill for farmers sped up, and they became even more eager to embrace whatever innovation promised to boost returns. Just as farm prices were cratering, Monsanto and others began promoting genetically altered seeds for corn and soybeans with cost-cutting promises, and this new technology swept the landscape. "These farmers are so desperate for profitability," Fred Stokes said, "they grab whatever is offered to them. Offering GM seeds is like selling them a bag of cocaine." His grain-growing colleagues in the Organization for Competitive Markets affirm that they have seen no bottom-line benefits from GM seeds. As agricultural experience has long demonstrated, the first farmers to adopt new production technologies will enjoy higher returns, but the effect soon wears off when everyone is using the same stuff. The result is still higher yields and greater productive capacity—more surpluses than the market can absorb.

Exports, as many farmers have figured out, are not going to save them. The logic promoted by agribusiness and the Agriculture Department—not to mention global-trade boosters in and out of government—was that greater efficiency would allow lower prices on U.S. crop exports and thus give U.S. farmers the edge to grab market share from other grain-growing nations. Roughly the opposite has occurred during the past thirty years, despite the inflated promises that accompany each new trade agreement (most recently with China). Agricultural economist Daryll Ray of the University of Tennessee has documented a stair-step decline in the U.S. share of global trade in corn, soybeans and wheat, starting in the 1970s. "What the past fifteen years have taught us is that lower crop prices do not cause competing exporters, including Canada, the European Union, Brazil, Argentina and Australia, to fold up shop and give the United States their market share," Ray explained. "When U.S. prices drop, our competitors quickly lower their export prices as well." Importing countries, he added, do not increase their food purchases significantly when supplies are plentiful and prices lower. Nations, like people, buy what they need, but they do not eat twice as much just because the food is cheap.

The more momentous consequence of the price collapse is that in the past few years it drove many more farmers into accepting the status of contract producers—growing crops or livestock under fixed-price contracts with the corporations. Richard Levins, an agricultural economist at the University of Minnesota, said these production contracts covered about $60 billion by 1997, almost one-third of farm-level crop and livestock sales, and have expanded greatly since. Mainstream authorities regard supply contracting as the future. "Old MacDonald's farm is being absorbed into what might be called New McDonald's Farms," Levins observed. In other words, farming begins to resemble a fast-food franchise to run a burger joint or an auto dealership. The operator buys the supplies and equipment from the brand-name company and produces to its uniform specifications. "They are going to put cattle in buildings, too," Levins predicted. "It's not there yet, but cattle will be raised indoors eventually."

While contract status will effectively end the entrepreneurial culture in farming, it also ostensibly frees small producers from the harrowing instabilities of market prices. Or does it? Farmers foresee that the supposed stability of contract farming will actually leave them utterly dependent on the handful of agribusiness firms and without alternatives. Neil Harl, a veteran agricultural economist from Iowa State University, explained: "Let's say we're down to two huge hog-slaughtering firms, and each is 90 percent vertically integrated. The new contract [offered to a hog-factory operator] is considerably less attractive than the expiring contract. The producer is told, Take or leave it. If the closest competitive option for hogs is 900 miles away—and is also heavily integrated—clearly a producer in that situation is likely to be squeezed."

Agriculture's emerging pattern of organization begins to resemble what is under way in other major sectors, including globalized manufacturing. The model is no longer the huge industrial behemoth but the "virtual corporation" that owns very little in hard capital assets itself—that is, factories—but organizes a complex, floating network of affiliated producers and subcontractors who adhere to its brand standards—think of Nike. One can predict that the consolidated food industry will likely respond to periods of slack demand in the same way the auto industry or shoe manufacturers do—dropping subcontractors, closing factories, discarding workers.

The deeper implications are about power, as Jeremy Rifkin explains in *The Age of Access*. If there is no other place for smaller producers to sell, then access to the network becomes the crucial privilege. And who exactly controls the access? Or has the power to expel and punish weaker partners? This is among the veils that a strong new antitrust doctrine must look behind.

Farmers at long last will find themselves in the very same predicament that confronted industrial workers in other sectors 100 years ago. Harl believes that, unthinkable as it sounds, farmers must sooner or later pursue labor's remedy—collective action—by organizing unions that restore their bargaining power and by creating producer cooperatives large enough to compete with the big guys. "There was stability in Russia," Harl mused. "Russian agriculture was stable because the center told everyone what to do. And we will get stability if Cargill tells us what to do. But is that what Americans want?"

Maybe they do. Most consumers have seemed at least indifferent. Why cry for small farmers, a *New York Times* feature asked, when modern consolidations are wiping out so many other local enterprises, from independent bookstores to neighborhood groceries? But aside from the questions of food quality and safety or social equity, there is another threat that consumers might ponder: If this nexus of collaborating corporations acquires the market power to control total farm output and stabilize prices, then it will also have the power to inflate food prices on behalf of greater profit. In the last act, cheap food disappears right along with the free market.

Who Pays for Fast Food?

The short answer is nearly everyone, one way or another, even those who have never encountered a Big Mac or extra-crispy KFC. The economies of scale gained from bigness do matter, but only up to a point. The real source of efficiency in consolidated agribusiness is a long-familiar operating principle of capitalist enterprise—push the true costs of production off the company's balance sheet and onto someone else. "They maintain their profitability by shifting costs off on the community," said William Weida, an economist at Colorado College who counsels many grassroots groups opposing hog factories. "You don't put in a proper lagoon. The costs of dealing with animal waste are avoided by the owners and shifted to the surrounding population as health problems, traffic, social problems and pollution—odors, chemicals and pathogens in air or water. You don't pay the worker more than you absolutely have to. You do take advantage of every public subsidy available. But the biggest cost issue is that hogs are a lot like humans and are sensitive to disease. That means the life of these projects is only about twelve years because the buildings become so contaminated they can't use them any longer. Too many hogs die. Then they pick up and leave, and the community is stuck with the damage."

Oddly enough, one of the government's most vigorous champions of supply-contract farming and the hog-factory system is the Federal Reserve, which is supposed to regulate money and credit, not agriculture. Its Center for the Study of Rural America at the Kansas City Federal Reserve Bank last spring sponsored a conference on rural economic development titled "Beyond Agriculture." Mark Drabenstott, the center's director, has relentlessly promoted the factory concept as the inevitable wave of the future and argues that corporate consolidation allows rural communities to put aside farm issues so they can pursue brighter prospects for development.

One speaker at the Fed conference, an Italian official from the Organization for Economic Cooperation and Development, suggested that small farmers may still be needed on the land, if only to protect the lovely landscape. "It is true in Tuscany," Mario Pezzini allowed, "that, if you remove all the olive trees, the beauty of the region will be destroyed."

A much grimmer portrait of the future was described by Professor Thomas Johnson, an agricultural economist from Missouri. Johnson warned the Fed conference of the emerging specter of "isolated rural communities" where most of the large factory farms and packinghouses are located. The food factories will operate with the most advanced technologies, yet local public services, especially education, will be minimal. Incomes will be significantly lower, populations stable or declining, the tax base weak and eroding. "These communities will rival inner cities as the primary destination of international immigrants," Johnson said. "These immigrants will largely work at close to minimum wages for value-added agricultural processing or other manufacturing firms." The pattern is already visible in rural backwaters and on Indian reservations—sites chosen by agribusiness on the assumption that very poor people will not object to anything that promises a little income.

In other words, this very sophisticated corporate system for food production is in the process of creating new pockets of poverty across prosperous America—places where people without much income or influence dwell in an environment that is ruined both physically and socially. If you think about history, this is what coal and steel and other emerging manufacturing industries did a century ago, when immigrant workers and others were clustered in coal camps and mill towns. Government is still dealing with the messes those industries left behind, and taxpayers will someday pay for the new ones that agribusiness is generating. In a variety of ways, cheap food assigns its true costs to many unwitting victims.

First, consider the situation of workers. The consolidating packinghouse industry first boosted its "efficiency" by breaking unions and busting down wages, next by drawing hapless immigrant workers into slaughterhouse jobs that were already dirty and dangerous. Then the companies sped up the assembly lines—and the Agriculture Department accommodated high-speed production by "modernizing" its own inspection system. Professor Ronald Cotterill, an antitrust authority at the University of Connecticut's Food Marketing Policy Center, described current working conditions as "now clearly more dangerous and debilitating than at any time since Upton Sinclair wrote *The Jungle*," in 1906. Some brave workers are rebelling. In Omaha, a joint organizing campaign led by the United Food and Commercial Workers and the Industrial Areas Foundation's church-based community organization, Omaha Together One Community, has signed up a majority of the workers at the ConAgra beef packinghouse. The workers are demanding union recognition.

Then there is public health. Salmonella poisoning has staged a comeback, thanks to the greater efficiencies in slaughterhouses and meat inspection. Just as the assembly line was sped up for workers, factory farms also speed up the birth-to-slaughter cycle of animals with heavy injections of growth-accelerating antibiotics and hormones. Europeans, fearful of the chemical residues in food, prohibit these practices, and the U.S. government responds by denouncing such concerns as barriers to free trade. No one really knows what the consequences will be for human health. The Organization for Competitive Markets warns: "It is likely that the rapid buildup of pathogens and chemicals in our surface water—much of which is due to the improper handling of animal wastes—will lead to some kind of major disease outbreak or health problems in the next few years." Health issues include overuse of antibiotics; the emergence of new, antibiotics-resistant pathogens; the effects on children of bovine growth hormone in milk products; and the risk of unintended genetic migrations from biotech seeds. The monarch butterfly, we are informed, may pay the price for GM corn. Government regulators often prove to be unreliable guardians of safe food. In Britain the threat of mad-cow disease was actively kept from the public until people started dying. In the United States, Aventis won EPA approval to sell its GM corn seeds by promising to keep the corn segregated from human consumption, but it went into taco shells.

There's also the issue of food security. Given the usual abundance of food, it's unsettling to hear agricultural experts explain how a sudden crisis could occur in the U.S. food supply. According to William Heffernan of Missouri, "Biotechnology eliminates diversity, and there's a lot of uncertainty about what results from the homogenization of breeds, the entropy of the gene pool, the concentration of production that generates new pathogens." He adds, "The control of the animal genetics pool is concentrating, and the genetic base for domestic animals is narrowing. For example, more than 90 percent of all commercially produced turkeys in the world come from three breeding flocks. The system is ripe for the evolution of a new strain of avian flu for which these birds have no resistance. Similar concerns exist in hogs, chickens and dairy-cattle genetics." Food security may also be threatened by the fragile economic condition of producers and extreme price swings. "If we had two droughts in a row like 1988," Daryll Ray of Tennessee warned, "we would see the farmers slaughtering their animals and we would have food shortages."

And finally there is the cruel treatment of animals. In slaughterhouses, Missouri hog farmer Keith Mudd told me, the line moves so fast that on occasion workers are sawing the legs off an animal that is not yet dead (anyone who doubts this should read Gail Eisnitz's exposé, *Slaughterhouse*). The Humane Farming Association, based in San Rafael, California, circulates a film on hog factories that provides stomach-turning glimpses inside the production system—sows dead or dying, chewing frantically on the bars and metal flooring because they have been made psychotic by close confinement, where they cannot root or even turn around. Their piglets are removed soon after birth and the sows are swiftly reimpregnated—high-speed birthing that continues until, sore and exhausted, the animal drops. The film also shows hog production in Sweden, where growth-accelerating antibiotics are forbidden by law and the animals are raised and fattened in natural settings and normal routines. Animal-rights advocates remind us of this admonition: The ways in which people treat animals will be reflected in how people relate to one another.

TRACTORS AND TREE-HUGGERS UNITE!

State Senator Paul Muegge from Tonkawa, Oklahoma, a grain and livestock farmer who chairs the State Senate's agriculture committee, joked about his odd reputation in Oklahoma politics. "I'm known as a wacko tree-hugger myself," he admitted. "Me and a friend figured out awhile back we can't beat these tree-huggers; they're everywhere.

So we started talking to them, and within a year we got some things worked out. We had alliances with family farmers and environmentalists on the hog-waste issue, and that coalition simply swept over the state." The white-haired Muegge is among those who encouraged the Organization for Competitive Markets to initiate the broader conversation on food.

The OCM vision statement doesn't attempt to strategize on the politics, but it lays out the big picture in persuasive detail and proposes some ambitious goals. Some of them are:

- *Reinvigorating antitrust enforcement.* If the Justice Department remains passive, state governments and private lawsuits can lead the way. Litigation should not only explore the breakup of existing consolidations but also develop a broader antitrust doctrine that encompasses producer prices and the antisocial consequences of monopoly power.

- *Stabilizing the production system.* OCM proposes a global food reserve, coordinated with other major grain-producing nations, that can reduce the highs and lows of price swings without re-establishing the old price-support system. Food reserves would also serve as the nation's "rainy-day fund," protecting against food-supply risks from weather or genetic catastrophes.

- *A whole-food system.* By involving consumers, rich and poor, in agriculture policy, the government would change directions fundamentally. Instead of subsidizing the industrialized system, public funds would go to farmers who are making the difficult transition to alternative farming, which is both sustainable and humane but which has lower yields. Agricultural research, including at some land-grant universities now corrupted by corporate sponsors, would refocus on social objectives. Campaigns to require honest food labeling and to eliminate dangerous working conditions and antibiotics would also be obvious priorities.

No one should have any illusions about how difficult it will be to reform our current food system—or how hard it is for country folks and city folks to put aside their usual differences and learn to do politics on the same page. Still, as Tom Linzey says, the food system has to change for our own good and for the future's. The farmers, like Fred Stokes and Paul Muegge, who have started the conversation are opening a door to new politics, brushing aside old stereotypes that divide the millions of Americans who ought to be allies. If kindred spirits will return the favor, something important—maybe even powerful—could unfold.

The meat packing industry's motto? Let them eat shit.

Bad Meat
from *The Nation* (9/16/02)
Eric Schlosser

In a summer full of headlines about corporate misdeeds and irresponsibility, ConAgra's massive recall in July stands apart. The defective product wasn't fiber optic cable, energy futures or some esoteric financial instrument. It was bad meat—almost 19 million pounds of beef potentially contaminated with E. coli O157:H7, enough to supply a tainted burger to at least one-fourth of the U.S. population. Unlike other prominent scandals, this one does not seem to involve any falsification of records, shredding of crucial documents or deliberate violation of the law. And that makes it all the more disturbing. The Bush Administration and its Republican allies in Congress have allowed the meatpacking industry to gain control of the nation's food safety system, much as the airline industry was given responsibility for airport security in the years leading up to the September 11 attacks. The deregulation of food safety makes about as much sense as the deregulation of air safety. Anyone who eats meat these days should be deeply concerned about what our meat-packing companies now have the freedom to sell.

At the heart of the food safety debate is the issue of microbial testing. Consumer advocates argue that the federal government should be testing meat for dangerous pathogens and imposing tough penalties on companies that repeatedly fail those tests. The meatpacking industry, which has been battling new food safety measures for almost a century, strongly disagrees. In 1985 a panel appointed by the National Academy of Sciences warned that the nation's meat inspection system was obsolete. At the time USDA inspectors relied solely on visual and olfactory clues to detect tainted meat. After the Jack in the Box outbreak in 1993, the Clinton Administration announced that it would begin random testing for E. coli O157:H7 in ground beef. The meatpacking industry promptly sued the USDA in federal court to block such tests.

E. coli O157:H7, the pathogen involved in both the Jack in the Box outbreak and the recent ConAgra recall, can cause severe illness or death, especially among children, the elderly and people who are immuno-suppressed. The Centers for Disease Control and Prevention (CDC) estimate that about 73,000 Americans are sickened by E. coli O157:H7 every year. An additional 37,000 are sickened by other dangerous strains of E. coli also linked to ground beef. At a slaughterhouse these pathogens are spread when manure or stomach contents get splattered on the meat.

The USDA won the 1993 lawsuit, began random testing for E. coli O157:H7 and introduced a "science-based" inspection system in 1996 that requires various microbial tests by meatpacking companies and by the government. The new system, however, has been so weakened by industry opposition and legal challenges that it now may be less effective than the old one. Under the Hazard Analysis and Critical Control Points plans that now regulate production at meatpacking plants, many food safety tasks have been shifted from USDA inspectors to company employees.

In return for such concessions, the USDA gained the

power to test for salmonella and to shut down plants that repeatedly failed those tests. Salmonella is spread primarily by fecal material, and its presence in ground beef suggests that other dangerous pathogens may be present as well. In November 1999, the USDA shut down a meatpacking plant for repeatedly failing salmonella tests. The Texas company operating the plant, Supreme Beef Processors, happened to be one of the leading suppliers of ground beef to the National School Lunch Program. With strong backing from the meatpacking industry, Supreme Beef sued the USDA, eventually won the lawsuit and succeeded this past December in overturning the USDA's salmonella limits. About 1.4 million Americans are sickened by salmonella every year, and the CDC has linked a nasty, antibiotic-resistant strain of the bug to ground beef. Nevertheless, it is now perfectly legal to sell ground beef that is thoroughly contaminated with salmonella—and sell it with the USDA's seal of approval.

This summer's ConAgra recall raises questions not only about the nation's food safety rules but also about the USDA's competence to enforce them. The USDA conducts its random tests for E. coli O157:H7 at wholesale and retail locations, not at the gigantic slaughterhouses where the meat is usually contaminated. By the time the USDA discovers tainted meat, it's already being distributed. On June 17 and 19, USDA test results showed that beef shipped from the ConAgra slaughterhouse in Greeley, Colorado was contaminated. But the USDA failed to inform ConAgra for almost two weeks. Meanwhile, the bad meat continued to be sold at supermarkets, served at countless restaurants and grilled at outdoor barbecues nationwide. Although the packages said "Freeze or sell by

06 18 02," Safeway supermarkets in Colorado held a two-for-one sale of the questionable ConAgra meat from June 19 to June 25.

Four days later the USDA informed ConAgra that it had distributed beef contaminated with E. coli O157:H7. ConAgra announced a "voluntary recall" of 354,200 pounds. Then health authorities noticed that people were getting severely ill, mainly small children in Colorado. A common symptom was vomiting and defecating blood. After consultations with the USDA, ConAgra expanded the voluntary recall on July 19 to include an additional 18.3 million pounds of beef processed at the Greeley plant between April 12 and July 11. About three dozen illnesses and one death have thus far been linked to ConAgra's meat. Based on previous E. coli outbreaks, perhaps twenty times that number of illnesses occurred without being properly diagnosed or reported. According to the most recent tally, less than one-tenth of the 18.6 million pounds of ConAgra's recalled meat has been recovered. The rest has most likely been eaten.

Throughout the recall, USDA officials praised ConAgra for how well it had cooperated with the government, offering little criticism or explanation of how this company had managed to ship thousands of tons of potentially contaminated meat for months. The USDA also deflected criticism of its own role in the outbreak; a Montana wholesaler had warned the agency in February that beef shipped from ConAgra's plant in Greeley was tainted. Instead of imposing a tough penalty on ConAgra, the USDA often seemed eager to shift the blame and responsibility to consumers. "If people cooked their food correctly," said Elsa

Murano, USDA under secretary for food safety, "a lot of outbreaks would not take place."

Although ConAgra apparently violated no laws, its behavior made clear where the real power lies. The recall of its meat was entirely voluntary. In an age when defective Happy Meal toys can be swiftly ordered off the market at the slightest hint of a choking hazard, the government can neither demand the recall of potentially deadly meat nor impose civil fines on companies that sell it. ConAgra has refused to disclose publicly which restaurants, distributors and supermarkets got meat from Greeley; federal law does not require the company to do so. Colorado health officials did not receive a list showing where ConAgra's meat had been distributed until the first week of August—more than a month after the initial recall. Health officials in Utah and Oklahoma did not receive that information from ConAgra until the third week in August. "I know it's here," an Oklahoma public health official told the *Denver Post* at one point, referring to the recalled meat. "But without knowing where it went, there's not a whole lot we can do." In future recalls, ConAgra now promises to do a better job of sharing information with state health authorities—even though the law does not require the company to do so.

ConAgra's meatpacking operations in Greeley are described at length in my book *Fast Food Nation,* and I've spent a great deal of time with workers there. For years they have complained about excessive line speeds. The same factors often responsible for injuries in a slaughterhouse can also lead to food safety problems. When workers work too fast, they tend to make mistakes, harming themselves or inadvertently contaminating the meat.

America's food safety system has been expertly

designed not to protect the public health but to protect the meatpacking industry from liability. The industry has received abundant help in this effort from the Republican Party, which for more than a decade has thwarted Congressional efforts to expand the USDA's food safety authority. According to the Center for Responsive Politics, during the 2000 presidential campaign meat and livestock interests gave about $23,000 to Al Gore and about $600,000 to George W. Bush. The money was well spent. Dale Moore, chief of staff for Agriculture Secretary Ann Veneman, was previously the chief lobbyist for the National Cattlemen's Beef Association. Elizabeth Johnson, one of Veneman's senior advisers, was previously the associate director for food policy at the NCBA. Mary Waters, USDA assistant secretary for Congressional relations, assumed the post after working as legislative counsel for ConAgra Foods.

It would be an understatement to say that the Bush Administration has been friendly toward the big meatpackers. During Congressional testimony this past spring, Elsa Murano, USDA chief food safety advocate, argued that her agency does not need the power to order a recall of contaminated meat. Nor did it need, she said, any new authority to shut down ground beef plants because of salmonella contamination.

The meatpacking companies don't want any of their customers to get sick. But they don't want to be held liable for illnesses either, or to spend more money on preventing outbreaks. The exemplary food safety system at Jack in the Box increases the cost of the fast food chain's ground beef by about one penny per pound. The other major hamburger chains also require that their suppliers provide meat largely free of dangerous pathogens—and that requirement has not yet driven the meatpacking industry into bankruptcy. Senator Tom Harkin has introduced two pieces of food safety legislation that would help fill some of the glaring gaps in the current system. The SAFER Meat, Poultry and Food Act of 2002 would give the USDA the authority to demand recalls of contaminated meat and impose civil fines on meatpacking companies. The Meat and Poultry Pathogen Reduction Act would place enforceable limits on the amounts of disease-causing bugs that meat can legally contain. Harkin's bills embody a good deal of common sense. Companies that produce clean meat should be allowed to sell it; those that produce dirty meat shouldn't. The Republican Party's alliance with the big meatpackers does not reflect widespread public support. The issue of food safety isn't like abortion or gun control, with passionate and fundamentally opposing views held by millions of American voters. When most people learn how the meatpacking industry operates, they're appalled. The outrage crosses party lines. Democrat or Republican, you still have to eat.

None of the recently proposed reforms, however, would prove as important and effective as the creation of an independent food safety agency with tough enforcement powers. The USDA has a dual and conflicting mandate. It's supposed to promote the sale of American meat—and protect consumers from unsafe meat. As long as the USDA has that dual role, consumers must be extremely careful about where they purchase beef, how they handle it and how long they cook it. While many Americans fret about the risks of bioterrorism, a much more immediate threat comes from the all-American meal. Until fundamental changes are made in our food safety system, enjoying your hamburgers medium-rare will remain a form of high-risk behavior.

This selection is from a memo that the U.S. Department of Agriculture distributed to meat inspectors in May 2002. Note the tone of the note—how would you like to receive this memo from your employer?—as well as its substance.

It's What's For Dinner
reprinted in *Harper's* (April 2003)
U.S. Department of Agriculture

GENERAL INFORMATION AND CONDUCT

There are many serious responsibilities you have assumed in your role as a Consumer Safety Inspector. You need to learn your role and work within the guidelines. We are anxious to help you know your role well.

You must understand the responsibility you accept when you stop the company's production processes by stopping the line. If a product that is going into the food supply has been directly contaminated and you can justify the production loss that will prevent its entrance into the food supply, then you will be supported, because that is in your scope of work.

Stopping production for "possible" cross contamination is unjustifiable unless you can verify that there is direct product contamination. Verification is OBSERVATION of gross contaminate, not SUSPECTED contaminate. This is the only criteria for justifying halting production.

You are justified to stop production if it is physically impossible for you to properly examine the product presented to you. That means, for example, that the tongue is on the hook backward, or the paunches are upside down. That does not mean a paunch that is right side up but twisted only slightly, or the weasand [esophagus] and bung [anus] up underneath the paunch or intestine. That is going to happen occasionally, and we can pull most of those organs out for proper examination without stopping production. You may be accountable for the time the company has lost if that lost production is not verifiable and the action not justifiable.

INSPECTION

You need to know about tolerable limits of dust, hair, hide, grubs, etc. Any amount of oil on the hocks is a minor defect. An oil spot on the rounds or other parts of the carcass less than two inches in diameter is also minor and can be trimmed on the moving line. The line should NOT be shut off for an oil problem.

You must learn the difference between active and healed pleural adhesions and pleuritis. Pleura may contain a layer of fat that gives them a thickened appearance, and they may even have blood clinging to them that, if you run your finger over them, will scrape away and does NOT need to be peeled out.

"Bunk bruises" are NOT bruises at all but degenerated fat in the brisket and of no pathological significance. They are sterile and do not involve surrounding tissue. They are not unwholesome. The company can trim those very nicely after chilling, and they do not get into the food supply.

There is ZERO TOLERANCE of contamination from ingesta, feces, and milk on the carcass at final presentation. We will allow the company a chance to trim it off on the moving line unless it is so excessive that it must be corrected with the line stopped. You are responsible for the time the line is off. Turning off the line must be justifiable and verifiable if we are to support your action. Remember,

YOU are accountable for this very serious responsibility of stopping the company's production. Be sure that supervisors can support your decision. Identifiable and verifiable ingesta or feces is as follows: a material of yellow, green, brown, or dark color that has a fibrous nature. Milk is a cream-colored to white fluid, not a clear fluid.

If you have unidentifiable material on the carcass and you are unsure what to do, you are instructed to apply a RETAIN/REJECT tag on the leading side of the carcass. It is unnecessary to cause significant loss of production. You don't have to decide what the unidentified material is, where it came from, or any remedy. That is outside your scope of work.

VISCERA TABLE

A contaminated liver needs one stamp for pet-food salvage if it is otherwise healthy. If there is a single isolated abscess that can be removed, stamp the salvageable end and make a slice for the company to know how much of the liver they can have for pet food. If there are no hepatic lymph nodes presented and NO OTHER PATHOLOGY, DO NOT stamp out the liver. It is still acceptable for human food.

Contamination with small amounts of ingesta on the paunch and small intestine which are salvaged by the company to be further processed to become edible does not always require condemnation.

Ingesta INSIDE the trachea is not contamination sufficient to condemn the heart. When an inspector upstream from you has made that determination and not stamped it, that inspector's judgment should not be overridden. That should be the rule: INSPECT YOUR OWN PRODUCT. Stay within your own scope of work.

Intact bladders still attached to the bung that are full of urine but not leaking are not contaminating anything, and nothing needs to be condemned. Leaking bladders are different, because either you see the urine leaking out or you don't. Did that urine contaminate something? How much was it? The whole carcass? Other edible viscera? Use good judgment.

Head chain

Condemn product affected by abscess and ingesta contamination on head and/or tongue and only one product in front and behind. DO NOT STOP LINE AND DO NOT WASH OUT HEAD CABINET.

Clumps of hair on head and/or tongue are NOT a major source of bacteria. If you must, you can put a spot of ink on the area. Someone down the line will trim it. DO NOT STOP THE LINE. This includes other trimmable lesions of head or tongue.

If pathology on head and/or tongue is sufficient to remove the carcass, you may stop the line, but only long enough to be sure you have proper identity of the carcass. Be reasonable about the time; it should only take a few seconds, not minutes.

If heads and tongues are not identified together properly and there is NO pathology, condemn the tongue. If the head has no ID and no pathology, condemn the head too. IF THERE IS SUFFICIENT PATHOLOGY OF EITHER HEAD OR TONGUE AND NO ID, SHUT OFF THE LINE UNTIL THE COMPANY HAS FOUND THE RIGHT CARCASS. (When they do and you are satisfied it is right, immediately start the line again.)

THEY POISON
OUR WORLD

with a quote by Monsanto

We have let corporations use our public space for their own gain—and they have proven horribly short-sighted. They pollute the water we drink, the food we eat and the air we breathe; they clutter and wear out our infrastructure and chop down trees in our national forests. They sell products that make us sick, and then lie about it. They commandeer our airwaves for profit, and smother our public and private spaces with their advertisements—which often portray corporations as caring stewards of the environment.

Corporations are literally killing us.

What really happened when the Exxon Valdez *hit Bligh Reef?*

A Well-Designed Disaster:
The Untold Story of the *Exxon Valdez*
from *The Best Democracy Money Can Buy* (2003)
Greg Palast

On March 24, 1989, the *Exxon Valdez* broke open and covered twelve hundred miles of Alaska's shoreline with oily sludge.

The official story remains "Drunken Skipper Hits Reef." Don't believe it.

In fact, when the ship hit, Captain Joe Hazelwood was nowhere near the wheel, but belowdecks, sleeping off his bender. The man left at the helm, the third mate, would never have hit Bligh Reef had he simply looked at his Raycas radar. But he could not, because the radar *was not turned on*. The complex Raycas system costs a lot to operate, so frugal Exxon management left it broken and useless for the entire year before the grounding.

The land Exxon smeared and destroyed belongs to the Chugach natives of the Prince William Sound. Within days of the spill, the Chugach tribal corporation asked me and my partner Lenora Stewart to investigate allegations of fraud by Exxon and the little-known "Alyeska" consortium. In three years' digging, we followed a twenty-year train of doctored safety records, illicit deals between oil company chiefs, and programmatic harassment of witnesses. And we documented the oil majors' brilliant success in that old American sport, cheating the natives. Our summary of evidence ran to four volumes. Virtually none of it was reported: The media had turned off its radar. Here's a bit of the story you've never been told:

- We discovered an internal memo describing a closed, top-level meeting of oil company executives in Arizona held just ten months before the spill. It was a meeting of the "Alyeska Owners Committee," the six-company combine that owns the Alaska pipeline and most of the state's oil. In that meeting, say the notes, the chief of their *Valdez* operations, Theo Polasek, warned executives that containing an oil spill "at the mid-point of Prince William Sound not possible with present equipment"—exactly where the *Exxon Valdez* grounded. Polasek needed millions of dollars for spill-containment equipment. The law required it, the companies promised it to regulators, then at the meeting, the proposed spending was voted down. The oil company combine had a cheaper plan to contain any spill—don't bother. According to an internal memorandum, they'd just drop some dispersants and walk away. That's exactly what happened. "At the owners committee meeting in Phoenix, it was decided that Alyeska would provide immediate response to oil spills in *Valdez* Arm and *Valdez* Narrows only"—not the Prince William Sound.
- Smaller spills before the Exxon disaster would have alerted government watchdogs that the port's oil-spill-containment system was not up to scratch. But the oil group's lab technician, Erlene Blake, told us that management routinely ordered her to

change test results to eliminate "oil-in-water" readings. The procedure was simple, says Blake. She was told to dump out oily water and refill test tubes from a bucket of cleansed sea water, which they called "the Miracle Barrel."

• A confidential letter dated April 1984, fully four years before the big spill, written by Captain James Woodle, then the oil group's *Valdez* Port commander, warns management that "Due to a reduction in manning, age of equipment, limited training and lack of personnel, serious doubt exists that [we] would be able to contain and clean up effectively a medium or large size oil spill." Woodle told us there was a spill at *Valdez* before the *Exxon Valdez* collision, though not nearly as large. When he prepared to report it to the government, his supervisor forced him to take back the notice, with the Orwellian command, "You made a mistake. This was not an oil spill."

SLIMEY LIMEYS

The canard of the alcoholic captain has provided effective camouflage for a party with arguably more culpability than Exxon: British Petroleum, the company that in 2001 painted itself green (literally: all its gas stations and propaganda pamphlets now sport a seasick green hue). Alaska's oil is BP oil. The company owns and controls a near majority (46 percent) of the Alaska pipeline system. Exxon (now ExxonMobil) is a junior partner, and four other oil companies are just along for the ride. Captain Woodle, Technician Blake, Vice President Polasek, all worked for BP's Alyeska.

Quite naturally, British Petroleum has never rushed to have its name associated with Alyeska's recklessness. But BP's London headquarters, I discovered, knew of the alleged falsification of reports to the U.S. government *nine* years before the spill. In September 1984, independent oil shipper Charles Hamel of Washington, D.C., shaken by evidence he received from Alyeska employees, told me he took the first available Concorde, at his own expense, to warn BP executives in London about scandalous goings-on in *Valdez*. Furthermore, Captain Woodle swears he personally delivered his list of missing equipment and "phantom" personnel directly into the hands of BP's Alaska chief, George Nelson.

BP has never been eager for Woodle's letter, Hamel's London trip and many other warnings of the deteriorating containment system to see the light of day. When Alyeska got wind of Woodle's complaints, they responded by showing Woodle a file of his marital infidelities (all bogus), then offered him payouts on condition that he leave the state within days, promising never to return.

As to Hamel, the oil shipping broker, BP in London thanked him. Then a secret campaign was launched to hound him out of the industry. A CIA expert was hired who wiretapped Hamel's phone lines. They smuggled microphones into his home, intercepted his mail and tried to entrap him with young women. The industrial espionage assault was personally ordered and controlled by BP executive James Hermiller, president of Alyeska. On this caper, they were caught. A U.S. federal judge told Alyeska this conduct was "reminiscent of Nazi Germany."

A WELL-DESIGNED DISASTER

CHEAPER THAN MANHATTAN

BP's inglorious role in the Alaskan oil game began in 1969 when the oil group bought the most valuable real estate in all Alaska, the *Valdez* oil terminal land, from the Chugach natives. BP and the Alyeska group paid the natives *one dollar*.

Arthur Goldberg, once a U.S. Supreme Court justice, tried to help the natives on their land claim. But the natives' own lawyer, the state's most powerful legislator, advised them against pressing for payment. Later, that lawyer became Alyeska's lawyer.

The Alaskan natives, the last Americans who lived off what they hunted and caught, did extract written promises from the oil consortium to keep the Prince William Sound safe from oil spills. These wilderness seal hunters and fishermen knew the arctic sea. Eyak Chief-for-Life Agnes Nichols, Tatitlek native leader George Gordaoff and Chenega fisherman Paul Kompkoff demanded that tankers carry state-of-the-art radar and that emergency vessels escort the tankers. The oil companies reluctantly agreed to put all this in their government-approved 1973 Oil Spill Response Plan.

When it comes to oil spills, the name of the game is "containment" because, radar or not, some tanker somewhere is going to hit the rocks. Stopping an oil spill catastrophe is a no-brainer. Tanker radar aside, if a ship does smack a reef, all that's needed is to surround the ship with a big rubber curtain ("boom") and suck up the corralled oil. In signed letters to the state government and Coast Guard, BP, ExxonMobil and partners promised that no oil would move unless the equipment was set on the tanker route and the oil-sucker ship ("containment barge") was close by, in the water and ready to go.

The oil majors fulfilled their promise the cheapest way: They lied. When the *Exxon Valdez* struck Bligh Reef, the spill equipment, which could have prevented the catastrophe, wasn't there—see the Arizona meeting notes above. The promised escort ships were not assigned to ride with the tankers until *after* the spill. And the night the *Exxon Valdez* grounded, the emergency spill-response barge was sitting in a dry dock in Valdez locked in ice.

When the pipeline opened in 1974, the law required Alyeska to maintain round-the-clock oil-spill-response teams. As part of the come-on to get hold of the Chugach's *Valdez* property, Alyeska hired the natives for this emergency work. The natives practiced leaping out of helicopters into icy water, learning to surround leaking boats with rubber barriers. But the natives soon found they were assigned to cover up spills, not clean them up. Their foreman, David Decker, told me he was expected to report one oil spill as two gallons when two thousand gallons had spilled.

Alyeska kept the natives at the terminal for two years— long enough to help Alyeska break the strike of the dock workers' union—then quietly sacked the entire team. To deflect inquisitive inspectors looking for the spill-response workers, Alyeska created sham emergency teams, listing names of oil terminal employees who had not the foggiest idea how to use spill equipment, which, in any event, was missing, broken or existed only on paper. When the *Exxon Valdez* grounded, there was no native spill crew, only chaos.

The Fable of the Drunken Skipper has served the oil industry well. It transforms the most destructive oil spill in history into a tale of human frailty, a terrible, but onetime, accident. But broken radar, missing equipment, phantom spill personnel, faked tests—all of it to cut costs and lift bottom lines—made the spill disaster not an accident but an inevitability.

I went back to the Sound just before the tenth anniversary of the spill. On Chenega, they were preparing to spend another summer scrubbing rocks. A decade after the spill, in one season, they pulled twenty tons of sludge off their beaches. At Nanwalek village ten years on, the state again declared the clams inedible, poisoned by "persistent hydrocarbons." Salmon still carry abscesses and tumors, the herring never returned and the sea lion rookery at Montague Island remains silent and empty.

But despite what my eyes see, I must have it wrong, because right here in an Exxon brochure it says, "The water is clean and plant, animal and sea life are healthy and abundant."

Go to the Sound today, on Chugach land, kick over a rock and you'll get a whiff of an Exxon gas station.

Everyone's heard of the big jury verdict against Exxon: a $5 billion award. What you haven't heard is that ExxonMobil hasn't paid a dime of it. It's been a decade since the trial. BP painted itself green and ExxonMobil decided to paint the White House with green: It's the number-two lifetime donor to George W. Bush's career (after Enron), with a little splashed the Democrats' way. The oil industry's legal stalls, the "tort reform" campaigns and the generous investment in our democratic process has produced a Supreme Court and appeals panels that look more like luncheon clubs of corporate consiglieri than panels of defenders of justice. In November 2001, following directives of the

Supremes, the Ninth Circuit Court of Appeals overturned the jury verdict on grounds the punishment was too dear and severe for poor little ExxonMobil.

The BP-led Alyeska consortium was able to settle all claims for 2 percent of the acknowledged damage, roughly a $50 million payout, fully covered by an insurance fund.

And the natives? While waiting for Exxon to make good on promises of compensation, Chief Agnes and Paul Kompkoff have passed away. As to my four-volume summary of evidence of frauds committed against the natives: In 1991, when herring failed to appear and fishing in the Sound collapsed, the tribal corporation went bankrupt and my files became, effectively, useless.

Coda: Nanwalek Rocks[*]

At the far side of Alaska's Kenai Fjord glacier, a heavily armed and musically original rock-and-roll band held lockdown control of the politics and treasury of Nanwalek, a Chugach native village.

---

[*] This diary of life in the native villages of the Prince William Sound was nearly censored out of *Index on Censorship*. The magazine had hired a guest editor for the "Tribes" issue, an amateur anthropologist. He'd been to the same group of Alaskan villages where I worked. The natives performed their special ceremony for him. Among themselves they call it "Putting on the feathers," in which they provide those quaint and expected lines that so please the earnest white men with 16mm Airflex cameras and digital tape recorders. The great white anthropologist wrote down "healing poems" about "our friend the bear." I imagined him with helmet and pukka shorts preserving in his leather notebook the words of the ancient, wizened Injuns. Stanley Livingstone meets Pocahontas.

It was my terrible, self inflicted misfortune to spoil this delicate idyll of the Noble Savage by my reporting that Alaskan natives are, in fact, very much like us, if not more so.

According to not-so-old legend, rock came to the remote enclave at the bottom of Prince William Sound in the 1950s when Chief Vincent Kvasnikoff found an electric guitar washed up on the beach. By the next morning, he had mastered the instrument sufficiently to perform passable covers of Elvis tunes. Of all the lies the natives told me since I began work there in 1989, this one, from the chief himself, seemed the most benign.

When I first went to work there in 1989, I sat with the chief in his kitchen, across from an elaborate Orthodox altar. Russian icons were spread the length of the wall. It was a golden day, late summer at the end of the salmon run, but the chief's eighteen-year-old nephew hung out in the bungalow watching a repeating loop of Fred Astaire movies on the satellite TV.

Fishing was just excellent, the chief assured me. He'd taken twelve seals that year. I didn't challenge the old man, legless in his wheelchair. Everyone knew he'd lost his boat when the bank repossessed his commercial fishing license.

The village once had eight commercial boats, now it had three. Besides, all the seal had been poisoned eight years earlier, in 1989, by Exxon's oil.

It took an entire month for the oil slick from the *Exxon Valdez* to reach Nanwalek. Despite the known, unrelenting advance of the oil sheet, Exxon had not provided even simple rubber barriers to protect the inlets to the five lakes that spawned the salmon and fed the razor clams, sea lions, bidarki snails, seals and people of the isolated village on the ice. But when the oil did arrive, followed by television crews, Exxon put virtually the entire populace of 270 on its payroll.

"The place went wild," Lisa Moonan told me. "They gave us rags and buckets, $16-something an hour to wipe off rocks, to baby-sit our own children." In this roadless village that had survived with little cash or store-bought food, the chief's sister told me, "They flew in frozen pizza, satellite dishes. Guys who were on sobriety started drinking all night, beating up their wives. I mean, all that money. Man, people just went berserk."

With the catch dead, the banks took the few boats they had, and Chief Vincent's sister, Sally Kvasnikoff Ash, watched the village slide into an alcohol- and drug-soaked lethargy. Sally said, "I felt like my skin was peeling off." Nanwalek's natives call themselves Sugestoon, Real People. "After the oil I thought, this is it. We're over. Sugestoon, we're gone unless something happens."

Sally made something happen. In August 1995, the village women swept the all-male tribal council from office in an electoral coup plotted partly in the native tongue, which the men had forgotten. Sally, who's Sugestoon name Aqni-aqnaq means "First Sister," would have become chief if Vincent, she says, hadn't stolen two votes. The rockers, Chief Vincent's sons, were out—so was booze (banned), fast food and the band's party nights in accordance with the new women's council cultural revolutionary diktats. The women returned native language to the school and replaced at least some of Kvasnikoff's all-night jam sessions, which had a tendency to end in drunken brawls, with performances of the traditional Seal and Killer Whale dances.

They put the village on a health-food regimen. "We're fat," says First Sister, who blames the store-bought diet which, since the spill, must be flown in twice weekly from city supermarkets. To show they meant business on the alcohol ban, the women arrested and jailed Sally's disabled Uncle Mack for bringing a six-pack of beer into the village on his return from the hospital.

On Good Friday 1964, the snow-peaked mountains of Montague Island rose twenty-six feet in the air, then dropped back twelve feet, sending a tidal wave through the Prince William Sound. At the village of Chenega, Chugach seal hunter Nikolas Kompkoff ran his four daughters out of their stilt house, already twisted to sticks by the earthquake, and raced up an ice-covered slope. Just before the wall of water overcame them, he grabbed the two girls closest, one child under each arm, ran ahead, then watched his other two daughters wash out into the Sound. Chenega disappeared. Not one of their homes, not even the sturdier church, remained. A third of the natives drowned. Survivors waited for two days until a postal pilot remembered the remote village.

Over the following twenty years, Chenegans scattered across the Sound, some to temporary huts in other Chugach villages, others to city life in Anchorage. But every Holy Week, these families sailed to the old village, laid crosses on the decaying debris, and Kompkoff would announce another plan to rebuild. Over the years, as the prospect of a New Chenega receded into improbability, Nikolas became, in turn, an Orthodox priest, a notorious alcoholic and failed suicide. He survived a self-inflicted gunshot to the head; however, he was defrocked for the attempt.

In 1982, Nikolas convinced his nephew, Larry Evanoff, to spend his life savings building a boat that could traverse the Sound.

Evanoff has four long scars across his torso. These wounds from Vietnam helped him get a government job as an air traffic controller in Anchorage, but he was fired when his union went on strike. Larry had lost both his parents in the earthquake and tidal wave.

Larry's boat was not finished until the subarctic winter had set in. Nevertheless, he sailed to remote Evans Island with his wife and two children, aged nine and fourteen. They built a cabin and, for two years, without phone or shortwave radio, one hundred miles from any road, lived off nearby seal, bear and salmon while they cleared the land for New Chenega. Over the next seven years, twenty-six of Chenega's refugee families joined the Evanoffs, built their own homes and, with scrap wood from an abandoned herring saltery, built a tiny church with a blue roof for Nikolas, whom they still called "Father."

On March 24, 1989, the village commemorated the twenty-fifth anniversary of the tidal wave. That night, the *Exxon Valdez* oil tanker ran aground and killed the fish, smothered the clam beds and poisoned all the seal on which Chenegans subsisted.

In mid-century, the average life expectancy for Chugach natives was thirty-eight years. They had next to nothing by way of cash and the state moved to take even that away. In the 1970s, new "limited entry" laws barred natives from selling the catch from their traditional fishing grounds unless they purchased permits few could afford. The natives did have tenuous ownership of wilderness, villages and campsites. In 1969, America's largest oil deposit was discovered on Alaska's north slope. The Chugach campsite on *Valdez* Harbor happened to be the only place on the entire Alaska coast that could geologically support an oil tanker terminal. Their strip of land grew in value to tens or even hundreds of millions of dollars. In June of that year, Chief Vincent's father, Sarjius, representing Nanwalek, and Father Nikolas, representing the nonexistent Chenega, agreed to sell *Valdez* to British Petroleum and Humble Oil (later called Exxon)—for the aforementioned one dollar.

The one-dollar sale was engineered by the Chugach's attorney, Clifford Groh. Before he moved on to his next gig as an oil company lawyer, Groh transformed the Chugach utterly and forever. No longer would Chugach be a tribe; Groh *incorporated* them.

The tribe became Chugach Corporation. The villages became Chenega Corporation and English Bay (Nanwalek) Corporation. The chiefs' powers were taken over by corporate presidents and CEOs, tribal councils by boards of directors. The Sound's natives, once tribe members, became shareholders—at least for a few years until the stock was sold, bequeathed, dispersed. Today, only eleven of Chenega's sixty-nine shareholders live on the island. Most residents are tenants of a corporation whose last annual meeting was held in Seattle, two thousand miles from the island.

I first met the president of Chenega Corporation, Charles "Chuck" Totemoff, soon after the spill when he missed our meeting to negotiate with Exxon. I found the twenty-something wandering the village's dirt pathway in soiled jeans, stoned and hungover, avoiding the corporate "office," an old cabin near the fishing dock.

Years later, I met up with Chuck at Chenega Corporation's glass-and-steel office tower in downtown Anchorage. The stern, long-sober and determined executive sat behind a mahogany desk and unused laptop computer. Instead of photos of the village, a huge map of Chenega's property covered the wall, color-coded for timber logging, real estate subdivision and resort development.

He had penned a multimillion-dollar terminal services agreement with the Exxon-BP pipeline consortium. For Chenega Island, a forty-six-room hotel was in the works.

In 1997, I returned to Chenega. It was the worst possible day for a visit. Larry was out on "pad patrol," leading a native crew cleaning up tons of toxic crude oil still oozing out of Sleepy Bay eight years after the *Exxon Valdez* grounding. They'd already lost a day of work that week for Frankie Gursky's funeral, an eighteen-year-old who had shot himself after a drink-fueled fight with his grandmother.

Larry and his team continued to scour the oil off the beach, his family's old fishing ground, but it wasn't theirs anymore. The day before, the corporation had sold it, along with 90 percent of Chenega's lands, to an Exxon-BP trust for $23 million.

"Corporation can't sell it," Larry said, when I told him about the check transfer. "People really can't own land." He rammed a hydraulic injector under the beach shingle and pumped in biological dispersants. "The land was always here. We're just passing through. We make use of it, then we just pass it on." Nanwalek also sold. Chief Vincent's son, leader of the Nonwalek Village rock band and director of the corporate board, arranged to sell 50 percent of the village land to an Exxon trust.

I was in corporate president Totemoff's office the day Exxon wired in the $23 million. When Totemoff moved out of the village, he announced, "I hope I never have to see this place again." Now he doesn't have to. I asked

Chuck if, like some city-dwelling natives, he had his relatives ship him traditional foods. "Seal meat?" He grinned. "Ever smell that shit? Give me a Big Mac any time."

Think Exxon paid for the clean-up after the 1989 Valdez *oil spill in Prince William Sound? Think again.*

Whatever It Takes

from *The Nation* (4/5/04)

Ashley Shelby

Shortly after the catastrophic 1989 *Valdez* oil spill in Prince William Sound, Exxon sent Don Cornett, the company's top official in Alaska at the time, to the fishing port of Cordova to reassure the fishers that the company would make things right. "You have my word," Cornett told them then. "I said it, Don Cornett. We will do whatever it takes to keep you whole. We do business straight."

No one in Cordova's Masonic Lodge tonight, where attorney Brian O'Neill has called a town meeting, has forgotten that promise, and no one has failed to notice that things haven't exactly worked out that way. O'Neill, a lawyer with the Minneapolis firm Faegre & Benson and the head of the legal team on this case, has, for ten years, returned to Cordova regularly to update his clients on the progress of the civil case against Exxon.

At this meeting, a man walks in late. He pours himself a cup of coffee and stands back near the kitchen, listening to his neighbors talk about how they now consider their wives' health insurance plans dowries and how the new definition of a high-liner is a fisherman whose wife has a good job. He listens to as much as he seems able, then turns to O'Neill and says, "Where in the hell is my money? That's what I want to focus on. If any of us knew we'd be having this meeting fourteen years later, we'd have liquidated and moved out. Maybe we should have."

The man's name is Phil Lian, and in 1988 he was one of the most successful fishers and businessmen in Cordova, fishing the sound and selling supplies to Cordova's fleet. His business was growing at 80 percent a year, and grossing $2 million a year. But after the spill, no one needed supplies because no one was going fishing. Today, his empty fishing-supply superstore, across the road from the Cordova Fisherman's Memorial, is a symbol of loss and matters left unresolved.

"We're going to get the award," O'Neill says. "In regards to your anger—"

"I don't like to call it anger," Lian says sharply. "I like to call it frustration."

"Well hell, I'm angry!" O'Neill shouts.

The story of Cordova is not just a sad tale of a few bad fishing seasons. It is the story of how corporations can use the legal system and the seeming apathy of the federal government to avoid responsibility for their actions. It's been ten years since a federal jury awarded the fishers and Natives on the sound $5.2 billion in punitive damages from Exxon, but not a single check from that award has been cut. Instead, Exxon has been fighting the verdict, employing hundreds of lawyers, filing countless appeals and effectively buying science that supports its claims. And even when ordinary people think they've finally won—that the final appeal has been denied—they haven't. Perhaps they never will. Says O'Neill, "They see me as part of a system that's failed them."

On March 23, 1989, Captain Joseph Hazelwood stepped onto the oil tanker *Exxon Valdez* having consumed, according to him, three vodkas on the rocks at various bars in the port city of *Valdez*. Affidavits from bartenders in the port, however, claimed the captain drank the equivalent of five doubles, or, in the words of the Court of Appeals for the Ninth Circuit, enough to make most people unconscious. The 11-million-gallon spill that occurred while he was in command eventually spread down 1,200 miles of coastline. The environmental damage was catastrophic. Cleanup crews watched in horror as otters scratched out their own eyes to rid them of oil. Justice Department teams recovered the carcasses of more than 36,000 migratory birds and a thousand sea otters, and believe they represent only a fraction of the actual numbers.

For a few months, the disaster was imprinted on the national consciousness. But as time passed, it was reduced to a few stubborn media images: an oiled otter, a tar-covered seagull, men in haz-mat suits spraying boulders with boiling water. An out-of-work commercial fisherman was never among the emblems. But the fishermen were long-term victims too. Cordova, once an exuberant fishing port of 2,600 where high-liners—a term reserved for the most successful commercial fishers—might bring in a couple of hundred thousand dollars or more a year, is depressed and Dickensian. Today, there isn't a single fisher in town who would be considered a high-liner by pre-spill standards; instead, former high-liners mend nets in cannery warehouses, and bartenders fill and refill beer glasses.

If the herring fishery had been closed one or maybe even two seasons, fishers say, they might have been able to bounce back; but there hasn't been a herring season for more than ten years.

On the sound, a commercial fishing permit is like a home—it is a fisher's greatest investment, something that stays in the family, an asset that accrues value. In 1988 there were fishers in Cordova whose permits were worth nearly a million dollars. Today, their permits—fishers often call them their "nest eggs"—have depreciated in value by a staggering 90 percent.

One day during Brian O'Neill's visit to Cordova, Jack Babic takes the lawyer on a ride around the sound in the purse seiner he once used during herring season. Jack and his wife, Heidi, are two of O'Neill's 32,000 clients. Babic made out well after the spill; Exxon hired local fishers to help with the cleanup, and the company paid well. The Babics took the money they made and bought a boat they hoped to pass on to their children. Then the herring seasons were canceled and the salmon prices dried up, and suddenly the Babics had no viable fishery and had to start thinking about how to manage their finances until the Exxon payments came through. Those payments always seemed just around the corner, and people planned their lives around them.

"I was born in this," Jack says. "I never wanted to do anything else. I think of the last fourteen years as a lost opportunity. You can't quantify it in terms of dollars." O'Neill asks Jack if he's angry. Jack keeps his eyes on the horizon, one hand draped over the steering wheel.

"I'm still angry," he finally says, "but how long can you be angry? I see people in this community living their lives in anger, and I don't want to live my life that way." He adds, "It's not a guaranteed thing that we'll be compensated. You just try to pick up the pieces and move on. Isn't that what we have a responsibility to do?"

"Eighteen to twenty-four months, and the final and whole settlement will be distributed," O'Neill says. It's clear Jack is doubtful. Does he believe O'Neill?

"I believe he believes it. I believe that damn company will find a way to put the skids on it. I can't say I totally believe him," Jack says. Heidi smiles at O'Neill and adds, "But I'm glad you believe it."

Later in the day, O'Neill pulls up to an old warehouse on Cordova's Cannery Row. Upstairs, two redheaded brothers, Robbie and Mike Maxwell, are mending nets. As local kids, fishing was the only thing they'd ever wanted to do; when they got older, they raised families on the good money they made during the season. Nowadays they still fish, but they don't make a living out of it, so they repair nets during the off-season.

"Let me ask you a question," Mike says to O'Neill. "'Punitive' means to punish, right?"

"You're right."

"So how does $5 billion hurt Exxon?"

"Five billion is more punitive than nothing," O'Neill says.

But is it? The *Anchorage Daily News* reported that while awaiting a final judicial decision, Exxon has earned enough in interest alone to pay the initial $5 billion award. "Each year Exxon delays payment of its obligation," the National Association of Attorneys General wrote in a 1999 letter to Exxon CEO Lee Raymond, "it earns an estimated $400 million from the difference between the statutory interest rate on judgments of 6 percent and the company's internal rate of return of about 14 percent."

When Exxon and Mobil presented a merger proposal to the Federal Trade Commission in 1999, many saw an opportunity for the federal government to put pressure on Exxon to pay the punitive fine. Yet few in Washington—and no one from Alaska's Congressional delegation—even tried. One legislator who did, Senator Slade Gorton, a Republican from Washington State, said in 1999, "We have an opportunity to make an indelible impression on what would be the largest corporation on Earth—that an oil spill like this must never happen again." The FTC approved the Exxon/Mobil merger in November of 1999.

"Who's being punished here?" Mike Maxwell asks O'Neill. "We are. Looking into the future, is my son going into fishing? Absolutely not."

"The best I can do," O'Neill says, "is to get the $5 billion. I can't put the sound back together."

"I would just love to collect the Exxon oil that is on our beaches," Mike says, "and dump those gallons of oil on the front yard of its corporate headquarters. It's been in my front yard for fourteen years."

Dr. Steven Picou, a professor of sociology from the University of South Alabama, has spent the past fifteen years studying the effect the Exxon spill has had on the towns of the sound, specifically Cordova. Over the years, his focus has slowly shifted from the effects of the environmental devastation on the fishermen to the sociological and psychological damage inflicted by the legal battle.

Picou's findings in Cordova were damning: A third of fishers were clinically depressed; approximately 37 percent exhibited symptoms of post-traumatic stress disorder.

Sixty percent of Cordova commercial fishers have had to take second jobs to make ends meet. Toxins, Picou was finding, had contaminated more than just the water; they had contaminated the town of Cordova.

"I think the vast majority of people in Cordova believed the reps from Exxon," Picou said. "But once the issue was transformed from how-to-get-out-of-the-media-limelight to how-to-get-in-a-position-to-protect-our-profit-margin-and-stock-value, then it changed overnight. They zipped up their purse strings, got out of town, and said, You'll find us in the courtroom."

The Chemical Industry's Bhopal Legacy

from AlterNet.org (12/3/03)

Gary Cohen

Nineteen years ago this week, families in Bhopal, India were awakened in the middle of the night by terrible burning in their eyes and lungs. Within minutes, children and mothers and fathers staggered into the street, gasping for air and blinded by the chemicals that seared their eyes. As they ran in terror, someone shouted that the Union Carbide pesticides factory had exploded, spewing poisonous gas throughout the city.

Soon thousands of people lay dead in the city's main roads. Every truck, taxi and ox cart was weighted down with injured and terrified refugees. No one in the emergency room at the city hospital knew what the toxic gases were or how to treat the thousands of patients that flooded into the hallways.

By morning, more than 5,000 people were dead, while a half million more were injured.

Bhopal has rightly been called the Hiroshima of the chemical industry. It not only tells the stark story of the human fall-out from a chemical factory explosion born of supreme negligence but offers up important lessons about the continuing failure of the chemical industry and government to address the security and public health threats posed by dangerous chemicals.

The day after the disaster, Union Carbide's CEO Warren Anderson flew to India to assess the damage his company had visited upon its Indian neighbors. He was promptly met at the airport and arrested. After a few days he was released and allowed to return to the United States. Anderson has not returned to India since. There is an outstanding warrant for his arrest and a pending criminal homicide case against him and other Carbide officials in the Bhopal courts. The Indian government has even issued extradition orders for Anderson, but the U.S. government has so far ignored the extradition request. This complete lack of respect for the law reinforces the image of the chemical industry as a renegade industry that is largely uncontrollable.

Nineteen years have passed, but today in Bhopal thousands of people remain sick from chemical exposure, while more than 50,000 are disabled due to their injuries. The amount of compensation Union Carbide paid to the survivors has not been enough to cover basic medicines, let alone other costs associated with various disabilities and inability to work. The sad reality is that we continue to learn about chemicals by exposing large numbers of people to them.

We have learned about dioxin contamination by poisoning American veterans and the entire Vietnamese population with Agent Orange. We have learned about asbestos by killing off thousands of workers to lung disease. And we have learned about the long-term effects of methyl-isocyanate (MIC) by spewing it across an entire city in India. There are many other examples of this kind of uncontrolled chemical experimentation. In most cases, the industry rarely pays the full cost of the massive damage it has caused.

The abandoned factory site in Bhopal remains essentially the same as the day that Carbide's employees ran for their lives. Sacks of unused pesticides lay strewn in storerooms; toxic waste litters the grounds and continues to leak into the neighborhood well water supply. The buildings themselves are ghostly, a rotting monument to the excesses of the pesticide revolution in India and the lack of corporate responsibility for its failures.

Officials at Dow Chemical, the new owners of Union Carbide, claim they have nothing to do with the ongoing disaster in Bhopal—neither the pending criminal case, the environmental contamination, nor the public health fallout. Yet Dow has set aside $2 billion to address Carbide's asbestos liabilities, another public health legacy of the former chemical giant.

The chemical industry has always viewed Bhopal purely as a public relations disaster; a powerful symbol that demonstrated the industry was a menace and a threat to

people's health and safety. In order to head off further regulation, the chemical manufacturers created a voluntary
program called "Responsible Care" with the logo, "Don't
Trust Us, Track Us." In this way, the industry has avoided
any serious restrictions on its chemicals for nearly 20 years.

During this time lapse, we have continued to learn more
about the dark side of the chemical revolution. We have
learned that today we all carry the chemical industry's toxic
products in our bodies. Every man, women and child in
America has a "body burden" of chemicals that are linked
to cancer, birth defects, asthma, learning disabilities and
other diseases. We are all guinea pigs in an epic uncontrolled chemical experiment run by Dow, Monsanto,
DuPont and other petrochemical companies.

If we woke up one morning and learned that this chemical invasion was the work of foreign terrorists, the federal
government would be completely mobilized to defend our
citizens from this chemical warfare threat. But because the
perpetrators are some of President Bush's most generous
contributors and ardent collaborators, we are left defense-
less as a nation against this chemical security threat.

Recently, it's become even harder to track the chemical
industry, since it has been working with the Bush Administration behind the veil of homeland security to conceal information about the "worst case disaster" for its facilities and
the health threat posed by its products. But the picture that
is emerging is a frightening one.

According to federal government sources, there are 123
chemical facilities nationwide that could kill at least one
million people if they accidentally exploded or were
attacked by terrorists. Some of these chemical factories
are located in major American cities and put as many as

8 million lives at risk. Yet the chemical industry continues to resist any meaningful regulation that would require it to replace the most dangerous chemicals with safer alternatives. A recent "60 Minutes" expose vividly showed that many facilities lack even the most basic security protection, yet the government is spending billions of our tax dollars looking for chemical terrorists overseas.

We don't have to look in Iraq for weapons of mass destruction. They are right here, in our neighborhoods, in our food and in our bodies.

On this 19th anniversary of the Bhopal disaster, survivors in Bhopal will march and make speeches and demand their basic rights to be free of chemical poisons, to be compensated for their damages, and to hold the chemical industry responsible for the world's worst industrial disaster.

Despite their ongoing victimization, people in Bhopal have not given up. Their protests are testimony to the triumph of memory over forgetting and the celebration of the human spirit over the rationalized tyranny of corporate profit margins and evasion of responsibility.

The Bhopal survivors are speaking for us as well. In the last two decades, Bhopal has come much closer to home. The chemical terror they experienced and the lack of care and respect they have received are a haunting reminder that we also live under a similar poison cloud.

Corporations are good at keeping secrets—especially discreditable ones.

What Monsanto Knew

from *The Nation* (5/29/00)

Nancy Beiles

In a small brick house strung year-round with Christmas lights, behind curtains made of flowered sheets, Jeremiah Smith is listening to his favorite preacher on the radio. As tonight's installment of the Gospels winds down, Smith, who has warm brown eyes and a shock of graying black hair, takes a seat at a table draped with a zebra-print cloth and piled high with papers and drifts back thirty years, to the brief period when he was a hog farmer. Like others in Anniston, Alabama, an industrial town with rural traditions, Smith used to raise vegetables and livestock in his yard to provide additional food for his family. "We were poor people," he says in a thick drawl. "We had to raise food ourselves. . . . We were trying to survive and live."

Smith planted potatoes and greens in his backyard. He also had a cow and rabbits, but most of his time and attention went to his hogs. In 1970 he had about fifty—too many for his small plot of land, so he led them, Pied Piper-like, past the old Bethel Baptist Church, the Lucky-7 Lounge and the labyrinth of pipes and smokestacks that surrounded the Monsanto chemical plant his father helped build, to a grassy hill where they could graze. Each evening before heading off to work the night shift at a pipe company, Smith would check on them, give them some feed and, when the need arose, he'd bring home some bacon.

One night, as he was feeding the hogs, a man from the

Monsanto plant drove up the hill in a flatbed truck and made him an offer: $10 apiece for the hogs and a bottle of Log Cabin whiskey. The offer was intriguing. Smith had begun to notice that something was wrong with some of his hogs anyway; their mouths had turned green. And Smith, ever in need of cash, could hardly afford to pass up $500. He sold. But for more than twenty years, he wondered what on earth a chemical company would want with his hogs.

> Problem: Damage to the ecological system by contamination from polychlorinated biphenyl (PCB).
> Legal Liability: Direct lawsuits are possible. The materials are already present in nature having done their "alleged damage." All customers using the products have not been officially notified about known effects nor [do] our labels carry this information.
>
> —Memo from Monsanto committee studying PCBs, 1969

People Jeremiah Smith's age are old enough to remember Monsanto's glory days in Anniston. The company provided well-paying jobs and helped nurture this friendly Southern town's sense of community. Residents used to marvel at the plant's well-manicured grounds, which the company sometimes let them use for Easter-egg hunts. Most never thought to connect Monsanto to some of the odder features of life in Anniston. Like the creek, known locally as "the ditch," which passed through town carrying water that ran red some days, purple on others and occasionally emitted a foggy white steam.

Public Image: The corporate image of Monsanto as
a responsible member of the business world genuinely concerned with the welfare of our environment will be adversely affected with increased
publicity. . . .

Sources of Contamination: Although there may
be some soil and air contamination involved, by far
the most critical problem at present is water contamination. . . Our manufacturing facilities sewered
a sizable quantity of PCB's in a year's time. . . .

—Monsanto committee memo, 1969

Over time, the residents of West Anniston, Alabama,
came to believe they had been silently poisoned for
decades by Monsanto. Many also believe that if the contamination had occurred in the more affluent (and
more heavily white) east side of town, there would have
been more scrutiny by the government. The change in
attitude was spurred by what at first seemed like a
straightforward real estate transaction between Monsanto and a local church.

In December 1995 Donald Stewart, a former state legislator who served briefly in the U.S. Senate, was taking some
time off from his legal practice when he received a phone
call from a former client, Andrew Bowie. Bowie, a deacon at
the Mars Hill Missionary Baptist Church, explained that a
Monsanto manager had approached him about buying the
church. "It doesn't seem like we're going to achieve a satis-
factory deal," Bowie told Stewart. "I think we need a
lawyer." Stewart agreed to help. "I thought it was a simple
case," Stewart says. "And then it just mushroomed."

Stewart soon learned that Monsanto wanted to buy the

church's property, which was across the street from its plant, because it had discovered high concentrations of PCBs in the area and was planning a cleanup. After an open meeting at the church, Stewart began fielding a flood of calls from concerned residents, who had a dizzying array of health problems they now attribute to the contamination. The neighborhood around the plant is populated by people with cancer, young women with damaged ovaries, children who are learning-impaired and people whose ailments have been diagnosed as acute toxic syndrome. (Medical studies have shown that PCBs cause liver problems, skin rashes and developmental and reproductive disorders in humans. The EPA says that, according to animal studies, they probably cause cancer.) In addition to the church, which filed its own suit against Monsanto, more than 3,000 Anniston residents who have high levels of PCBs in their blood and on their property have filed suit against the company since 1996, alleging that beginning in the sixties, the company knew it was introducing PCBs into the environment, knew the hazards of doing so, failed to inform the community and tried to conceal what it had done.

Monsanto denies the allegations. While it concedes that much of Anniston is contaminated by PCBs, the company says its chemical discharges were negligible—and maintains that it did not fully understand how PCBs affected the environment at the time they were released. "As soon as we discovered there were PCB discharges from the plant, we began our operations to limit and hopefully eliminate those discharges," says Bob Kaley, director of environmental affairs for Monsanto's now spun-off chemical division. "At the time, there were no federal regulations with regard to PCBs. . . . Everything was done voluntarily, and there was really almost no understanding of the effect of PCBs on the environment and human health." Kaley adds, "I think as we've moved forward in the past thirty years, there are potentially some effects at high levels in the environment. But we do not believe even today that there are concerns for human health at those environmental levels."

The case is beginning to attract the attention of environmental activists, 150 of whom will be taking a bus tour of the contaminated areas this month. The EPA is currently considering whether to order a federally monitored cleanup, and it may declare the area a Superfund site. The likelihood of that is enhanced by PCBs' number-six spot on the agency's list of toxic substances at contaminated sites.

Monsanto lawyers have had plenty of practice defending against liability, since the company has been named as a co-defendant in dozens of PCB suits across the country. The company's track record in court on this front is excellent; while Monsanto has settled a few suits, it has succeeded in getting the vast majority of complaints—most of which have been brought by companies that purchased the chemicals from Monsanto—thrown out by arguing that these companies knew what they were getting into.

But the Anniston case stands out in the annals of PCB litigation in the extent of damage to property and people it alleges. It is also among the first brought by ordinary citizens rather than sophisticated corporations. And this time Monsanto will have to confront its own paper trail in court. The black binders that the plaintiffs' lawyers have stuffed full of internal memorandums and reports, branded "Hot Documents" and "Hottest Documents" with yellow Post-it notes—many of which have never been seen by the public but which will become public record when the trial begins—make this an especially difficult defense to mount.

Karen McFarlane lives in plain view of the plant. It's a mild morning in February, and Karen didn't sleep much last night. Clothed only in a T-shirt and underwear, with a sweater draped over her lap, she lights her first cigarette of the morning—a bent Basic—and promptly drops it on the shaggy blue rug. Dakota, Karen's 16-month-old, is playing with the severed head of a Barbie knock-off and there's not much to eat in the house. But Karen has other worries. Outside, a chain-link fence, six feet high and capped by barbed wire, surrounds the gray Buccaneer trailer where she lives with her husband, Ryan, and their five children, blocking access to gray-green fields once populated by neighbors and small businesses that have been chased away by PCB contamination. "I never thought I'd say it, but I just want to get away from here," says Karen, who has lived in Anniston her whole life.

She has PCBs in her body fat. According to tests done by a local doctor, Ryan's blood has nearly triple the level considered "typical" in the United States; for Tiffany, their 6-year-old, it's double. Nathan, 8, has severe developmental problems, and everyone in the family suffers from respiratory problems and the skin rashes associated with PCB exposure. Chris, Karen's 11-year-old son, who's home from school with an upset stomach and is splayed out on the couch, lifts his Panthers basketball T-shirt to reveal brownish-red blotches climbing up the sides of his chest. "It smells like decaying flesh," Ryan warns. "Like it's rotten."

Most of their friends and family have already left, but the McFarlanes can't afford anything other than the small dirt lot where they park their trailer. Karen was recently hospitalized for respiratory-stress disorder and had two strokes at age 30. Her most recent Pap smear was abnormal, but she says she's too scared to have a follow-up exam. Ryan, who has small pink growths dotting his neck, wistfully talks of going to an oncologist for a full cancer screening, something he's unlikely to get soon because he doesn't have health insurance. The McFarlanes are stuck in a place where, according to the Alabama Department of Public Health, cancer rates are 25 percent higher than in the rest of the state.

Anniston was founded as a company town. In 1872, Samuel Noble, a British-born businessman, and Daniel Tyler, a Union general and a cousin of Aaron Burr, established Woodstock Iron in a then-barren outpost at the foot of the Appalachian Mountains. The company built a church, a schoolhouse and a general store. To guarantee the moral fiber of their fabricated utopia, the townspeople threw away their whiskey bottles, declared their own Prohibition and erected a fence around the town's perimeter, creating one of the nation's earliest gated communities. During World War I, chemical producers arrived, and in 1929, the Theodore Swann Company became the nation's first maker of PCBs, nonflammable chemicals that lubricate industrial systems that generate heat. By 1935 the Monsanto Company recognized PCBs as big business and bought Swann's Anniston facility. For close to forty years, Monsanto sold PCBs to companies like General Electric and Westinghouse, helping them insure that webs of electrical wires wouldn't burst into flames.

In the sixties Monsanto encountered a serious threat to its success. While chemical manufacturers throughout the country were scrutinizing the environmental impacts of their products amid growing pressure to reduce emissions, a team of Swedish researchers discovered PCBs in wildlife. For every electrical wire kept from overheating, some of the chemical had been escaping. This discovery, which received wide publicity in 1966, raised concerns for Monsanto, which worried that it would usher in governmental regulations limiting PCB use. "Truly the PCBs are a worldwide ecological problem," declared a company memo that included a list of concerns under the heading "Business Potential at Stake on a Worldwide Basis."

At the time, the government had not yet declared PCBs to be hazardous to human health, but suspicions had been growing for quite a while. As early as 1937 the medical community was examining PCBs to see if they were a public health hazard—a study published that year in the *Journal of Industrial Hygiene and Toxicology* suggested links between PCBs and liver disease. In the mid-fifties Monsanto researchers and executives began writing confidential memos describing their fears about the chemicals' toxic effects, but they drafted plans for continuing to sell them despite these suspicions. In 1956 Monsanto considered the chemicals toxic enough to give workers protective gear and clothing, and encourage them to hose off after each shift. Along with other chemical manufacturers, the company publicly expressed skepticism about PCBs' association with disease, but over the next decade the evidence became harder and harder to dismiss. In 1968 the links between PCBs and disease won wide credibility when residents of a Japanese town were harmed by consuming PCB-contaminated rice oil. Subsequent studies published in leading medical journals

showed that PCBs damage the immune system, the reproductive system and the nervous and endocrine systems.

Monsanto had hundreds of millions in PCB sales to
lose if regulators placed restrictions on their use. By
1969 the company established a committee to keep
abreast of the state of knowledge on PCBs. The issue
was beginning to look like "a monster," in the words
of one former executive.

> Make the Govt., States and Universities prove their
> case, but avoid as much confrontation as possible. . . .
> We can prove some things are OK at low concentra-
> tion. Give Monsanto some defense. . . . We can't
> defend vs. everything. Some animals or fish or insects
> will be harmed. . . . The Dept. of Interior and/or state
> authorities could monitor plant outfall and find
> [discharges] of chlorinated biphenyls at . . . Anniston
> anytime they choose to do so. This would shut us
> down depending on what plants or animals they
> choose to find harmed. . . .
> —Monsanto researcher, September 1969

At issue in the lawsuit is whether the company was aware
of the extent of the PCB contamination and whether it
could have protected or warned the community. Many of
the answers may be found in the documents.

In the late sixties Monsanto began keeping track of its
PCB discharges in an attempt to reduce emissions.
According to the company's July 1970 progress report,
Monsanto was dumping about sixteen pounds a day of
PCB waste into the town's waterways. It was a significant
amount, but in the closed world of Monsanto executives,

it almost seemed like good news—the year before, the company had been dumping about 250 pounds a day.

Monsanto went on the offensive, reporting to regulators at the now-defunct Alabama Water Improvement Commission that it was finding PCBs in the water near the plant. But the regulators, according to a company memo, agreed that "all written effluent level reports would be held confidential by the technical staff and would not be available to the public unless or until Monsanto released it." Monsanto never did.

To predict whether federal or state regulators would find the chemicals to be a threat to the environment or human health, Monsanto began commissioning animal toxicity studies; the results, in the early seventies, didn't look good. "Our interpretation is that the PCBs are exhibiting a greater degree of toxicity in this study than we had anticipated. . . . We have additional interim data which will perhaps be more discouraging," a company executive wrote. "We are repeating some of the experiments to confirm or deny the earlier findings and are not distributing the early results at this time."

Testing continued, but the results didn't get any better. In 1975 the lab submitted its findings from a two-year study of PCBs' effects on rats. An early draft of the report said that in some cases, PCBs had caused tumors. George Levinskas, Monsanto's manager for environmental assessment and toxicology, wrote to the lab's director: "May we request that the [PCB] 1254 report be amended to say 'does not appear to be carcinogenic.'"

The final report adopted the company's suggested language and dropped all references to tumors.

Anniston residents got their first glimpse of Monsanto's

troubles with PCBs in late 1993. A contractor doing dredging work on the nearby Choccolocco Creek noticed largemouth bass with blistered scales. Tests showed the fish contained extremely high levels of PCBs. Around the same time, the Alabama Power Company broke ground on land it had acquired from Monsanto in the sixties, opening up a PCB landfill that bled black tar. Alabama Power insisted that Monsanto take back the land and reported its discovery to the Alabama Department of Environmental Management. Testing ordered by ADEM and carried out by Monsanto found that a wide swath of West Anniston and local waterways were highly contaminated with PCBs. Soon after, the company made its quiet buyout offer to the church.

The contamination came as news to residents, but Donald Stewart quickly discovered that Monsanto had known about it for decades. "There have been some big bonanzas," Stewart says of the internal company documents he has collected. "Someone's going to have to sit down somewhere in the bowels of that company and make it right."

Since Stewart had never handled a case like this before, he enlisted the help of a Mississippi firm and Kasowitz, Benson, Torres & Friedman, a New York firm that represented Liggett in the tobacco suits. Even with all that legal firepower, Stewart still has a formidable task ahead. "It just seems these folks have the skill and the capability to avoid having somebody pin the tail on their donkey. I mean, they've just been able to walk away from it," he says. "I can't wait to get before a jury to say, 'Well, this is what happened.' I'm looking forward to hearing how they're going to explain this away."

Early in 1970, we established a target of 10 ppb [parts per billion] of PCBs in our plant waste streams which we expected to achieve by the third quarter 1971. No specific target was established for the quantity of PCBs we could tolerate in the atmosphere. During the year as the plant gained tighter control of known sources of PCB pollution, it became increasingly obvious that the high levels would continue because of the PCBs trapped in the soil and in the sewer systems. Clean-up of these sources can be economically impractical.

—Former Monsanto plant manager,
January 1971

Adam Peck, one of Monsanto's lawyers, isn't sweating it. The company, which spun off its chemical division as a stand-alone firm, Solutia, in 1997, assigned an environmental manager to lead a $30 million cleanup focusing on everything from a landfill where 150-200 million pounds of PCB waste are buried to waterways and contaminated land in the neighborhood. Beginning with the Mars Hill church, the company began buying out small businesses and residents in West Anniston. They bulldozed buildings, laid thick plastic tarps over the contaminated soil and covered them with clean soil. The company plans to convert some of the contaminated land into a wildlife refuge. It has built perching posts near the landfill to attract purple martins, and recently released salamanders into a pond that catches runoff water from the landfill.

In Peck's mind, these activities demonstrate convincingly that the corporation has behaved responsibly. "Our position is that when a jury hears all the evidence they will conclude that Monsanto and Solutia acted responsibly in the manufacture of PCBs and in efforts to remediate," he says. "I think liability will be for a jury to determine. We have offered to acquire property. We've offered to clean property. What does that mean? Does that mean we acted responsibly or that we should have done more?" After a pause, he adds, "I'm not sure what more we could have done."

Peck says Monsanto didn't notify the community about the PCB releases years ago because at the time there wasn't sufficient understanding of how the chemicals migrated through the environment. Yet one of the documents Stewart obtained, a sample Q&A on PCBs produced by Monsanto for its customers in 1972, reads in part: "PCB is a persistent chemical which builds up in the environment. It, therefore, should not be allowed to escape to the environment." Peck continues: "And if you think about it from the perspective of the plant manager and the folks who were there at the time, the levels that were escaping the plant were extremely small compared to the levels that those guys were working with on a daily basis. They weren't worried for their own health. Why should they be thinking the minute levels that are escaping are of any concern to anybody outside there?" The protective gear worn by workers, Peck insists, was simply routine.

Ryan McFarlane is lumbering across the dirt lot outside his trailer. Overweight and easily winded, he moves slowly past a broken trampoline to a set of wire pens that house his chickens. Undersized and lethargic, they huddle in the corners of the rusty pens, occasionally exhaling a thin cluck. For years, Ryan raised chickens for food. But these days, knowing they are probably contaminated, and since his health problems have kept him from working for the past five years, Ryan keeps chickens around to give him something to do.

Until the PCB contamination came to light, the McFarlanes, like many of their friends and former neighbors, regularly ate fish from the creeks, and chicken and vegetables raised in their yards. They might have given the practice up long before if Monsanto had told Jeremiah Smith in 1970 when it bought his hogs that it made the purchase because it was worried that people were eating PCB-contaminated pork. (Monsanto admits that the hogs were later shot and buried, although the company contends that its concern about PCB contamination was secondary to its concern about the hogs' trespassing on its property.) The Agency for Toxic Substances and Disease Registry, a division of the U.S. Department of Health and Human Services, completed a health study in Anniston in February, which found that PCB exposure in the town is a public health hazard. It also suggested that eating local pork, fish and chicken has been a major source of PCB contamination. The EPA says eating PCB-contaminated food is one of the most dangerous means of exposure because PCBs biomagnify, or increase in intensity, as they travel up the food chain.

Residents are anxiously awaiting the EPA's decision on whether to order a federal cleanup. "All they want to do, seem like, is study, study, study, we got to study some more," says one plaintiff in the case. The lawsuit is also taking longer than residents anticipated. Two weeks before the case was to go to trial, in March 1999, Monsanto appealed to the state Supreme Court to establish procedural rules for the circuit court. Now, more than a year later, the Court still hasn't returned its rulings. In the meantime, Stewart prepares for trial and works on other cases. He's hoping the jury will award compensatory damages for the property contamination and punitive damages for the fear the exposure has engendered. He also wants Monsanto to pay for regular health screenings. Early settlement talks went nowhere, both sides say.

Monsanto did settle the original suit on behalf of the Mars Hill congregation. It made no admission of guilt but paid $2.5 million to rebuild the church at another location. "In the Mars Hill case they protested all the time that they didn't do a thing," Stewart says. "Then they paid $2.5 million for a church they said was worth $400,000. Sounds like they did something, to me. Now, I'm just a small-town country lawyer, but I wonder how they arrived at that decision."

They Said It . . .

"There is little object in going to expensive extremes in limiting discharges."
—an internal Monsanto memo after the company in 1969 discovered PCB levels 7,500 times the legal limit in an Anniston, Alabama creek

Multi-national corporations love doing business with dictators.

Nigeria Crude

from *Harper's* (June 1996)

Joshua Hammer

To fly into the Niger Delta is to fall from grace. From the air, the silvery waters seem peaceful. Dubbed "The Venice of West Africa" in 1867 by British explorer Winwood Reade, the Delta stretches 290 miles along the Atlantic coast from the Benin River in the west to the Cross River in the east. In between, the powerful Niger feeds an intricate network of tributaries and creeks that partition sandbars and mangrove islands into cookie-cutter shapes as they meander toward the Gulf of Guinea.

Yet far beneath the belly of the airplane, oil fields mottle the landscape, their rigs ceaselessly pumping crude and natural gas from deep underground. The gas burns incessantly in giant geysers of flame and smoke, and at night the flares that ring the city of Port Harcourt and fishing villages deep within the mangrove swamps cast a hellish glow. As the smoke from the flares rises above the palm trees, methane and carbon dioxide separate from the greasy soot. The gases rise but the grime descends, coating the trees, the laundry hanging on lines, the mud-daubed huts, and the people within. There is nothing pure left in Nigeria.

In May of 1995, I traveled to Nigeria to scout the front lines of the struggle for the country's soul that pits the indigenous peoples of the Delta against Royal Dutch/ Shell, other petroleum producers, and the military government. It is a conflict that threatens the fabric of Nigerian society, and by that I don't mean the political fabric—

which, like most African nations, was never much more than a crazy quilt of hundreds of tribal groups haphazardly stitched together by colonial governments—but the character of the people. Easy oil money has created a culture of corruption that, even for Third World military dictatorships, is breathtakingly epic. It wasn't just that on a short drive out of Port Harcourt my taxi driver was stopped twelve times by police demanding bribes, or that the military was exporting its methods of intimidation, graft, and outright thievery to Liberia as part of its U.N. "peacekeeping" duties there, or that foreign businesses have to anticipate extra expenditures to cover kickbacks and payoffs. It was that in Nigeria, even the innocent are sullied, their expectations lowered, their complicity expected, perhaps even inevitable. Crude oil, once viewed as the means of Nigeria's ascent to greatness, had instead greased the skids into chaos.

The latest manifestation of Nigeria's descent was the trial of Ken Saro-Wiwa, a member of a Delta tribe called the Ogoni, who six years ago began organizing his people against the petroleum producers and the military regime. His efforts earned him a Nobel Peace Prize nomination and landed him—along with fourteen other members of the Movement for the Survival of the Ogoni People, or MOSOP—in prison on trumped-up charges that he ordered the murder of four Ogoni chiefs who had disagreed with his increasingly militant actions. I was to attend the trial later in my visit, and although the government had preordained his guilt, the question was larger than whether Saro-Wiwa would be executed or merely imprisoned indefinitely. The question was whether one man, dead or alive, had started an indigenous revolt against the tenth-largest, and the most profitable, corporation in the world, or, in the long view, had failed to prevent that company from poisoning his country.

I hired a small skiff at the Port Harcourt waterfront. Five minutes down the Bonny River the sounds of the city were lost to the whine of the outboard and the syncopated percussion of a tropical downpour. For three hours, as I crouched beneath a thick tarpaulin, the boat threaded through a network of creeks, overtaking fishermen in canoes—their paddles rhythmically dipping into the coffee-colored water—river taxis, oil barges, and ghost ships scuttled among the mangroves. Herons and egrets flapped by, and occasionally telltale plumes of smoke from gas flares wafted above the trees. At last I arrived in Okoroba: a cluster of weather-beaten, rain-sodden wooden huts and dugout canoes huddled around a splintered pier. Six years ago, Shell had dredged a canal through Okoroba to reach a new well. Since then, the company had yet to produce oil but it had tapped deep reserves of frustration and rage.

Paramount chief Steven Joel Engobila, a near-toothless man in a black bowler hat, sat on a battered cushioned sofa in his dim hut. Its walls were bare except for a faded 1991 Shell Oil calendar. He led me outside for a tour of Okoroba. Heavy rain had turned the dirt alleys into quagmires; filthy, naked children ran out of huts, excitedly screaming "Oibo!" (white man). The village had no electricity, no paved roads, no shops, and a primary school with broken wooden chairs and a leaking roof. A trip to the nearest doctor took four hours by canoe. As we walked across a swamped soccer field, sinking to our ankles in the muck, Engobila ran through a list of Shell's misdeeds. The canal builders had knocked down the village health center, he said, flattened most of the village's coconut palms, and damaged the local fishing industry by flooding freshwater creeks with salt water.

"We tried to grow new coconuts, but they died. We don't know why," he said. Shell had paid a few dollars' compensation for the destroyed trees, built a water tank, and contracted with a local firm to construct a new health center, but the workers had abandoned the structure after a few months. "This is empty public relations," Engobila said, waving his hand at the roofless concrete-block building. "Shell brought us nothing but anguish." The chief felt powerless. "We are ignorant people. What can we do?" Most people in the region were so destitute, Engobila admitted, that they lived in constant hope that an oil spill would bring them even a small settlement from the company.

It is nearly impossible to overstate Shell's role in Nigeria. Today, under the terms of its OPEC quota, Nigeria produces about 2 million barrels of crude a day, bringing about $10 billion a year to the military junta and accounting for about 97 percent of export revenues. Half of that total is pumped by Shell, making the company by far the dominant economic force in Nigeria. The relationship between the company and the country is not exactly colonial. Colonialism is unwieldy, expensive, and risky. Shell, like the multinationals in Mexico and Indonesia, merely recognizes a good business climate when it sees one, and that is all it chooses to see. That much, Nnaemeka Achebe, Shell's polished and articulate general manager and the highest-ranking Nigerian in the company, cheerfully admitted when I visited him in his plush Lagos office with sweeping views of the Gulf of Guinea. "For a commercial company trying to make investments, you need a stable environment," Achebe said. "Dictatorships can give you that. Right now in Nigeria there is acceptance, peace, and continuity."

In truth, Nigeria has never really known peace. This country of 100 million people, whose boundaries were established by the British in 1914, is a pastiche of more than 250 ethnic groups, and between many of them are ancient, even violent divisions of language, religion, and culture. Violence escalated with the arrival of the Dutch and British, who used the Delta waterways to build the largest slave trade in West Africa. But these revenues paled in comparison with what followed. In 1937, the British government gave Shell D'Arcy, as the Anglo-Dutch company was then called, the exclusive right to prospect for oil. For more than two decades, exploration parties traveled by raft, canoe, barge, and on foot through the malarial swamps of the Delta, conducting seismographic surveys and core drilling. Wildcatters struck their first commercial deposits in 1956. During the following decade, as Nigeria gained independence from Great Britain, Shell laid pipelines through the Delta and opened the Bonny Island oil terminal downriver from Port Harcourt.

At that time, Nigeria was poised to become the undisputed leader of Africa. In addition to huge deposits of crude, the country had rich farmland, an educated population, and a democratic government. Its three dominant tribes—the Hausa-Fulanis in the Muslim north, the Yorubas in the west, and the Ibos in the east—were proud, artistic people with histories dating back a thousand years. Wole Soyinka and Chinua Achebe stood at the vanguard of an African literary renaissance.

Over the past generation, however, the promises of Nigeria have given way to disappointment and failure. In 1966, a military dictatorship from the northern Hausa-Fulani tribe seized power, and northern-dominated juntas have ruled the country for twenty-six of the thirty years since. They have profited enormously from the country's vast oil resources while deepening the misery of just about everyone else.

Immediately after the Hausa-Fulanis seized power, the Ibos led the Biarran region—which included the Delta, home of the Ogoni, Ogbia, Ijaw, and Andoni minority tribes—into a bloody revolt that lasted three years. After the Ibos were routed in 1970, Shell and the government were free to enter into a joint venture known as the Shell Petroleum Development Company of Nigeria, or SPDC. Shell put up the bulk of exploration and equipment costs, and in return it got to export 30 percent of the crude oil pumped, with 55 percent going to the government and the rest to two European companies, Elf and Agip. (American oil companies also have operations in Nigeria.) Collective gross oil revenues mushroomed from $600 million in 1973 to $26 billion in 1981.

While Shell and the other companies did all the work, the government sat back and collected its share of the profit. Between 1970 and 1974, the portion of government revenue derived from oil production jumped from 26 percent to 82 percent, about where it remains today. This surge in oil profits transformed Nigerian politics. Controlling the country now meant access to an ever-filling jackpot, and the "Kaduna Mafia," the Muslim-dominated military-industrial cabal named after a city in Nigeria's north, rose to unchallenged power. Officials awarded themselves billions of dollars' worth of inflated government construction contracts, lined their pockets with lucrative kickbacks, and transformed the British system of indirect rule through local chiefs into ethnic rivalry, nepotism, and institutionalized graft. Today the country is far better known for its heroin traffickers and financial scam artists than for its novelists.

The new wealth also created new poverty. While the average Nigerian scrapes by on less than $300 a year—down from about $1,200 in 1978—the country's oil elite dwell in lavish compounds with fleets of Mercedes, imported food and wine, and fat overseas bank accounts. According to Western diplomats, when oil prices soared during the Gulf War, former leader General Ibrahim Babangida reported no corresponding rise in the federal income; the equally kleptocratic current dictator, General Sani Abacha, has also siphoned off billions of dollars in oil profits. Meanwhile, the junta dropped any pretense of accountability to the people. In June 1993, Babangida annulled Nigeria's democratic presidential election. Five months later, Abacha, a participant in three previous coups who is known by his ritual scars and fondness for epaulets, seized power, abolished all democratic institutions and regional governments, shut down newspapers, and jailed most of the opposition, including the winner of the 1993 presidential election, Moshood Abiola. Such corruption, and the resultant neglect of infrastructure and development, has only furthered Nigeria's dependence on petroleum. Agriculture, which once accounted for 90 percent of export income, is in ruins. Nigeria's cities, swollen by the mass migration from rural areas during the 1970s oil boom, are smog-choked zones of anarchy.

Such as Port Harcourt. The city, home of Shell's Eastern Division headquarters, has swelled in population in the last twenty-five years from 80,000 to over a million. Lured by the promise of money, nearby tribespeople walked away from their fields and fisheries only to find themselves living here in concrete hovels in the shadow of glass office buildings and billboards advertising cellular phones and direct TV. A miasma of pollution hangs over potholed streets teeming with oil tankers, fertilizer trucks, overcrowded buses, and secondhand foreign imports known as tokumbos. Barefoot teenage vendors weave through the seemingly endless traffic jams, known as "go slows," hawking welcome mats, cap guns, hangers, Q-tips. They compete with polio victims who thrust their twisted limbs through car windows, pleading, "Mastah. Please, Mastah, just give me five naira only."

Known in imperial times as the Garden City, Port Harcourt today is dirty and denuded; virtually the only oasis is Shell Camp, a heavily guarded compound where 180 expatriate (and some high-ranking Nigerian) Shell executives live in air-conditioned luxury, amidst manicured lawns, tennis courts, and a golf course, as if in some far-flung fragment of Sacramento. Contact with ordinary Nigerians is intentionally limited: on workdays, executives travel by company car to the division headquarters, and from there by helicopter to oil facilities throughout the Delta.

Except for the gates, visitor badges, and security checks, Shell Camp could have been a location for a 1950s family sitcom, but outside the compound's fences was a very different story. By May of 1995, Ken Saro-Wiwa was in prison, the government had closed Ogoniland to outsiders, and troops had beaten foreign reporters attempting to get in. MOSOP members who were not already in jail were living semi-clandestinely in a kind of anxious limbo; no one was eager to act as my guide into their homeland.

Eventually Batom Mitee, a bearded, bespectacled man in his late thirties whose brother Ledum was on trial with Saro-Wiwa, agreed to escort me the next morning to the epicenter of the resistance, though he dared not cross the border in my company. I set out in a truck conspicuously marked "Liverpool School of Tropical Medicine," sitting next to bona fide medical personnel and clutching a set of fake credentials; Mitee followed in another vehicle. At 8:00 A.M. it was already pushing 90 degrees; the air was thick with swamp decay and diesel exhaust.

When we reached the border an hour later, the soldiers demanded a small payoff and waved us through. In Ogoniland's Gokana district, I met up with Mitee in his home village of Kegbara Dere. Here was a place and a people utterly subservient to the production of oil. High-pressure oil pipes snaked amid plots of yam and cassavas, past mud-brick huts, even through people's yards; I watched as one woman climbed over a tangle of pipes to get to her front door.

Ogoniland has a population of 500,000 crammed into 400 square miles. It contains ninety-six oil wells, four oil fields, one petrochemical plant, one fertilizer plant, and two refineries. By some estimates, the region has produced about 600 million barrels of crude during the past forty years. But despite the billions of dollars it has provided to Shell and various military regimes, Ogoniland has no hospitals, few jobs, one of the highest infant-mortality rates in Nigeria, and a 20 percent literacy rate. Moreover, frequent blowouts and leaking pipes have damaged crops and streams, sometimes irreparably; Ogoniland suffered 111 oil spills between 1985 and 1994. (Shell claims that 77 of those spills were the result of sabotage.)

"In the old days in Gokana you could fish, farm, and survive without money," said Mitee. We were sitting beside an abandoned natural-gas flare; until increasingly violent protests caused Shell to cease operations in Ogoniland in 1993, it had spewed a toxic cloud of smoke and flame 100 feet into the air above Kegbara Dere twenty-four hours a day. "But oil exploration spoiled the creeks and the seas, and you can't fish like you did before. We used to have a lot of land, but Shell made much of that unusable. Also, there's never been any family planning here, so there's growing pressure for land. My father has five sons—we can't all have his land. So we have to look for jobs. But there aren't any jobs. Everybody is suffering."

It was in this landscape that I began to apprehend what had compelled Ken Saro-Wiwa to confront the perversion of Nigeria. Born in the Khana district of Ogoniland in 1941 to a tribal chief, Saro-Wiwa attended mission schools, eventually winning a scholarship to the University of Ibadan, near Lagos, He served as administrator of the Bonny Island oil depot during the Biafran war, and between 1968 and 1973 he was a regional commissioner for education. When his militant views on Ogoni rights got him sacked, he launched successful real estate and grocery businesses, a publishing company, and a writing career that made him famous throughout Nigeria. His first novel, *Sozaboy: A Novel in Rotten English*, was an antiwar tale about a village youth recruited into the rebel army during the Biafran conflict. Later came *On a Darkling Plain*, an autobiographical account of the Biafran war, and

Basi and Company, a TV sitcom watched by 30 million Nigerians that lampooned the country's get-rich-quick attitude. But a political role beckoned. "Ken had this idea from the time he was fifteen," says Batom Mitee. "He wanted to create a campaign modeled after the American civil-rights movement, with mass protests, sit-ins, boycotts, vigils. He started mobilizing in 1990."

For decades, Shell had pumped oil in the Delta virtually free of burdensome environmental regulations. There were few or no requirements to conduct environmental impact studies, recycle oil waste, or lay subterranean oil pipes instead of cheap aboveground pipes. According to Greenpeace, between 1982 and 1992, 37 percent of Shell's spills worldwide—amounting to 1.6 million gallons—took place in the Delta. And according to data compiled for Shell by the World Wide Fund for Nature and leaked to the British newspaper the *Independent*, 76 percent of the natural gas pumped up with crude in Nigeria is burned off—compared with 20 percent in Libya, Saudi Arabia, or Iran; 4.3 percent in the United Kingdom; and 0.6 percent in the United States. Each year, gas flares in Nigeria emit 34 million tons of carbon dioxide and 12 million tons of methane, making petroleum operations in Nigeria the biggest single cause of global warming, according to the *Independent*.

The Ogonis claim that the gas flares cause acid rain that kills crops and fouls drinking water. But they have no legal recourse to fight the destruction of their environment. In 1978, the military declared all land in Nigeria the property of the federal government, freeing the petroleum companies from troublesome negotiations with locals sitting on top of oil. Four years later, the government agreed to allocate 1.5 percent of federal revenues to the 12 million people living in oil-producing areas. In 1990, after the paramilitary police—known as the Kill and Go Mob—massacred more than fifty residents of Umuechem who were demanding that Shell provide them with potable water and scholarships, the figure was raised to 3 percent. But most of the money has been siphoned off by corrupt officials, and Shell has shown little initiative to make reparations itself. In the nearly forty years that it has pumped oil in Ogoniland, Shell has by its own calculation put in only $2 million worth of improvements, including a smattering of schools and some medical equipment.

About the same time as the Umuechem massacre, Saro-Wiwa launched the Movement for the Survival of the Ogoni People with a handful of other members of Ogoniland's educated elite. They drafted an Ogoni Bill of Rights and demanded $10 billion in reparations from Shell and a measure of political autonomy for Ogoniland. Matching incendiary rhetoric with organizational skill, Saro-Wiwa became MOSOP's spokesperson. He was by all accounts a magnetic speaker, calling Shell's operations "genocide" and "systematic extermination," and urging the Ogonis to fight for their rights. On January 4, 1993, Saro-Wiwa drew international attention to their cause by leading a peaceful protest march of 300,000 people through Ogoniland.

Yet like so much in Nigeria, how dedicated Saro-Wiwa was to pacifism is a matter of great dispute. Against the wishes of other MOSOP leaders, Saro-Wiwa formed a more radical youth wing of the movement. Sabotage and threats to Shell workers increased; in January 1993, Shell ceased manned operations in Ogoniland, a move that cost the company and the government 28,000 barrels of crude oil a day. Although that amount was just 3 percent of oil production in Nigeria, MOSOP's actions signified unprecedented defiance of the junta, which feared that another secessionist movement was brewing in the Delta. The general manager of SPDC asked the government to protect Shell's installations across the Delta. During the summer of 1993, the government began replacing Ogoni police officers with officers from different ethnic groups, who prompted neighboring tribes into a series of attacks that left thousands of Ogonis dead or homeless.

In response, Saro-Wiwa called for the Ogonis to boycott the upcoming democratic presidential election, a tactic that widened schisms between the elite and the younger, poorer activists. Four MOSOP officers resigned, leaving Saro-Wiwa in charge of the organization. Ogoniland was quickly polarized, with many Ogoni activists becoming increasingly angry at the region's "traditional chiefs," hereditary leaders who oversaw the local distribution of government jobs and oil-cleanup, road, and construction contracts. When the chiefs warned Ogoni youths to desist from violence, posters appeared throughout the region branding the chiefs "vultures" and calling for their punishment. "MOSOP was changing the traditional structure," said Dr. David Owens Wiwa, Ken's younger brother. "Those who benefited from the old establishment, from government contracts, were seen as depriving the people of their due."

Revenge against the "vultures" could be harsh. Priscilla Vikue, the director-general of the Ministry of Education in Port Harcourt, was one of those branded a collaborator by Ogoni militants. "The youths requested that I resign my government appointment," she told me. "I refused. That's when they burned my house to the ground, along with those of six traditional chiefs."

Saro-Wiwa always publicly maintained that he sought to restrain the troublemakers, even asking the Nigerian military to arrest certain "hoodlums," but Vikue and other members of the elite who testified against him maintain that his anti-establishment rhetoric fueled the youths' actions. "I complained to Saro-Wiwa," said Vikue. "I said, 'Have you heard what they did to me? To my house?' He said, 'Look, Priscilla, there is a revolution in Ogoniland. You'd better go with it because heads will roll.' I was shocked," Vikue said. "He told the people they were qualified to live like kings and queens, that they would all be millionaires. And the people were unemployed. They believed him. I told him, 'You're misleading them. Not everyone can drive a Mercedes.' "

By 1994, the government had decided to escalate its efforts against MOSOP. A May 5 internal memo authored by Major Paul Okuntimo, head of the regional arm of the military, the Rivers State Internal Security Force, warned of what was to come: "Shell operations still impossible unless ruthless military operations are undertaken for smooth economic activities to commence. . . . Recommendations: Wasting operations during MOSOP and other gatherings making constant military presence justifiable. Wasting targets cutting across communities and leadership cadres especially vocal individuals of various groups." Four hundred more troops were sent to Ogoniland, and the memo notes that the government was pressuring the oil companies to underwrite the operation. "This is it," Saro-Wiwa told Greenpeace after the memo was leaked to MOSOP. "They are going to arrest us all and execute us. All for Shell."

Saro-Wiwa's prediction may have been melodramatic,

but it was also prescient. Shortly before noon on May 21, 1994, the traditional chief of the village of Giokoo hosted at his palace a meeting of about 100 other Ogoni chiefs and supporters. The event had been well publicized, and many young Ogonis were suspicious that the chiefs were planning to collaborate with the military to quell MOSOP. Suddenly, recalled eyewitness Al-Haji Kobani, "there was the sound of a loud motorcycle outside. A guy came in and said, 'Ken has been arrested on the way to a political rally.' Three minutes later the place was surrounded by over 2,000 people. There was no escape route. They removed our wristwatches, shoes, belts, and everything that was in our pockets. They escorted about 50 people to safety. Then the rest were left in the hall for killing. They attacked us with bottles, stones, iron bars, and machetes. I tried to talk sense to them. But they said, 'Ken Saro-Wiwa is going to bring us a kingdom.' "

Al-Haji's brother Edward Kobani, a Gokana chief, former Rivers State government official, and one of MOSOP's founders, was killed on the spot by a rake driven into his skull. The other victims, all erstwhile friends of Saro-Wiwa's who broke with him in 1993, were Albert Badey, a former secretary to the Rivers State government; Chief Samuel Orage, a former Rivers State commissioner, an Ogoni chief, and the brother-in-law of Saro-Wiwa's wife, Maria; and his brother, Chief Theophilous Orage, also a traditional leader. All three were chased down and murdered at a nearby market. According to witnesses, the killers stuffed the corpses inside a Volkswagen, doused them with gasoline, and set them on fire.

The chief's palace in Giokoo remains a monument to the violence unleashed by MOSOP. All of its louvered windows were smashed, and shams of glass covered the veranda. I could still make out faint bloodstains on the eggshell-blue walls of the large living room—the spot where Edward Kobani died. Overturned easy chairs, broken glass, cooking pots, leaves, and empty bottles of schnapps—a traditional gift to village chiefs littered the bare cement floor. A narrow hallway led to the juju shrine behind the house to which Al-Haji Kobani crawled during the mayhem, managing to save himself. Inside the shrine, chameleons scurried over sacks of cement, more empty schnapps bottles, and a pile of rodent skulls. As I looked over the palace, the intoxicating mixture of euphoria and rage that drove the killers seemed almost palpable. Rousing the Ogoni masses from passivity and despair, Saro-Wiwa had filled them with a sense of entitlement and rancor toward the old order. He may have been miles from the scene of the killings in Giokoo, but he was, in some way, responsible.

One day after the killings at Giokoo, a brigade from the Rivers State Internal Security Force stormed into Ogoniland, arrested MOSOP activists, and allegedly murdered and raped hundreds of civilians. Major Paul Okuntimo, the author of the secret "wasting" memo, led the troops. He was later implicated by one of his own soldiers in the rape of at least two women.

After I left Giokoo, I went to visit Okuntimo at his family's bungalow at the Bori military camp in Port Harcourt. He had a disarmingly charismatic presence—muscular, handsome, and well-spoken. Wearing a white jogging suit and smiling, he invited me into his house. Faded Christmas ornaments, wedding photos, and a plaque proclaiming MY FAMILY IS COVERED WITH THE BLOOD OF JESUS decorated the dusty, dark living room. Promoted to lieutenant colonel as a reward for his achievements in Ogoniland, Okuntimo is said to be planning a career in the evangelical Christian ministry when he retires from the army.

He disappeared into a back room and emerged five minutes later dressed in crisp fatigues. Then we climbed into his Toyota Land Cruiser and roared down a rutted dirt road to the headquarters of the military's Second Amphibious Brigade. Soldiers snapped to attention as he strode into his office, which was dominated by portraits of General Abacha and the army chief of staff. Okuntimo sat down behind an empty desk and leaned forward. "Look," he began, assuming a tone of restraint. "The Ogoni organization was established in good faith. But their nonviolent campaign metamorphosed. These young vigilantes took over the leadership, they set up roadblocks, they seized weapons from police stations, they began executing anyone they viewed as the enemy. At a certain point, Saro-Wiwa simply lost control.

"There was no relationship between the army and Shell. There were no discussions before the operation," he insisted. I asked Okuntimo about the admissions of some of his troops, cited in a Human Rights Watch/Africa report, that they had gunned down dozens of civilians on his orders. He laughed dismissively, and if he was lying— and I believe that he was—then it was accomplished with ease. "Where did I throw the corpses? In the creeks? They would float. Did I bury them? They could dig them up. These are all lies spread by Ogoni sympathists."

On May 17, 1995, I took a seat in the upstairs gallery of a small, high-ceilinged courtroom in a secure government compound in downtown Port Harcourt where Saro-Wiwa and fourteen other Ogoni activists, including top officials and members of the youth wing, were facing capital murder charges for having incited the killings at Giokoo. Frayed red carpets, peeling plaster walls, and forty whirring ceiling fans gave the courtroom a sad, neglected feeling. Two dozen soldiers armed with automatic weapons lined the walls, guarded the entrance, and peered in the windows from the garden outside. On the dais sat the three judges—two civilians in gray suits and a uniformed lieutenant colonel with a doctorate in criminology. Their verdict was unappealable, pending confirmation by General Abacha.

At one o'clock, the shuttered prison van carrying Saro-Wiwa and his codefendants arrived from the military barracks where they'd been detained for one year. Saro-Wiwa's appearance hushed the murmur of journalists and the families of the defendants and victims. He was a tiny, compactly built man, no more than five foot three, and wore gold-rimmed glasses, a brightly dyed green, blue, and white caftan, and leather sandals. Obviously in deteriorating physical condition, he leaned on a carved wooden cane as he slowly wobbled toward the dock. The day's first prosecution witness, a former MOSOP official, recounted a meeting in late 1993 during which Saro-Wiwa had allegedly ordered the murder of the four chiefs at Giokoo. The story sounded rehearsed and implausible. Saro-Wiwa pointedly ignored him, keeping his face buried in a United Nations report on military abuses in Ogoniland. One by one, prosecution witnesses took the stand. None would make eye contact with the defendants; each intoned the same rote account.

Midway through the proceedings the judges called a

brief recess, and two of Saro-Wiwa's defense attorneys ush-
ered me out of the courtroom. In a dimly lit lounge down
the corridor, Saro-Wiwa sat on a couch smoking a pipe,
surrounded by a dozen soldiers and policemen. He
looked at the policemen nervously, then stood up, balanced himself on his cane, and shook my hand. "Did you
get my letter?" he whispered. I nodded. The day before, he
had had a ten-page handwritten reply to a dozen questions of mine smuggled out of jail. In it, he denied insti-
gating the murders, claimed his movement was entirely
nonviolent, and accused the government of framing him.
"These people are criminals," he told me with a dismissive
wave. "They're going to find me guilty. So I don't even
bother to listen to the testimony. I'm not going to let these
goons have any advantage over me." Moments later, the
soldiers cut him off and escorted me from the lounge. I
returned to the courtroom, but my hope that the proceedings would clarify Saro-Wiwa's complicity in the escalating
violence in Ogoniland had evaporated. Whatever trans-
gressions he had committed—and I don't believe that
ordering the murder of the four chiefs was among them—
Saro-Wiwa would get no fair hearing in this court. Of the
nineteen prosecution witnesses called, two of the most
damaging would later admit to having been bribed by the
junta. In June, the defense team, led by pro-democracy
activist Gani Fawehinmi, resigned en masse, claiming that
the trial was rigged. Fawehinmi was almost immediately
arrested and was held for two weeks.

Six months later, on November 10, Saro-Wiwa and the
eight other prisoners who had been duly found guilty
were awakened at dawn, chained at their ankles, and
driven from Bori military camp to the central prison of

Port Harcourt. There they were herded into a bare cell. A few minutes later, Saro-Wiwa was called into the records room. As a sobbing priest performed last rites, he was made to sign a register and surrender his remaining property: a purse in which he kept his pipe and tobacco. Wearing a loose-fitting gown and bathroom slippers, he was handcuffed and shuffled off to the gallows. A few minutes before noon, a black cloth sack was placed over his head and he mounted the gallows. The pit into which Saro-Wiwa fell was only thirteen feet deep, and the fall failed to break his neck. It took him twenty minutes to die. The execution was videotaped, the cassette sent by courier to General Abacha, as proof that the Ogoni leader was really dead.

When the BBC broadcast the news of Saro-Wiwa's hanging, thousands of Ogonis wandered into the streets, disoriented and distraught. Within hours, the Nigerian military deployed 4,000 troops throughout Ogoniland, beating anyone caught mourning in public. In the week following the executions, the United States, Canada, South Africa, and several European countries withdrew their ambassadors. At the behest of British prime minister John Major and South African president Nelson Mandela, the Commonwealth of former British colonies suspended Nigeria. Even the Organization of African Unity, which once had greeted Idi Amin with standing ovations, expressed dismay.

That same week Shell announced it would put up the bulk of $3.8 billion to build a natural-gas plant on Bonny Island. The announcement suggested that, in ordering the executions, Abacha had taken a calculated gamble. Even from the seclusion of his presidential mansion at Aso

Rock, the dictator surely knew the killings would disgust the world and possibly provoke sanctions. Yet, for Abacha, international opprobrium was a fair exchange for internal stability. Abacha probably could have predicted too that despite calls for an oil embargo from civil-rights leaders around the world, neither the United States, which imports almost half of the oil produced by Nigeria, nor any other country found the resolve to do it.

One month after the executions, I returned to Shell's Nigerian headquarters on Lagos Island. Shell was running full-page ads in the *New York Times* saying: "Some campaigning groups say we should intervene in the political process in Nigeria. But even if we could, we must never do so. Politics is the business of governments and politicians. The world where companies use their economic influence to prop up or bring down governments would be a frightening and bleak one indeed. Shell. We'll keep you in touch with the truth." But despite this bit of corporate agitprop, the company was under siege; the public relations desk was blanketed with faxes from around the world deploring the company's environmental record in the Niger Delta and its failure to prevent Saro-Wiwa's hanging.

General manager Nnaemeka Achebe again welcomed me into his office, though his demeanor was far less chipper than when we had met the previous spring. He pointed out that after the death sentences were announced on October 31, Shell's chairman, Cor Herkstroter, had sent a personal letter to Abacha requesting mercy. Going further than that, Achebe explained, would have compromised Shell's "business principles." "Obviously we have significant economic power in the country," Achebe said.

"Yet we must be mindful not to interfere with local politics and be a government of some sort. . . . We're helping the cake grow bigger, and how that the cake is divided is up to the people to decide."

Achebe ticked off a list of development projects Shell was undertaking in the Delta. (In 1995, the company spent $9 million on improvements to the region, three times what it spent in 1990.) At the top of Achebe's list was the new gas plant, which would liquefy the natural gas, thus reducing pollution. "It's in the best interest of Nigeria for the project not to collapse," Achebe said. "The whole local economy around Bonny will benefit—small contractors, welders, electricians."

Shell's newfound interest in the environment and economy of the Delta is not surprising. During the past three years MOSOP has spawned at least half a dozen imitators, including the Ijaw National Congress and the Movement for Reparation to the Ogbia, and protests have paralyzed Shell's and other oil companies' operations in dozens of Delta locations. In one recent month alone, 5,000 people in Izere besieged Shell oil wells to protest the state of the roads and to demand a water project; hundreds of protesters in neighboring Olomoro seized a Shell flow station and hijacked eighteen vehicles belonging to Seismograph Services Ltd., a Shell contractor; and a convoy of villagers in canoes from Opuama took control of a Chevron drilling platform, demanding compensation for pollution. Protests were costing Shell and the other oil producers millions of lost barrels a year. "Shell is the victim in this," insisted Achebe. "We are caught in a situation where the communities can't get at the real target—the government—to express their grievances, so they attack us."

And so Shell was making amends to these little villages because, for now, it was in its best interest to do so. It was a payoff, a way of buying a measure of peace, of silencing the fax machines and the college kids camping out in front of the company's London headquarters. A few clinics and some asphalt was a small price to pay for continuing to operate without accountability.

In Port Harcourt and Ogoniland, meanwhile, the regime was trying to mute the local press and obliterate any trace of Saro-Wiwa's influence. In the absence of reliable information, rumors flourished. The executioners were said to have poured acid on the corpses of the Ogoni nine to speed their decomposition and discourage Ogoni activists from attempting to take possession of the bodies. When I tried to visit Saro-Wiwa's grave in a weed-choked cemetery in central Port Harcourt, I was escorted away by a phalanx of soldiers and brought before Colonel Dauda Musa Komo, who had supervised the executions.

Komo denied me permission to see the grave but said that the military should be commended for having treated the bodies with respect. "We buried each one in a coffin in his own grave. We could have just thrown them all in a pit," he said. "We have no regrets. We don't owe anybody an explanation."

To counter reports of military repression in Saro-Wiwa's home region, the regime had launched a propaganda campaign and insisted on providing me with a government escort, Fidelis Agbiki, the glib young press secretary to the Rivers State military administrator. "Everything is completely normal in Ogoniland," Agbiki cheerfully assured me as we passed one of the roadblocks set up at intersections throughout the region. "Most Ogonis stopped supporting Saro-Wiwa a long time ago."

But at a primary school in the Ogoni village of Beta, I met Principal M. A. Vite, a dapper, middle-aged man. He fidgeted behind a battered wooden desk in the stifling heat, nervously peering toward the front gate, where Agbiki waited in the government Peugeot. Around Vite sat a dozen Ogoni teachers: shabbily dressed men with solemn faces. "If you have a brother and your brother is killed—that's how we feel," Vite said, as his colleagues nodded and murmured in agreement. "But the moment we express anger they may say, 'Kill all of them.' It's futile to face machine guns with empty hands."

"If the military sees two or three people gathering, they may imprison you. If you wear black, they may beat you," said a science teacher who refused to give his name. "If you carry newspapers, they will seize them. Our headmaster was arrested last week as a warning to us not to discuss Ken in the classroom. Pastors were arrested because they prayed for Ken Saro-Wiwa. They take away people every day."

In the five months since I left Nigeria, the government has jailed hundreds of minority and pro-democracy activists, union and human-rights leaders, journalists, teachers, and lawyers. The State Department has warned that Nigeria's human-rights record is deteriorating, noting that "police and security services commonly engaged in extrajudicial killings and excessive use of force to quell antimilitary and prodemocracy protests." Shell set up a commission to investigate environmental destruction, but the head of the commission quickly resigned, citing his doubts about its impartiality. On March 12, the Clinton Administration announced that it had been trying to persuade U.S. businesses and foreign governments to stop all investment and freeze Nigerian assets. Resistance to this proposal was so strong that the harshest sanction that seemed possible was a ban on Nigerian participation in the Olympics. On that same day, incidentally, Shell announced that one of its joint ventures with the Nigerian government had made a major offshore oil discovery. The discovery was no coincidence. If "Bongo 1" and other deep-water reserves prove commercially viable, Shell and the government could abandon mainland production in turbulent areas. Lacking an effective venue for protest, the plight of the Nigerian people could easily be ignored. In the Delta, the hospitals would crumble, the ramshackle schools would rot and fall, and the half-built roads would slowly be swallowed up by the swamps.

We sometimes forget that we are the environment—we are nature itself. Ergo, corporations that pollute the world pollute us.

Pollution of the People
from AlterNet (5/8/03)
Stacy Malkan

Chemical contamination of water, air and food supplies has been documented for decades, but only recently have scientists begun to uncover details about the industrial pollution of a much more intimate site: our bodies.

It should come as no surprise that industrial chemicals

are running through our veins. Industry reported dumping 7.1 billion pounds of hazardous compounds into the air and water in the United States in the year 2000, according to the most recent Toxic Release Inventory, a U.S. Environmental Protection Agency (EPA) program that tracks only a subset of industries.

But not until recently, with advances in the technology of biomonitoring, have scientists been able to accurately measure the actual levels of chemicals in people's bodies.

Now, with the recent release of the largest-ever biomonitoring study by the U.S. Centers for Disease Control and Prevention (CDC), and a new peer-reviewed study by independent researchers, scientists know more than they ever have about a new evolutionary phenomenon: the universal chemical body burden of people.

"This is irrefutable proof that humans carry around scores of industrial chemicals, most of which have never been tested for human health effects," says Jane Houlihan, vice president of research at the Washington D.C.-based Environmental Working Group (EWG), and lead author of one of the studies.

Most of these chemicals did not exist in the environment, let alone in human bodies, just 75 years ago.

The $450-billion chemical industry has responded with assurances that the mere presence of chemicals in people is no proof of harm, but critics say the human population is the unwitting test subject of a dangerous and unprecedented chemical experiment.

CHEMICAL LOAD

The new CDC "National Report on Human Exposure to Environmental Chemicals," released in January, is the largest set of body burden data ever collected in the U.S. and the first time chemical exposure by age, race and sex has been analyzed on a national scale. CDC tested the blood and urine of a nationally representative group of Americans for the presence of 116 toxic chemicals—all of which were found in people.

"This report is by far the most extensive assessment ever made of the exposure in the U.S. population to environmental chemicals," says CDC Deputy Director Dr. David Fleming. "It's a quantum leap forward in providing objective scientific information about what's getting into people's bodies and how much."

Public health experts say one of the most disturbing findings is that children had higher body burdens than adults of some of the most toxic chemicals, including lead, tobacco smoke and organophosphate pesticides.

"This is a concern because of the potential of toxic chemicals to interfere with development," says Dr. Lynn Goldman, a former EPA official and a professor at the Johns Hopkins University School of Public Health.

Children had double the level of adults of the pesticide chlorpyrifos (known as Dursban)—a chemical that animal studies indicate has long-term effects on brain development if exposure occurs early in life. Dursban was the most widely used insecticide in the United States until the EPA banned its use in households a year ago, although some uses remain legal. Other organophosphate pesticides, also linked to neurological and nervous system damage in animal studies, remain in widespread use.

Children were also disproportionately exposed to some of the most toxic phthalates, the CDC found. Phthalates—

a class of industrial chemicals used in polyvinyl chloride (PVC) plastic, cosmetics and other consumer products—cause a spectrum of health effects in animal studies, including damage to the liver, kidneys, lungs and the reproductive system, particularly the testes of developing males.

CDC also identified some spikes among ethnic populations. The insecticide DDT, banned in the 1970s in the United States, was found in Mexican Americans at triple the levels present in the general population.

CDC found mercury at the highest levels in African-American women of childbearing age, and the study confirmed that 5 to 10 percent of all U.S. women of childbearing age already have enough mercury in their bodies to pose a risk of neurological damage to their developing babies.

CDC plans to release more body burden data every two years, including more information about potential sources of mercury, phthalates and other chemicals of particular concern.

A CLOSER LOOK

If the CDC report provides a panoramic view of the body burden of the U.S. population, another new study by the Environmental Working Group released in January offers a close-up snapshot at what individuals are carrying around in their bodies.

EWG looked for 210 chemicals in nine people and created a personal body burden profile for each—putting a human face, as well as a corporate face, on the problem.

Using peer-reviewed studies and various government health assessments, the report links the chemicals to potential health effects and found that, on average, each person's body had 50 or more chemicals that are linked to cancer in humans or lab animals, considered toxic to the brain and nervous system, associated with birth defects or abnormal development, or known to interfere with the hormone system.

The report also connected the chemicals to 11,700 consumer products, and to 164 past and current manufacturers.

So the study showed, for example, that Andrea Martin, 56, of Sausalito, California, contained at least 95 toxic chemicals in her body at the time of the test, which she likely ingested from scores of consumer products that are manufactured by Shell, Union Carbide, Exxon, Dow and Monsanto, among others.

"I was shocked at the breadth and variety of the number of chemicals. I was outraged to find out that without my permission, without my knowledge, my body was accumulating this toxic mixture," Martin says.

Martin appeared in a full-page ad announcing the body burden report that ran in the *New York Times* in January. Her photo was stamped with the headline: "Warning: Andrea Martin contains 59 cancer causing industrial chemicals."

She also happens to have cancer. At 42, Martin was diagnosed with an advanced case of breast cancer, underwent aggressive treatment and later contracted cancer in the other breast. A year ago, she was diagnosed with a large malignant brain tumor.

"My body biology is susceptible to cancer," Martin surmises. She has been asked if she thinks her chemical body burden caused the disease. "No one can say for sure, but no one can say it hasn't either," she says. "We deserve to know what toxins are in our bodies. We have a right to know what health effects these chemicals have."

The Unknown and the Chemophiles

Unfortunately, for everything scientists now know about which chemicals are in the environment and in people, there is much more they don't know about the effects on human health.

"Just because a chemical can be measured doesn't mean it causes disease," says Dr. Richard Jackson, director of the CDC's National Center for Environmental Health. The new CDC data offers "no new health effects information, no new understanding of the health effects from chemicals," Jackson says. "But it moves the science forward to increase this understanding."

The majority of people in the United States mistakenly believe that the government tests chemicals used in consumer products to make sure they are safe, according to an opinion poll recently conducted by the Washington Toxics Coalition.

The chemical industry also makes public claims to that effect. "Chemicals are evaluated by government scientists before being used, and there are precautions in place to help keep us safe from both natural toxins and modern chemicals," said a statement of the American Chemistry Council (ACC), the trade group for the biggest chemical manufacturers, issued in response to the CDC study.

However, most of the 75,000-plus chemicals in use today have never been evaluated for health effects. Most industrial chemicals in use today are regulated by the minimal health and safety standards of the Toxic Substances Control Act (TSCA), which assumes chemicals are safe until they are proven hazardous. TSCA does not require chemical companies to conduct health or safety studies prior to putting a chemical on the market, or to monitor chemicals once they are in use.

EWG accuses the chemical industry of creating the lax regulatory situation. "Chemical companies are pressuring our elected leaders to restrict new research and block common sense safeguards," says the *New York Times* ad paid for by the environmental group.

The ACC blasted the ad as an attempt to "put bogus words in the mouths of the men and women who make essential and life-saving products that we rely on every day" and said that "chemical makers support additional government research and also are spending millions of dollars every year in collaboration with government scientists on research into the relationship between chemicals and health."

Industry points to its voluntary efforts to improve health and safety performance, and says that significant reductions in chemical releases have occurred under the Responsible Care program, a voluntary program established by the ACC in 1988 in response to criticism of industry's environmental record.

But a recent study by Duke University associate professor Michael Lenox found that some members of Responsible Care are releasing more toxic substances into the environment than non-members, prompting Lenox to criticize the voluntary program as a failure.

In responding to the CDC report, industry has focused on the small levels of chemicals detected by biomonitoring. "It is remarkable that modern chemistry allows CDC scientists to measure incredibly small amounts of certain nutrients, natural food chemicals and modern chemicals in our bodies," says the ACC.

Elizabeth Whelan, president of the industry-funded American Council on Science and Health (ACSH), counsels that people "should remember the basic tenet of toxicology—the dose makes the poison"—a phrase used often by industry to make the point that small doses are not harmful.

The EWG report points out that science has evolved considerably since that phrase was coined in the sixteenth century. "Toxic effects don't require high doses," says EWG's Houlihan. For instance, low doses of lead or mercury at specific stages of fetal development or infancy have been shown to cause permanent health problems.

Much of the evidence of the toxicity associated with the chemicals detected by the body burden reports comes from animal studies. And many of the same health effects turning up in the animal studies are also on the rise in the human population.

The probability that a U.S. resident will develop some type of cancer at some point in his or her lifetime is now 1 in 2 for men, and 1 in 3 for women, according to the American Cancer Society. Many forms of cancer are on the rise in humans, including breast, prostate and testicular cancers, according to the National Cancer Institute.

Reproductive system defects and major nervous system disorders are also increasing in humans. Hypospadias, a birth defect of the penis, doubled in the United States between 1970 and 1993 and is now estimated to affect one of every 125 male babies born. Reported cases of autism are now almost 10 times higher than in the mid-1980s, according to some recent studies.

For all those diseases, there is data that either suggests or demonstrates that environmental factors may be contributing to the increase, and chemical exposures may be part of that picture, scientists say.

"There is an epidemic of breast cancer and there is an epidemic of many chronic diseases in this country and the question is, what is the contribution of this body burden that we are all bearing?" asks Michael Lerner, one of the EWG test subjects and the founder of Commonweal.

Industry counters the health worries with accusations that "chemophobics" are using the CDC study to further a political agenda.

Steven Milloy, frequent defender of the chemical industry and columnist for FoxNews.com, accused environmentalists of using the information in the CDC report to "terrorize us with yet another junk science-fueled campaign intended to advance their mindless anti-chemical agenda."

Industry defenders say that people should feel reassured by the information released by CDC. "Thanks to the CDC report, we're now more certain than ever that the synthetic chemical amounts we are routinely subjected to are trivial. We ought to feel safer than ever," said Todd Seavey of ACSH.

But industry critics question why industry has the right to contaminate people with products that may be harmful, and say industry should be held liable for chemical trespass.

"If somebody comes onto my land, it's trespassing, but companies can put 85 toxic substances into my body without my permission and tell me there is nothing I can do about it. That can't be right," says Charlotte Brody, RN, 54, director of the Washington, D.C.-based environmental group Health Care Without Harm and one of the nine subjects tested for the EWG report.

"OUTRIGHT BANNING WORKS"

Two encouraging findings in the CDC report point toward at least one solution to the toxic body burden in humans. The levels of cotinine (a marker for tobacco smoke) decreased in children by 58 percent, while exposure to unsafe levels of lead declined among children under age 5 from 4.4 percent to 2.2 percent—although there is debate over whether any level of lead is really safe.

The CDC also reported decreasing levels in the general population of DDT and PCBs, two substances banned in the 1970s.

"It appears that regulation, and in fact outright elimination or banning, works," says Dr. Peter Orris, director of the Occupational Health Services Institute at the University of Illinois. "These are all examples of regulatory action on the part of the government which we not only can applaud, but we now have data indicating that this works and is an effective means of social policy."

Orris says the CDC data should help set priorities for public health action.

"We need to move ahead, rapidly ahead, with mercury and other regulations," he says, including ratification of the Stockholm Treaty on Persistent Organic Pollutants (POPS). "These problems are global and not local." The United States has yet to ratify the POPS Treaty, an international agreement to ban 12 of the most harmful pollutants based on their known human health effects.

EWG recommends reform of TSCA, which the environmental group says is "so fundamentally broken that the statute needs to be rewritten." The group recommends that the chemical industry be made to disclose all internal studies about the environmental fate, human contamination and health effects of chemicals, and to thoroughly test all chemicals found in humans "for their health effects in low-dose, womb-to-tomb, multi-generational studies" focused on known target organs.

The CDC will, at least, continue to provide scientists and activists with more information about the extent of human contamination for years to come. The agency's $6.5-million biomonitoring study is "budgeted to continue at the same rate every two years into the indefinite future," says the agency's Pirkle.

The CDC plans to add new chemicals, and solicit input from other government agencies, environmental groups and industry about how to make the data more useful.

In the meantime, many activists say there is enough information available now to warrant regulations to protect people, particularly children, from industrial chemicals.

"We need to change the way of manufacturing products, shifting from protection that industry gets to protection of the consumer," says test subject Martin. She advocates for a "better safe than sorry" approach that requires manufacturers to test for safety before they are allowed to introduce chemicals into commerce.

"The fact that we are walking toxic dumps is literally the result of decisions made long ago and is not an inevitability of modern life," she says. "If there is intelligence to come up with new chemicals and come up with modern conveniences, the same intelligence exists to make it safe."

THEY ARE INHUMAN

<small>FIXING THE ROTTEN CORPORATE BARREL</small>
BY JOHN CAVANAGH AND JERRY MANDER—443

Corporations, for all their power, aren't alive—they don't think or feel or know anything. *And yet, somehow, we have ceded to these literally inhuman monsters control over our lives. They are subsuming our culture, our civilization, our very selves. Our only defense is to defend and nurture our humanity—our capacity for anger, for love, for experience itself. The fight against corporate power is a fight for our very lives.*

Fixing the Rotten Corporate Barrel

from *The Nation* (12/23/02)

John Cavanagh & Jerry Mander

The global corporations of today stand as the dominant institutional force at the center of human activity. Through their market power, billions of dollars in campaign contributions, public relations and advertising, and the sheer scale of their operations, corporations create the visions and institutions we live by and exert enormous influence over most of the political processes that rule us.

It is certainly fair to say, as David Korten and others have, that "global corporate rule" has effectively been achieved. This leaves society in the daunting position of serving a hierarchy of primary corporate values—expanding profit, hypergrowth, environmental exploitation, self-interest, disconnection from communities and workers—that are diametrically opposed to the principles of equity, democracy, transparency and the common good, the core values that can bring social and environmental sustainability to the planet. It is a basic task of any democracy and justice movement to confront the powers of this new global royalty, just as previous generations set out to eliminate the control of monarchies.

The first step in the process is to recognize the systemic nature of the problem. We are used to hearing powers that be—when faced with an Enron or WorldCom scandal—explain them away as simple problems of greedy individuals; the proverbial few rotten apples in the barrel; the exception, not the rule. In reality, the nature of the corporate structure, and the rules by which corporations routinely operate, make socially and environmentally beneficial outcomes the exception, not the norm.

Public corporations today—and their top executives—live or die based on certain imperatives, notably whether they are able to continuously attract investment capital by demonstrating increasing short-term profits, exponential growth, expanded territories and markets, and successful control of the domestic and international regulatory, investment and political climates. Questions of community welfare, worker rights and environmental impacts are nowhere in the equation. Given such a setup, Enron's performance, like most other corporate behavior—especially among publicly held companies—was entirely predictable, indeed, almost inevitable. Enron executives were only doing what the system suggested they had to do. Corporations that can successfully defy these rules are the rare good apples in an otherwise rotting barrel.

That such structural imperatives should dominate the global economic system and the lives of billions of people is clearly a central problem of our time; any citizens' agenda for achieving sustainability must be rooted in plans for fundamental structural change and the reversal of corporate rule.

New Citizen Movement

Around the world, the spectrum of anticorporate activity is broad, with strategies ranging from reformist to transformational to abolitionist. Reformist strategies include attempts to force increased corporate responsibility, accountability and transparency, and to strengthen the role of social and environmental values in corporate decision-making. Such strategies implicitly accept global corporations as here to stay in their current form and as having the potential to function as responsible citizens.

A growing number of activists reject the idea that corporations have any intrinsic right to exist. They do not believe that corporations should be considered permanent fixtures in our society; if the structural rules that govern them cannot be fixed, then we should seek alternative modes for organizing economic activity, ones that suit sustainability. These activists seek the death penalty for corporations with a habitual record of criminal activity. They also demand comprehensive rethinking and redesign of the laws and rules by which corporations operate, to eliminate those characteristics that make publicly traded, limited-liability corporations a threat to the well-being of people and planet.

Possibly the most visible and growing arm of this anticorporate movement is the one that focuses on the corporate charter, the basic instrument that defines and creates corporations in the United States. Corporations in this country gain their existence via charters granted through state governments. As the landmark research of Richard Grossman and Frank Adams of the Program on Corporations, Law and Democracy (POCLAD) has revealed, most of these charters originally included stringent rules requiring a high degree of corporate accountability and service to the community. Over the centuries corporations have managed to water down charter rules. And even when they violate the few remaining restrictions, their permanent existence is rarely threatened. Governing bodies today, beholden to corporations for campaign finance support, are loath to enforce any sanctions except in cases of extreme political embarrassment, such as has occurred with Enron, Arthur Andersen and a few others. Even then, effective sanctions may be few and small.

At the same time, corporations have obtained many rights similar to those granted human beings. American courts have ruled that corporations are "fictitious persons," with the right to buy and sell property, to sue in court for injuries and to express "corporate speech." But they have not been required, for the most part, to abide by normal human responsibilities. They are strongly protected by limited liability rules, so shareholder-owners of a corporation cannot be prosecuted for acts of the institution. Nor, in any meaningful sense, is the corporation itself vulnerable to prosecution. Corporations are sometimes fined for their acts or ordered to alter their practices, but the life of the corporation, its virtual existence, is very rarely threatened, even for great crimes that, if carried out by people in many states of the United States, might invoke the death penalty.

Of course, it is a key problem that these "fictitious persons" we call corporations do not actually embody human characteristics such as altruism or, on the other hand, shame—leaving the corporate entity literally incapable of the social, environmental or community ideals that we keep hoping it will pursue. Its entire structural design is to advance only its own self-interest. While executives of corporations might occasionally wish to behave in a community-friendly manner, if profits are sacrificed, the executive might find that he or she is thrown off the wheel and replaced with someone who understands the rules.

State charter changes could alter this. State corporate charter rules could set any conditions that popular will might dictate—from who should be on the boards, to the values corporations must operate by, to whether they may buy up other enterprises, move to other cities and countries, or anything else that affects the public interest. In Pennsylvania, for example, citizen groups have initiated an amendment to the state's corporation code that calls for, among other things, corporate charters to be limited to thirty years. A charter could be renewed, but only after successful completion of a review process during which it would have to prove it is operating in the public interest. In California a coalition of citizen organizations (including the National Organization for Women, the Rainforest Action Network and the National Lawyers Guild) petitioned the attorney general to revoke Unocal's charter. Citing California's own corporate code, which authorizes revocation procedures, the coalition offered evidence documenting Unocal's responsibility for environmental devastation, exploitation of workers and gross violation of human rights. While this action has not yet succeeded, others are under way.

Revoking a charter—the corporate equivalent of a death sentence—begins to put some teeth into the idea of accountability. Eliot Spitzer, Attorney General of New York, declared in 1998: "When a corporation is convicted of repeated felonies that harm or endanger the lives of human beings or destroy our environment, the corporation should be put to death, its corporate existence ended, and its assets taken and sold at public auction." Although Spitzer has not won a death sentence against a habitual corporate criminal, he has taken up battle with several giants, including General Electric.

Even if corporations were to be more tightly supervised, that would not be enough to change society. Such actions must be supported by parallel efforts to restore the integrity of democratic institutions and reclaim the resources that corporations have co-opted. But tough charters and tougher enforcement would be a start.

ALTERNATIVES

Names like Exxon, Ford, Honda, McDonald's, Microsoft and Citigroup are now so ubiquitous, and such an intimate part of everyday life, that it is difficult for many people in the industrial world to imagine how we might live without them. But there are hundreds of other forms of economic and business activity. And by whose logic do we need transnational corporations to run hamburger stands, produce clothing, grow food, publish books or provide the things that contribute to a satisfying existence?

Transition to more economically democratic forms becomes easier to visualize once we recognize that many human-scale, locally owned enterprises already exist. They include virtually all of the millions of local independent businesses now organized as sole proprietorships, partnerships, collectives and cooperatives of all types, and worker-owned businesses. They include family-owned businesses, small farms, artisanal producers, independent retail stores, small factories, farmers' markets, community banks and so on. In fact, though these kinds of businesses get very little government support, they are the primary source of livelihood for most of the world's people. And in many parts of the world—notably among agricultural and indigenous societies—they are built into the culture and effectively serve the common interest rather than the favored few. In the context of industrial society, the rechartering movement and the parallel efforts to eliminate "corporate personhood" and exemptions from investor liabilities are important steps in a similar direction, seeking to alleviate the dominance of institutions whose structural imperatives make it nearly impossible for them to place public interest over self-interest.

An I Hate Corporate
America *Timeline:*

Nate Hardcastle

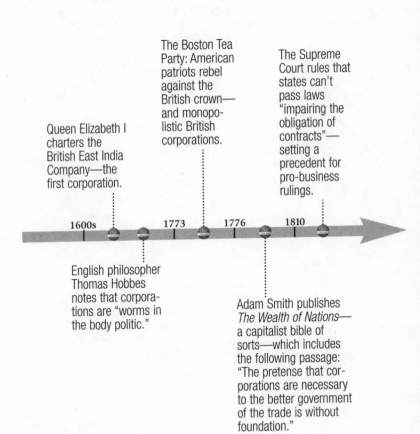

Queen Elizabeth I
charters the
British East India
Company—the
first corporation.

The Boston Tea
Party: American
patriots rebel
against the
British crown—
and monopo-
listic British
corporations.

The Supreme
Court rules that
states can't
pass laws
"impairing the
obligation of
contracts"—
setting a
precedent for
pro-business
rulings.

1600s   1773   1776   1810

English philosopher
Thomas Hobbes
notes that corpora-
tions are "worms in
the body politic."

Adam Smith publishes
The Wealth of Nations—
a capitalist bible of
sorts—which includes
the following passage:
"The pretense that cor-
porations are necessary
to the better government
of the trade is without
foundation."

AN *I HATE CORPORATE AMERICA* TIMELINE

Abraham Lincoln warns: "corporations have been enthroned. . . . An era of corruption in high places will follow and the money power will endeavor to prolong its reign by working on the prejudices of the people . . . until wealth is aggregated in a few hands . . . and the republic is destroyed." (Remember that the next time you hear a Republican say he represents the party of Lincoln.)

Thomas Jefferson says, "I hope we shall crush in its birth the aristocracy of our moneyed corporations, which dare already to challenge our government to a trial of strength and bid defiance to the laws of our country."

Congress passes the Sherman Antitrust Act to restrict corporate power.

| 1812 | 1832 | 1864 | 1886 | 1890 | 1901 |

The Supreme Court, invoking the 14th Amendment (originally intended to protect former slaves) defines corporations as legal "persons," giving them all the rights and liberties of individuals.

President Andrew Jackson kills the corrupt Second Bank of the United States.

The Monsanto Corporation is founded to manufacture saccharin—the first in the company's long line of cancer-causing and otherwise unhealthy products, including PCBs and Agent Orange.

AN *I HATE CORPORATE AMERICA* TIMELINE

Upton Sinclair publishes
The Jungle, which
exposes the horrifying
practices of the meat-
packing industry and
leads to the first major
federal consumer protec-
tion legislation, the Pure
Food and Drug Act.

A truckload of
Monsanto fertilizer
explodes, killing
more than 500
people in one of
the chemical
industry's first
major disasters.

DuPont and General Motors
first develop ozone-layer-
destroying chlorofluorocar-
bons (CFCs).

1906   1919   1920s   1921   1947   1953

Harry F. Sinclair of the Mam-
moth Oil Corporation and
Edward L. Doheny of the Pan-
American Petroleum and
Transport Company bribe Sec-
retary of the Interior Albert Fall
for access to Wyoming's
Teapot Dome oil fields.

Shareholders sue Henry Ford over
his plan to build a new factory: he
wanted to employ as many people
as possible instead of distributing
dividends. The court rules for
shareholders, on the grounds that
a corporation's sole purpose is to
make money for shareholders.

The United Fruit
Company backs a
right-wing coup in
Guatemala.

AN *I HATE CORPORATE AMERICA* TIMELINE

January
Republican president and war hero Dwight Eisenhower warns: "In the councils of government, we must guard against the acquisition of unwarranted influence, whether sought or unsought, by the military industrial complex. The potential for the disastrous rise of misplaced power exists and will persist. We must never let the weight of this combination endanger our liberties or democratic processes. We should take nothing for granted."

General Electric hires a new pitchman: Ronald Reagan.

The first Wal-Mart opens in Rogers, Arkansas.

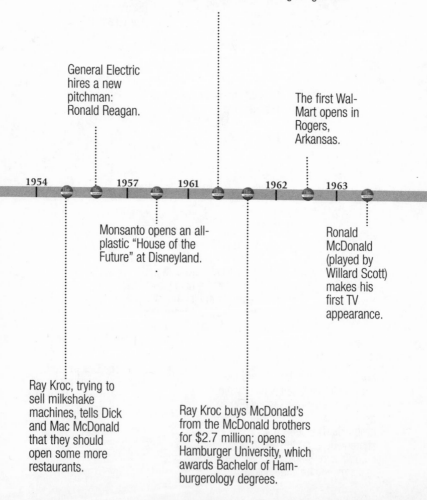

1954   1957   1961   1962   1963

Monsanto opens an all-plastic "House of the Future" at Disneyland.

Ronald McDonald (played by Willard Scott) makes his first TV appearance.

Ray Kroc, trying to sell milkshake machines, tells Dick and Mac McDonald that they should open some more restaurants.

Ray Kroc buys McDonald's from the McDonald brothers for $2.7 million; opens Hamburger University, which awards Bachelor of Hamburgerology degrees.

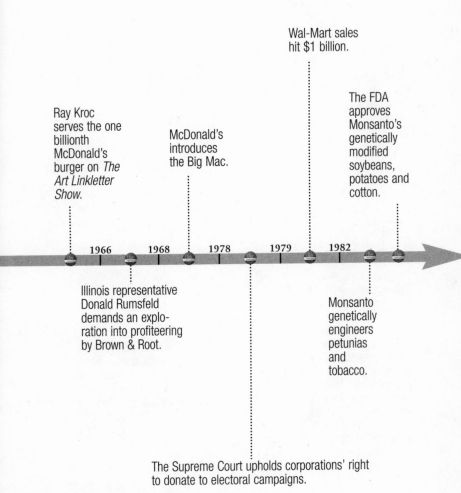

Wal-Mart sales
hit $1 billion.

The FDA
approves
Monsanto's
genetically
modified
soybeans,
potatoes and
cotton.

Ray Kroc
serves the one
billionth
McDonald's
burger on *The
Art Linkletter
Show.*

McDonald's
introduces
the Big Mac.

1966   1968   1978   1979   1982

Illinois representative
Donald Rumsfeld
demands an explo-
ration into profiteering
by Brown & Root.

Monsanto
genetically
engineers
petunias
and
tobacco.

The Supreme Court upholds corporations' right
to donate to electoral campaigns.

AN *I HATE CORPORATE AMERICA* TIMELINE

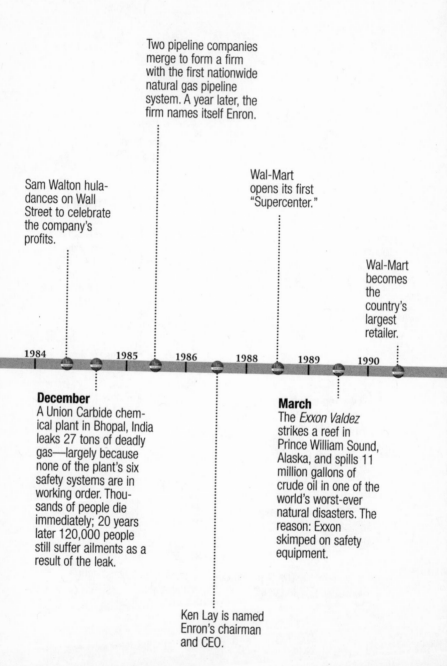

Two pipeline companies merge to form a firm with the first nationwide natural gas pipeline system. A year later, the firm names itself Enron.

Wal-Mart opens its first "Supercenter."

Sam Walton hula-dances on Wall Street to celebrate the company's profits.

Wal-Mart becomes the country's largest retailer.

1984   1985   1986   1988   1989   1990

December
A Union Carbide chemical plant in Bhopal, India leaks 27 tons of deadly gas—largely because none of the plant's six safety systems are in working order. Thousands of people die immediately; 20 years later 120,000 people still suffer ailments as a result of the leak.

March
The *Exxon Valdez* strikes a reef in Prince William Sound, Alaska, and spills 11 million gallons of crude oil in one of the world's worst-ever natural disasters. The reason: Exxon skimped on safety equipment.

Ken Lay is named Enron's chairman and CEO.

Octogenarian Stella Liebeck gets third-degree burns on her groin after spilling super-hot McDonald's coffee in her lap. She receives skin grafts and spends a week in the hospital. She sues after the company offers $800 in compensation. Jurors award her $2.9 million after discovering that McDonald's knew its coffee had severely burned more than 700 people in the past. The award is reduced to $480,000 on appeal.

April
Sam Walton dies.

December
Wal-Mart weekly sales hit $1 billion.

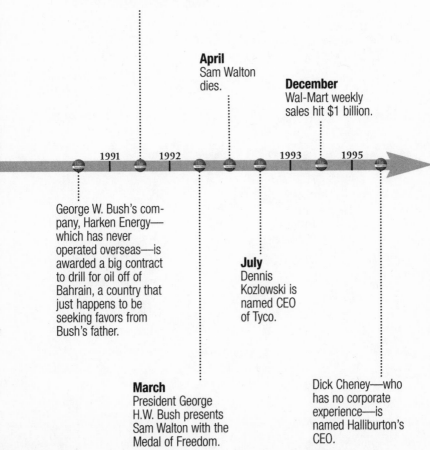

1991   1992   1993   1995

George W. Bush's company, Harken Energy—which has never operated overseas—is awarded a big contract to drill for oil off of Bahrain, a country that just happens to be seeking favors from Bush's father.

July
Dennis Kozlowski is named CEO of Tyco.

March
President George H.W. Bush presents Sam Walton with the Medal of Freedom.

Dick Cheney—who has no corporate experience—is named Halliburton's CEO.

AN *I HATE CORPORATE AMERICA* TIMELINE

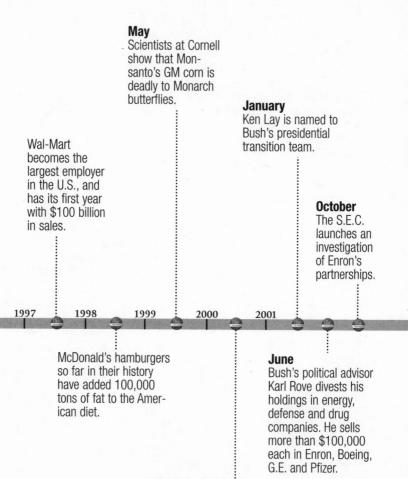

May
Scientists at Cornell show that Monsanto's GM corn is deadly to Monarch butterflies.

January
Ken Lay is named to Bush's presidential transition team.

Wal-Mart becomes the largest employer in the U.S., and has its first year with $100 billion in sales.

October
The S.E.C. launches an investigation of Enron's partnerships.

1997 1998 1999 2000 2001

McDonald's hamburgers so far in their history have added 100,000 tons of fat to the American diet.

June
Bush's political advisor Karl Rove divests his holdings in energy, defense and drug companies. He sells more than $100,000 each in Enron, Boeing, G.E. and Pfizer.

Ken Lay contributes more than $290,000 to Bush's presidential campaign.

AN *I HATE CORPORATE AMERICA* TIMELINE

September
Georgia's state government discovers that 10,261 children of Wal-Mart employees are enrolled in the state's low-income child health insurance program. (That's one enrolled child for every four employees in the state.)

May
Internal Enron documents reveal that the company profited enormously from California's energy crisis.

December
Enron files for bankruptcy.

Ken Lay resigns as Enron's CEO.

2002

November
Enron reports that it has overstated earnings since 1997 by $567 million.

February
The Government Accounting Office sues Dick Cheney to make him reveal the connections between Enron and the Bush administration's energy task force.

Former Tyco CEO Dennis Kozlowski and CFO Mark Swartz are indicted for stealing more than $170 million from the company to finance their extravagant lifestyles. Kozlowski's take includes an $18 million decorating bill for his company-owned New York apartment, an interest-free $19 million loan to buy a house in Boca Raton, and $11 million for art and other furnishings.

January
The Justice Department confirms that it has begun investigating Enron.

June
Dennis Kozlowski resigns from Tyco under heavy criticism.

AN *I HATE CORPORATE AMERICA* TIMELINE

A Pentagon audit finds that Halliburton has overcharged more than $61 million for gas deliveries.

November
Former HealthSouth CEO Richard Scrushy—proud owner of a Lamborghini, a 92-foot yacht and paintings by Picasso and Renoir—is indicted for directing a $2.7 billion fraud designed to boost the firm's stock price.

January
Pentagon auditors accuse Halliburton—contracted to provide soldiers' meals—of billing $16 million for meals that were never served.

2003

2004

December
Wal-Mart shopper Patricia Van Lester is knocked unconscious during a stampede spurred by a sale on DVD players.

July
Ken Lay surrenders to federal agents.

Halliburton earns $3.9 billion from military contracts.

October
South Carolina's Democratic Party considers allowing corporations to sponsor its presidential primary.

Acknowledgments

Many people made this anthology.

At Thunder's Mouth Press and Avalon Publishing Group: Thanks to Will Balliett, Maria Fernandez, Nate Knaebel, Linda Kosarin, John Oakes, Michael O'Connor, Susan Reich, David Riedy, Mike Walters, and Don Weise for their support, dedication and hard work.

Thanks also are due to the dozens of people who generously took time to help us find and obtain rights. Special thanks to Habiba Alcindor at *The Nation*, Raegan Carmona at Andrews McNeel Universal, Eleyna Fugman at AlterNet and Tyler Moorehead at *The Ecologist*.

Finally, I am grateful to the writers and artists whose work appears in this book.

Permissions

PERMISSIONS

be accessed at http://www.thenation.com. • "Wal-Mart Values" by Liza Featherstone. Reprinted with permission from the December 16, 2002 issue of *The Nation*. For subscription information, call 1-800-333-8536. Portions of each week's *Nation* magazine can be accessed at http://www.thenation.com. • "Union Blues at Wal-Mart" by John Dicker. Reprinted with permission from the July 8, 2002 issue of *The Nation*. For subscription information, call 1-800-333-8536. Portions of each week's *Nation* magazine can be accessed at http://www.thenation.com. • "The Burger International" by Liza Featherstone. Copyright © 1998 by Liza Featherstone. Reprinted by permission of the author. • "Tyson's Moral Anchor" by Eric Schlosser. Reprinted with permission from the July 12, 2004 issue of *The Nation*. For subscription information, call 1-800-333-8536. Portions of each week's *Nation* magazine can be accessed at http://www.thenation.com. • "Global Agenda" by William Greider. Reprinted with permission from the January 31, 2000 issue of *The Nation*. For subscription information, call 1-800-333-8536. Portions of each week's *Nation* magazine can be accessed at http://www. thenation.com. • "The Last Farm Crisis" by William Greider. Reprinted with permission from the November 20, 2000 issue of *The Nation*. For subscription information, call 1-800-333-8536. Portions of each week's *Nation* magazine can be accessed at http://www.thenation.com. • "Bad Meat" by Eric Schlosser. Reprinted with permission from the September 16, 2002 issue of *The Nation*. For subscription information, call 1-800-333-8536. Portions of each week's *Nation* magazine can be accessed at http://www.thenation.com. • "A Well-Designed Disaster: The Untold Story of the Exxon Valdez" from *The Best Democracy Money Can Buy* by Greg Palast. Copyright © 2003 by Greg Palast. Reprinted by permission of the Diana Finch Literary Agency. • "Whatever It Takes" by Ashley Shelby. Reprinted with permission from the April 5, 2004 issue of *The Nation*. For subscription information, call 1-800-333-8536. Portions of each week's *Nation* magazine can be accessed at http://www.thenation.com. • "The Chemical Industry's Bhopal Legacy" by Gary Cohen.

Bibliography

The selections used in this anthology were taken from the sources listed below

Alexander, Max. *Man Bites Log.* New York: Carroll & Graf, 2004.

Beiles, Nancy. "What Monsanto Knew." Originally published by *The Nation,* May 29, 2000.

Brownlee, Shannon. "Plunder Drugs." Originally published by *The Washington Monthly,* March 2004.

Burton, Bob and Andy Rowell. "Disease Mongering." Originally published in *PR Watch,* first quarter 2003.

Cavanagh, John and Jerry Mander. "Fixing the Rotten Corporate Barrel." Originally published by *The Nation,* December 23, 2002.

Cohen, Gary. "The Chemical Industry's Bhopal Legacy." Originally published by AlterNet, www.alternet.org, December 3, 2003.

CorpWatch. "Houston, We Have a Problem: An Alternative Annual Report on Halliburton." www.corpwatch.com.

Dicker, John. "Union Blues at Wal-Mart." Originally published by *The Nation,* July 8, 2002.

Featherstone, Liza. "The Burger International." Originally published by *The Left Business Observer,* November, 1998.

Featherstone, Liza. "Wal-Mart Values." Originally published by *The Nation,* December 16, 2002.

Fitrakis, Bob and Harvey Wasserman. "Diebold's Political Machine." Originally published by *Mother Jones,* March 2004.

Gorelick, Steve. "It's the Corporate Economy, Stupid." Originally published by *The Ecologist,* June 22, 2002.

Greider, William. "Global Agenda." Originally published by *The Nation,* January 1, 2000.

Greider, William. "The Last Farm Crisis." Originally published by *The Nation,* November 20, 2000.

Hammer, Josh. "Nigeria Crude." Originally published by *Harper's,* June 1996.

Jewell, Michael. "USA Inc." from *The I Hate Republicans Reader.* New York: Thunder's Mouth Press, 2003.

Johnston, David Cay. "Profits Trump Patriotism" from *Perfectly Legal.* New York: Portfolio, 2003.

Malkan, Stacy. "Pollution of the People." Published by AlterNet, www.alternet.org, July 7, 2004.